W9-AEP-444

PHILOSOPHICAL EXPLORATIONS
A Series Edited by George Kimball Plochmann

Ancient Tragedy and the Origins of Modern Science

by

MICHAEL DAVIS

SOUTHERN ILLINOIS UNIVERSITY PRESS

CARBONDALE AND EDWARDSVILLE

Library of Congress Cataloging in Publication Data

Davis, Michael Peter, 1947–
    Ancient tragedy and the origins of modern science / by Michael Peter
Davis.
        p.   cm. — (Philosophical explorations)
    Bibliography: p.
    Includes index.
    ISBN 0-8093-1390-1
    1. Science—History.   2. Science—Philosophy.   3. Sophocles.
Ajax.   4. Descartes, René, 1596–1650. Discours de la méthode.
5. Plato. Meno. I. Title. II. Series.
Q124.6.D38   1988
190—dc19   87-21275
                                                                        CIP

WITHDRAWN

for my parents

I grow old always learning many things.

Count no man happy until he dies.

—Solon

Contents

Foreword
George Kimball Plochmann

T HIS VOLUME OF MODEST size but very substantial import consists of commentaries on three diverse texts, with a *Vorspiel* on portions of a fourth. What are termed commentaries are, of course, efforts of many sorts, some being concerned partly if not almost wholly with questions of orthography, punctuation, families of manuscripts or editions and printings, and similar matters. (Whether these should be called commentaries in any primary and proper sense is something else to be considered.) A second kind is dedicated to supplying historical events thought relevant to the composition of the text, or anticipations of the text in previous authors or in the same author, or biographical backgrounds, the latter often verging upon detailed psychological analysis of the writer as a way of explaining his writings. Strictly speaking, these two types, valuable as they are, should be called adventitious, and they form a contrast with the third, which elucidates the meanings of terms, weighs the possible truth or falsity of statements, and judges the validity of the arguments, all through back-and-forth references to the composition as a whole, the nature of what is written about, its large structure, and its intent, declared or implied. If we take the first three—terms, statements, and arguments—as the materials of the text and the rest as contributing to its form, then striking a balance between the form and matter would seem to be the obligation laid upon commentators pursuing their task in this most comprehensive yet essential way.

An important text, being an individual thing, houses an infinite number of characteristics; there is no limit to the aspects, whether vital or incidental, that can be listed or at least queried about. The greater the originality of the text discussed, the greater the chance of its being *sui generis* and the larger the variety of true propositions assertible of its nature, its expressed thoughts; for its message falls into no readily identifiable species of human discourse with their conventions and parameters, however much its outward dress may be the same—comedy, summa, sonnet, or whatnot. Certainly each of the three chief texts treated by Professor Davis is one of a kind, if we account for both form and content, regardless of the fact that it is easy to list many relatives close enough in conventional structures to be called by the same names, tragic drama, semiautobiographical treatise, and dialogue. Preeminent in the author's discussions of these is his power to seek out and distinguish the unique messages of each of them and to show that following Aristotle in the theory of tragedy will carry one but part way into Sophocles' *Ajax*, that taking literally the interpretations of modern historians of science will be of limited assistance in reading the Cartesian *Discourse on Method*, and that accepting the word of well-received commentators, European and American, may be insufficient to guide one in detecting and explicating all the subtleties of Plato's *Meno*. The sort of commentary that Professor Davis writes is, so to speak, a very private affair, an intimate communion with the written words of far-off, long-gone thinkers who in turn had intimate communion with their own pages and wax tablets.

It would be foolish to claim that the approaches in the present book are wholly without parallels; the author acknowledges freely his indebtednesses. But he has, along with his firm rejection of all information he considers extraneous to his main purposes, created a highly coherent interpretation of each of the texts just named (and of parts of Plato's *Symposium* as well), and has succeeded also in binding these together so that their common topics are revealed, their teachings compared and contrasted.

The *Symposium* in its prologue and in the two speeches selected raises many issues pertinent to love, hate, and strife, concepts bearing much weight in the *Ajax* and the other texts. In a dialectical, not a chronological, sequence the playwright adds preoccupation with the self, so that the triad now turns into self-pity, self-loathing, and self-slaughter. He adds the *polis* as well, and this combination again generates political solidarity, its dispersion, and civil conflict. All six of these doubled concepts are expressions, varied and often at serious odds with one another when manifested in life, of the struggle for autonomy that marks the human condition, personal and public. The *Ajax* is a strange drama about a second-greatest warrior who attempts to annihilate an entire Greek military force, is diverted by sudden madness, and who upon regaining his senses realizes that the only possible vengeance will be against himself, eventually leading to a further dilemma built around the political issue of rites to be accorded in the burial of a suicide.

To do more than suggest the character, let alone the details of modern science, in anything less than a multivolume encyclopedia is naturally out of the question, but a brief introduction to its nature and primary connections lies in the chapters in which one sees René Descartes through the eyes of Professor Davis or, just as properly, Davis through those of Descartes. Discussion of almost all the technical details that have occupied scientists following after the father of French philosophy—or, as the French would have it, the father of modern philosophy everywhere—that is, the equations, proofs, experiments, surveys, reports, lie outside the *Discourse on Method*. Many of the principles animating the scientific labors of the past three centuries are nevertheless given a hearing in that little text, a handbook on clear thinking, an autobiographical sketch, an ethical and quasi-political tract, and a tiny review of some work being done or that should be done. Had the book been called *Confessions of a Wayfarer* the title would have fitted as well. Its personal aspects—brought out convincingly in the present commentary—have been echoed more often in the autobiographies of scientists than in the treatises that caused their lives to be memorable enough to give their self-revelations point and popular acceptance in the first place.

The *Ajax* pits the good of the individual against that of the group and the *polis*. The *Discourse on Method* asks how virtues, both intellectual and moral, can be acquired, and along the way discusses the relation of opinion to knowledge. In its tussles over both virtue and knowledge the *Meno* very adroitly treats the problems that permeate both the old Greek drama and the seventeenth-century free-flowing little treatise, bringing their many diversified issues close together. Thirty Stephanus pages of profound, tortuous, varied thought, no more, the *Meno* succeeds in asking how virtue is acquired, moving on to the nature of virtue itself, indicating that in the special context marked out by the dialogue the answer should lie both in the congenital equipment of the human soul and also in the degree to which decisions are appropriate to political exigencies. Yet this very political virtue falls shorts of knowledge— of mathematical certainty. Plato hints that a real question remains: Which participant in it, the highly suspect Meno, the self-righteous Anytus, or the questing Socrates, actually practices this kind of human goodness, which is based upon right opinion, nothing more.

Thomas Wolfe remarks at the very outset of *Look Homeward, Angel* that every book is in some sense an autobiography, and if he is right then the emphasis of Professor Davis upon the psychic and cosmic realities that each text probes, and that are implied in his own examination of them, is peculiarly, fundamentally autobiographical. The three texts are not merely a set of utterances for a masked actor to project from an open stage, or a list of instructions for neophyte scientists, or a highly structured conversation supposedly taking place in some Athenian courtyard. Rather they are, all three, testaments to the humanity and thus the autonomy of three thinkers, one at a time; each has his aspirations and hopes, fulfilled or forlorn, for overcoming the obstacles put in his way by the implacable gods, by partly inscrutable nature, or by the disjointed *polis*. There are dark shadows in all three texts, and the author of this book has penetrated that darkness.

Ancient Tragedy and the Origins of Modern Science is, then, no mere account of some classics that its author happened to read and admire; a sound principle runs threadlike all through. It is this, that at the very center of each text is the lesson that Coleridge, something of a Platonist but certainly no Cartesian, put so well:

> I may not hope from outward forms to win
> The passion and the life, whose fountains are within.

The writer of these three commentaries has an honesty, depth of perception, and sense of urgency that bespeak a mind taking these examples of tragic theater, exact science, and ethical philosophy seriously as writings, but only because he sees them in their close attachment to life itself.

Acknowledgments

BOOKS ARE AS LITTLE autonomous as human beings. This book, no exception, is the result of many debts. The chapter on Plato's *Meno* owes much to the interpretation of Leo Strauss presented in a course on the dialogue at the University of Chicago in the spring of 1966. While I did not attend the course, studying a transcript provided the direction for my own understanding of the *Meno*. Richard Kennington's interpretation of Descartes' *Discourse on Method* presented in articles, classes, and in private conversation was decisive for my reading of the *Discourse*. The measure of what I have learned from Kennington about Descartes cannot adequately be indicated by citation. His work deserves to be the standard against which to measure all other Cartesian scholarship. Finally, Seth Benardete and I read the *Ajax* together in the fall of 1980. He also kindly made available to me his notes for the course he offered on the play in the summer of 1981. I am doubly grateful. A good deal of the first chapter emerged first in conversations with him. Benardete especially helped me to understand the importance of enmity in the play, and the importance of Hades. The degree to which these two figure in my own argument gives some small indication of the extent to which I am indebted to him.

Several people read all or part of this work at various of its stages. I want especially to thank for their thoughtful comments Robert Berman, Ronna Burger, Richard Velkley, and, once again, Seth Benardete. My wife, Susan Davis, has read or listened to this work with helpful criticisms at every stage of its composition. I am also grateful to George Kimball Plochmann, Professor Emeritus of Philosophy at Southern Illinois University, and editor of the present series. Virtually every page of this book has been improved by his criticisms. Sarah Lawrence College generously provided two grants for the preparation of the manuscript. Chapter 2 originally appeared in somewhat different form as "Politics and Madness" in *Greek Tragedy and Political Theory*. I thank the University of California Press for permission to include it in this volume.

*Ancient Tragedy and the
Origins of Modern Science*

I

Introduction

Many the uncanny things, but nothing comes more uncanny
than man.

—Sophocles, *Antigone* 332

IF A GOOD BOOK is like an animal,[1] its parts fitting together with the same
necessity as the parts of a living body, an introduction would seem to be at
best superfluous and, at worst, like an autopsy performed in order to prove
that the patient is alive. What applies to introductions should apply equally
to interpretations, and so to books about books. Nevertheless, this is a book
about three other books: Sophocles' *Ajax*, Descartes' *Discourse on Method*,
and Plato's *Meno*. While by any account they are important, alive, there is
no end of argument about what gives them life. That they have purposes is
clearer than the nature of the purposes they have. Purposiveness and obscurity
mixed in this way make them seductive. The three are bound together by
virtue of being meant to be examples of what they are about. Because their
own seductiveness is meant to be taken as paradigmatic for what is in general
seductive, these books demand interpretation at the same time that they wish
to call attention to the fact that they demand interpretation. If animals, they
are peculiarly self-conscious animals.

Still, one might wonder whether something more than willfullness is responsible for placing interpretations of such different books together. They
are not connected historically. Two are from Greek antiquity; one is from
seventeenth-century France. Two are written by men acknowledged to be
philosophers, one by a tragic poet. Plato and Sophocles use characters, and
say nothing in their own names. Descartes' discourse is written in the first
person singular; he speaks *only* in his own name. On the surface, the three
are not connected thematically. At first glance an autobiographical account
of the founding of the modern scientific method, a dialogic inquiry into the
way virtue is acquired and a tragedy about a hero's madness look to be

altogether unrelated. An introduction would justify itself if it were to justify a second glance.

The most distinctive product of our age is its science, modern science. It was once called the "new" science of nature, which implies that it had a beginning, a genesis. Its founders were a group of men who self-consciously rejected the understanding of nature which they took to be the teaching of antiquity. If science as we understand it is modern, tragedy is not. It seems to grow poorly in modern soil. Ancient tragedy and modern science appear at odds, perhaps even incompatible. But why should that be the case unless there is something incompatible about the worlds they describe? Ancient tragedy and modern science can be paired because they represent alternative answers to the same question. They are both concerned with the question of human autonomy.

Descartes is in general most famous as the founder of modern philosophy and in particular as the author of the sentence "I think; therefore I am."[2] Yet, this, his Archimedean fixed point for moving the world, is initially formulated in a negative way. Descartes cannot deny that he thinks, because even doubting that he thinks is a form of thinking, but that means that our first awareness of ourselves is as doubting, as fundamentally incomplete and imperfect creatures. Modern science is the edifice built on this foundation, its goal, "to render us like masters and possessors of nature."[3] Cartesian science, then, must be understood as a response to this awareness of fundamental imperfection, as an attempt of an essentially incomplete creature to render itself whole. The goal of Descartes' new mathematical physics is autonomy.

Formulated in this way, the issue central to the founding of modern science is very close to the issue that preoccupies ancient tragedy. Sophocles' Ajax is a man who wishes to be autonomous. He will take no assistance from the gods; he thinks that virtue assisted is not virtue at all. Ajax demands that the world perfectly reflect and reward superior virtue, that it be perfectly purposive. Like Descartes he "sees" the connection between mastery of nature and autonomy. Assuming his autonomy, he must assume certain things about nature. When he is passed over in favor of Odysseus in the contest for Achilles' armor, Ajax attempts to slaughter the whole Greek army in revenge. He is prevented from this act of extreme brutality by the intervention of Athena who clouds his vision so that he sees the Greek herds and herdsmen as that army. His action is not villainous. Ajax's perfectly purposive world can recognize neither chance nor the intervention of gods. Being passed over for Odysseus cannot be understood as bad luck in a world in which luck has no status. In a world without chance the good, the instruments of purposiveness, can fail only when failing to exert themselves, that is, only when they are not good. Sophocles' *Ajax* is a play about the absolute character of morality in a world without chance, and it is a play which shows the brutality of such a world. This is a world in which a man would slaughter his commrades in their sleep for failing to recognize his virtue. The beauty of tragedy is its presentation of the moral necessity of chance. Descartes' attack on chance is therefore necessarily an attack on the world as tragedy describes it.

It is not exactly novel to claim that autonomy is the goal of human life. Whether individually or collectively, self-sufficiency as the goal of life has its place in ancient philosophy (e.g., Plato's *Philebus* 19c, Aristotle's *Ethics* 1125a12–16 and *Politics* 1252b27–30), in tragedy quite apart from the *Ajax* (e.g., *Antigone* 332–75), and in Machiavelli's modern science of politics, not to mention Descartes' new science of nature. It is the meaning of the longing for the state of nature and for the experience of the simple sentiment of one's own existence in revery in Rousseau, and it is explicitly at the heart of our moral being in Kant. It is behind issues as apparently diverse as "absolute wisdom" in Hegel, the "withering away of the state" in Marx, and both the "will to power" and the "eternal return of the same" in Nietzsche.

The desire for autonomy is at the heart of what it means to be human, and yet the desire for autonomy is not autonomy. It is perhaps closer to a hatred of being ruled. The obstacle for any project to attain autonomy is that on the one hand no assistance can be received from without, for that would be heteronomy. On the other hand, to attain autonomy from within means to be autonomous already. For that reason Nietzsche saw the problem as "*wie man wird was man ist*," or how one becomes what one is.[4] To be a god might be possible; to become a god is something more difficult.

To become more than you are means necessarily to turn on yourself. The obstacle to any willing is always what is already present, the given. When we turn our wills on ourselves what is given with apparent finality is our past. We are what we are largely because of what we have been. As it seems impossible to change what we have been, it seems impossible to control what we are. Autonomy is therefore limited by the past, and so by time, the nature of which is to pass. Even a turning against the past, attempting to annihilate it, is a sign of dependence on it. We become enslaved by what we hate.

This understanding of the problem of autonomy is largely Nietzsche's.[5] His solution is that each must become responsible for his own past. The only way to become a "self-propelled wheel" is to be one's own parent. Therefore the hardest project for the will is the willing of the "eternal return of the same." If what is about to happen at any moment has happened already an infinite number of times and what has just happened will be repeated an infinite number of times the difference between past and future is confused. To think of myself as the cause of my own future will mean that I am the cause of the recurrence of that future, and so of my own past. The radical character of Nietzsche's solution is a sign of the radical character of the problem. He sees that human autonomy would ultimately require the reconciliation of eternity and temporality, being and becoming, God and man. Nietzsche proclaimed that God is dead but recognized that the same human will which once unconsciously made the son of God and God the same might now understand itself as it once understood God.

All of this is reflected in rather ordinary ways in our everyday lives. Parents commonly hold themselves responsible for things that their children have done. And yet if they are responsible they cannot be responsible, for if they were responsible for their children, they would be in turn the responsibility of their parents. Their humanity guarantees membership in two families, the one they come from and the one they make. Adolescence seems such a tumultuous time of life because it is the felt version of being simultaneously caused and cause. The one means dependence, the other autonomy.

The attempt to be the complete cause of one's fate is the subject of ancient tragedy. Only by committing the most criminal of acts, parricide and incest, can Oedipus collapse the difference between his two families and become whole. His past, the given, becomes confused with that of which he is the cause. The problem of Oedipus is in this way the same as the problem for which the eternal return of the same was meant as a solution. It is also what motivates us to attempt the mastery and possession of nature. Human beings are characterized by their desire to become gods. But anyone who longs to become a god is not a god, and cannot become one. Human life seems to be the essentially self-contradictory desire for autonomy. It seems doomed to frustration.

The human desire for autonomy is experienced as a lack, pointing rather to what we do not want than to what we do want. The desire to be free comes into view first as the desire not to be ruled. It is predictable, then, that when thwarted such a desire should give way to anger. If what thwarts us is perceived as having a will, our anger will be directed toward other men, our enemies. In this way the desire for autonomy is connected to righteous indignation, to justice, and ultimately to the whole of political life. In the extreme case such anger will be directed at the gods. If what thwarts us is perceived as lacking a will, then our anger will be directed at nature, and perhaps at our own natures. It is too simple, and at the same time revealing, to say that the first possibility is the concern of tragedy and its alternative that of modern science. It is too simple because the gods necessarily become an issue for science, as nature necessarily becomes an issue for tragedy. The *Discourse on Method* is at heart antithetical to Christianity, and yet it is a book that takes on the form of Christian apologetics, not in spite of its hostility to Christianity, but because Descartes recognizes that the Christian teaching of the fall of man provides the proper form for the understanding of the problem of human autonomy. The tragedy of Sophocles' *Ajax* begins with his failure to acknowledge the gods. Among other things this means that Ajax cannot understand the difference between convention and nature.

Both the *Discourse on Method* and the *Ajax* are concerned with the problem of autonomy, the former in connection with the new science and the latter in connection with tragedy. But what has Plato's *Meno* to do with this pair? There are a number of hints. Socrates, for example, alludes to Meno's preference for "tragic" answers after Meno has expressed his satisfaction with a particularly "scientific" definition of color (76e). Meno, who is admittedly very beautiful (76b–c, 80c), is also demonstrably vicious (compare 75b with 76a–b); Plato uses Meno's very being to suggest a split between the beautiful and the good. Finally, the gods become thematic insofar as the original question "How is virtue acquired?" receives as its answer divine dispensation. Platonic dialogues resist summary. It is therefore not self-evident that the central concern of the *Meno* is the problem of autonomy, or that Plato has understood before the fact the intimate connection between ancient tragedy and modern science. However, that Plato knows quite well that the two problems are one will be evident from a glance at the *Symposium*.[6]

The *Symposium* immediately strikes us as strange. It is a dialogue about erotic love presented by way of a frame narration. The narrator, Apollodorus, is a self-righteous and angry man who shows his love of Socrates by hating everyone else (172c–173a, 173d–e). In scolding those to whom he is narrating for not living the philosophic life, Apollodorus displays missionary zeal. Philosophy has become for him not so much an irresistible activity as a way to salvation, a moral project. Apollodorus is pushed to philosophy by an awareness of a lack in himself, not pulled to it by its own attractive power. He does not so much love wisdom as hate incompleteness. His nature is our first encounter with what proves to be a fundamental, if indirect, issue in the *Symposium*: *thumos*, anger or spiritedness.[7]

Thumos is both opposed to and connected with *erōs*. The first sign of this fact is the manner in which the conversation of the *Symposium* is supposed to have been transmitted. Apollodorus was not present himself; he heard the account from another lover of Socrates, Aristodemus. As described in the *Symposium*, Aristodemus looks just like the god Eros (173b). In his behavior toward Socrates he shows himself to be a genuine lover (174a–d). Is the dialogue we hear the speech of Aristodemus or is it that of Apollodorus, the speech of *erōs* or of *thumos*? It is clearly both; the two are outwardly indistinguishable. The *Symposium* is a dialogue in which speeches are given in praise of *erōs*, but a speech in praise of *erōs* is not necessarily an erotic speech. To seek to justify *erōs* as the "solution" to the human problem is not to have "fallen" in love. It is rather like deciding that what one really needs is to fall in love. This tension between *erōs* and *thumos* is alluded to by Socrates (174b–c) when he compares the setting of the dialogue, dinner at Agathon's house, to another dinner described in the second book of Homer's *Iliad*,[8] a dinner held for the purpose of planning a war. The *Symposium*, on the surface erotic, is beneath the surface a preparation for war.

The first words of the *Symposium* are crucial in this connection. The words, *dokō moi*, literally, "I seem to me," are uttered by the angry Apollodorus. They are obviously extremely self-regarding and point to the fact that it is possible for me to make an object of myself for myself, to be self-conscious. Autonomy can be a goal for us only because we both love ourselves as we are and seek to make ourselves over. The expression *dokō moi* occurs only three times in the dialogue: here at the beginning introducing the whole account of *erōs*, again at the outset of Eryximachus' speech (186a) raising the question of the relation of *erōs* and art (*technē*), and then in the mouth of Zeus in Aristophanes' speech (190c) introducing an ultimately tragic "solution" to the problem of human *hubris*. Aristophanes and Eryximachus are connected by a comical event (185c–e). When Aristophanes' turn comes he cannot speak owing to a bad case of hiccoughs. Eryximachus, the doctor, prescribes some cures and offers to speak in his stead. The speeches of the two men are therefore interchanged, and so in his oblique way Plato is indicating that they are in some way interchangeable. What the two prove to share with the speech of the angry Apollodorus is that all contain attempts to right an undesirable situation by means of a kind of violence. All prove to contain instances of *thumos*. *Thumos* is the connection between tragedy and science. This issue is most visible in Aristophanes' speech.

Aristophanes presents a myth to account for the origin of *erōs* (189c–193d). Men, he says, were originally spherical in shape. We came in three sexes: male, female and androgyne. We had two faces, four arms, four legs and two sexual organs. We could move either by walking erect as we do now or by extending our members and circling like wheels. Aristophanes is not altogether clear, but it seems as though females laid eggs on the ground where males deposited their sperm. What *is* clear is that there was no sex. These circle-men attack the gods for reasons very dark except that they have "lofty thoughts" (*megala phronēmata*), a phrase earlier in the *Symposium* (182c) associated with tyrannicide. As is always the case when one attacks the gods, the circle-men lose. Zeus decides to punish them by splitting them down the middle so that they will be both weaker and more numerous. That way he will increase the numbers of his worshippers and decrease their potential trouble-making. It is by way of introducing this elegant solution to his problem that Zeus says *dokō moi*—I seem to me. However, Zeus has failed to foresee that these half-men would be so consumed with longing for their sundered halves that upon finding them they would spend all their time hugging and longing to become whole again, so that they would completely forget to eat. To keep the race from dying out Zeus moves our primal ancestors' sexual organs to the front and changes their manner of reproduction so that in this rebellious act of hugging one thing will lead to another, and the result will be not the death of the species but its reproduction. This is the origin of *erōs*.

On the basis of this brief sketch a few remarks can be made. The myth seems at first to be an account of *erōs* as the longing of our impaired natures for their original wholeness. The problem is that it does not explain why the circle-men were so dissatisfied as to revolt in the first place. If we were originally whole why were we rebellious? If our deepest longing is to return to our original condition that condition ought to have been one in which we were content. That Aristophanes' account rests on a paradox of this sort is confirmed by an interpretation of the details of his myth. It becomes clear on several levels that no "other half" exists or ever existed. In any case it is clear that beginning in the second generation there is in principle no possibility of another half. We are born as halves to which there is no natural completion. The significance of this fact is that were we to find what we thought to be our other half, even were we to recombine we would not be satisfied.

For Plato's Aristophanes, then, *erōs* is the illusion that a particular beloved would make us whole and happy, and *erōs* is the essence of man as we know him. *Erōs* saves us from despair. It gives us hope, and it is this hope which makes us happy, paradoxically happier than the circle-men who rebelled against the gods. They rebelled not out of any positive desire for anything, but out of a negative sense of their own incompleteness. Unable to bear not being gods, the circle-men are pushed, not pulled out of paradise. Original man, born of cosmic gods of a pre-Promethean age, is like pre-Promethean man, without hope. Aristophanes' view, then, seems to be that *erōs* is a useful illusion rooted in something deeper, something closer to a general sense of discontent aroused not by looking without, but by looking within. Self-reflection is what is revealed by the expression *dokō moi*, and it is coupled with a general sense of discontent. To overstate it, for Aristophanes *erōs* seems to be a form of *thumos*. In the myth, after cutting the circle-men in half, Zeus orders Apollo to sew them up, gathering the extra skin together like a purse and then to turn their heads toward the wound (190e–191a). Apollo's "gift" thus makes it possible both to couple and to see our navels, the signs of our mortality. The true "gift of Apollo," as his name suggests, is Apollodorus, the angry narrator. *Erōs*, as the attempt to cure the wound of mortality, is an unself-conscious attempt to become autonomous. All love is rooted in self-love, and self-love is just a complicated form of resentment of what is other.

Aristophanes, however, takes us still deeper. *Erōs* is a longing to couple with another human being in order to overcome one's own partiality, in order to become whole. According to Aristophanes' account this wholeness is so desirable as to make us willing to merge completely with our beloved. But this sacrifice of the self in a larger whole is not different in kind from what the political community demands of its citizens. This is the context in which Aristotle cites Aristophanes' speech in *Politics* Book II (1262b10–13).[9] And Aristophanes in the *Symposium* makes a point of connecting the activities of male halves to politics (192a). *Erōs* is indeed a longing for wholeness, but the "objective correlative" of this wholeness is not a circle-man but the *polis*, the political community. The *polis* is a unit in which the self is necessarily suppressed, and ultimately in the perfect *polis* would be lost. There is no difference in principle between combining with one to overcome one's incompleteness and combining with many for the same end. The political community is therefore a vehicle for human autonomy. But insofar as the *polis* is a coming together for the sake of autonomy it is a new rebellion against what the gods represent. Rebelling against our lack of autonomy is a rebellion against the role that chance plays in our lives.

This solution to our incompleteness brings problems of its own. The wholeness of the political order is altogether reactive. The ugly core of patriotism is hatred of what is other. In addition, to form this artificial whole requires obedience to the law. Men must submit to the rule of law for the sake of autonomy or freedom. That is the true meaning of Zeus' knife, that we can be free only by submitting to Zeus, to conventional law. This has rather obvious difficulties as a way to autonomy. The *polis* originates in a longing for freedom, but it can at best be a partial overcoming of our impaired condition. The law is a constant reminder that we must relinquish some of our freedom in order to be free. Political life is, therefore, both the vehicle and the obstacle to human autonomy. But as genuine autonomy is not something that can be approximated (one cannot be almost a god), and as the *polis* originates in this longing for autonomy, the *polis* is at its core tragic. Aristophanes' comedy conceals a deeper tragedy.

The limit to the *polis* as a solution to the human longing for autonomy is death, the sign that we are ultimately incomplete and dependent creatures.

Thumos is really a sense of indignation at the fact that we will die. Love of immortality is rooted in this indignation. *Thumos* makes its home most naturally in the political sphere, but, as Aristophanes' speech makes clear, to fight mortality requires more than the *polis*. This need to go beyond political life is the root of both Cartesian science and Christianity, and is anticipated by Plato in the speech of Eryximachus, the doctor, who utters the third *dokō moi*. In reversing the order of the speeches here we simply follow Plato's hint that although cosmology appears before politics, it is in fact derivative.

It is at first difficult to understand why Eryximachus' utterance belongs with the other two. He is a rather unprepossessing man, solid but without much dash, and not particularly harsh or angry. The clue to his inclusion is the dramatic date of the *Symposium*. At about the time of Agathon's victory with his first tragedy in the year 415 (the *Symposium* is of course a celebration of that victory) the Hermes statues, traditional symbols of the democracy, were defaced. In the subsequent inquiry evidence of other defacings and of profanations of the mysteries was discovered. Along with Phaedrus and Alcibiades, Eryximachus was charged.[10] According to Thucydides those involved were said to be young men enjoying themselves after they had had too much to drink, a description not altogether inappropriate to the *Symposium* itself.[11] Like Aristophanes, Eryximachus has something to do with an attack, albeit a failed one, on the gods. His is the first speech to point to the true dimensions of the problem. *Erōs* has to do with longing for freedom, with not being threatened from without. True autonomy, therefore, would require full mastery of the whole, a sort of universal tyranny. Accordingly, Eryximachus' speech is an attempt to give an account of an art, or *technē*, dealing with the whole.

Eryximachus says "I seem to me (*dokō moi*) to have seen from medicine, my own art (*technē*), how great and wondrous the god is, and how his reach extends to everything concerning both human and divine matters" (186a–b). Love has cosmic consequences (the divine seems for Eryximachus to include all that is not human). At the same time he discovers the universality of the sway of *erōs* by looking to himself, to his own art. This dual perspective is the heart of the problem with his speech. Eryximachus takes over this problem from the previous speaker.

> Well, it seems necessary for me, since Pausanias, although starting his speech beautifully, did not sufficiently end it, that I must try to put an end on the speech. Since Eros is double, it is beautiful to divide him. (186a)

Pausanias had divided *erōs* into that which is *kalos*, beautiful or noble, and that which is *aischros*, ugly or base (180c–e), but finally could not justify his sexual appetites on the basis of his account of the beautiful love. Indeed, his praise of the beautiful *erōs* was so elevated as to make it impossible for him to justify any form of sexual activity whatsoever. Pausanias' motive was altogether at odds with the content of his praise. His speech consequently needed a *telos*, an end or purpose, and so Eryximachus begins with an understanding of the necessity to give due regard to the body and its individual passion. While an account removing from love all selfishness is no longer about love, the distinction between noble and base would seem to require that *erōs* be directed toward more than bodily pleasure. The body which Eryximachus restores as the locus of love must therefore be interpreted anew.

To begin with medicine, a remedial *technē*, is to begin with the body as defective. Its sick and healthy elements wage war against each other. The noble *erōs* at first seems grounded in the conditions for the gratification of the healthy elements of the body, the base in those of the diseased. Health, however, is presented as the consequence of medicine, "knowledge of the erotic matters of the body with regard to repletion and evacuation" (186c–d). Since any element of the body may desire either repletion or evacuation, these objects of *erōs* cannot be used to distinguish the base from noble love. Repletion and evacuation, the alternating beloveds of the body, are in themselves neutral to the distinction between health and sickness. On this account both base *erōs* and noble seem equally natural—the distinction between them artificial. Only from the perspective of the body as a whole is it possible to talk about health and disease, but then it becomes necessary to find a standard outside of the body to support the distinction between noble and base. Eryximachus must therefore change his ground. The body is not the lover and repletion and evacuation the beloveds; rather, within the body is an opposition of lovers. Medicine has as its task the harmonizing of this opposition. However, none of the elements within the body, strictly speaking, love this harmony which is thus not a natural beloved, but, as the result of *technē*, artificial. The body, at odds within itself, does not even desire that the struggle cease. Neutral *technē* effects a desirable, but unnatural, peace. Eryximachus, therefore begins his account with medicine because the body is by nature sick. It does not know what it desires as a whole, because it is naturally many and only artificially whole. Our original condition here, no less than in Aristophanes' speech, is one of sickness and disharmony in which we are not even capable of diagnosing our malady. Only a godlike doctor (Eryximachus points out at 186e that medicine has divine origins) could provide the proper perspective for our cure. It is no wonder, then, that Eryximachus plans to praise *erōs* and his art simultaneously. It would seem that without medicine, *erōs* would be a tragic, perpetual longing with no possibility of satisfaction.

On the other hand, the problem is not so easily solved as the structure of Eryximachus' speech indicates. After the introduction of the problem of the double love the speech divides roughly into three parts, each of which then treats its subject in a double manner. Eryximachus discusses medicine (186c–187a) as both diagnostic or theoretical and as applied or practical. He then discusses music (187a–188a) first as theoretical, the science of proportion, and then as practical. Finally (188a–e), he discusses astronomy as the science of the heavens, including what we would call meteorology, and divination as the "science" by which we influence the gods. The structure seems at first haphazard, but each part makes the next part necessary. By making *erōs* a cosmic principle applying to body as such and not simply human or animal bodies, the range of the *technē* which deals with *erōs* must also be extended. Medicine must give way to a science dealing with harmony as such. One wonders, then, why Eryximachus did not simply introduce mathematics. The answer seems to have something to do with his twofold intention. The praise of his art requires that medicine be reinterpreted as the science of proportion, but the praise of pederastic *erōs* requires that he not leave the human sphere altogether behind. The distinction between theoretical and practical, first present in the section on medicine, is repeated here on the level of music. By calling theoretical music, not mathematics, the science of proportion, Eryximachus conceals the fact that the only art or science able to provide an account of harmony sufficiently neutral to be applicable indifferently to all elements of the cosmos is indifferent to those elements. Eryximachus saw that Pausanias' speech had to be given a *telos*, an end, but he is hard-pressed to provide one. He does not know whether he wishes to use the noble love to harmonize the conflicting base loves, in which case, by virtue of its neutrality, it ceases to be love, or to harmonize the noble and base loves in which case the noble love ceases to be noble. Effecting harmony, let us say mastery of nature, requires a science not hindered by the erotic, hence biased, character of human vision. Such a science, powerful because it has no *telos*, is for the same reason directionless. One does not really know what a harmony is unless one can *hear* it, even though hearing it guarantees that one has heard imperfect harmony. Practical music is important for Eryximachus because it marks his recognition that theoretical music, where "as yet the double love is not" (187c), is not the science he is seeking. The highest science would have to combine the neutrality of mathematics with purposiveness.

A science designed to bring harmony to the whole of the cosmos would have to deal with all bodies, near and far. Astronomy is the diagnostic or theoretical part of this science. It reveals to us that there are remote things which have important effects on us. Through astronomy we are able to learn of forthcoming floods, droughts, and so forth, but it is only diagnostic. It enables us to predict disasters of all kinds, but to prevent them we would have to possess a science, comparable to practical medicine and practical music, that is capable of manipulating the heavens. For this reason Eryximachus is forced to end his speech with the *technē* of divination, represented here as a sort of business relation between gods and men. Aristophanes began with godlike men who were then split down the middle, disharmonized. Eryximachus began with the natural disharmony of man, and ends with the *technē* which is supposed to make him godlike. Aristophanes is necessary to correct Eryximachus' failure to think through the question of the possibility of this final *technē*. In the absence of evidence to the contrary we must assume that the gods to whom Eryximachus would appeal are the gods of the city, the Olympian gods. But his belief in them is at best questionable. Eryximachus, one of those implicated in the profanation of the mysteries, is a sophisticated member of the Athenian intellectual set.[12] Still, his appeal to the gods, however ironic, is necessary because Eryximachus' praise of *technē* has reached its limit in chance (chance is, of course, responsible for Eryximachus' speaking when he does). That it should master chance would be the highest praise of *technē*, but in the end Eryximachus cannot bestow such praise. He fails to give an account of a science which could master the whole from within, and so is forced to invent the "science" of divination. Knowing how to manipulate the gods gives us a kind of control over what they control. But Eryximachus is forced, therefore, to appeal to the very gods against whom it is necessary to rebel if one is to be autonomous. Feeling himself at the mercy of chance, he invents beings more powerful than he to master chance. Thereafter he is at the mercy of these beings.

Eryximachus is not conscious of the tragedy of his speech—the conflict between his cosmic account and his human preference. This lack of self-consciousness is indicated in the drama of the dialogue. He begins his speech by prescribing several cures for Aristophanes' hiccoughs. The prescription calls for much sneezing and gargling. Since Aristophanes is cured by only the most radical application of these cures, and then only after some time (189a), it is obvious that Eryximachus' sober and somewhat pedantic speech has been accompanied throughout by an array of sound effects guaranteed to produce laughter. He seems not even to be aware of this comedy of opposition. This inability to recognize the comic character of his own art has something to do with his failure to grasp the tragedy of his attempt in praising his art to push it beyond he limits of what is possible.

Eryximachus fails, but he does point the way. His speech points to the fundamental problem for a science which sets as its goal the mastery and possession of nature: to achieve a perspective from which any such mastery is possible while not undermining the perspective from which it is desirable. This science would be a response to the injustice of our original, that is, our present, condition, and would understand itself as an alternative to politics as a means to autonomy. Recognizing the gods or God as both an obstacle to and a model for the transformation of nature, this science would represent a primal rebellion against the way things are, against the given. It is not rash to suggest that Descartes takes up this Eryximachean project for righting the injustices of the natural order. Eryximachus did not understand the tension between his praise of his art and his erotic disposition because he failed to understand what it means that all men must have an erotic disposition of some sort—a partial perspective. As one can never simply separate oneself from nature, any attempted mastery of nature will always have a double concern. The *pursuit* of autonomy reveals this doubleness, and provides the connection between the two great themes of the *Discourse on Method*, Christianity and mathematical physics.[13]

What, then, is it that ancient tragedy and modern science share which justifies their pairing? Both are reflections of, and reflections on, the attempt to extend human dominion to the whole, and so, to politicize the whole. Sophocles' Ajax sees the *polis* as the whole. Descartes will be concerned with the human tendency to see the whole as a *polis*. Both encounter the difficulty which we have seen in outline in Plato's *Symposium* and which will prove central to the *Meno*. Both need the gods as a measure of what it would mean to rule the whole while at the same time resenting the gods as signs of our inabililty to rule the whole. The ability to say *dokō moi*, I seem to me, makes the human striving for autonomy possible, while appearing to make its achievement impossible. Ancient tragedy and modern science are both expressions of this theological-political problem.

2

Ancient Tragedy: Sophocles' Ajax[1]

Ajax feared to measure himself against Achilles and defied
Jupiter, because he knew Achilles and did not know Jupiter.

—Rousseau, *Emile* IV

SOPHOCLES' *AJAX* IS SIMPLE—on the surface. Ajax is a big, strong, dependable, not very imaginative or bright warrior, second best only to Achilles
in the *Iliad*. His valor is unquestionable and unalterable. Ajax is not fickle;
he is steady and steadfast, always there to defend when the Greeks are attacked.
A great defensive fighter, Ajax is celebrated for his seven-fold shield. When
Achilles is killed it is not surprising that Ajax expects to be acknowledged
as the best remaining warrior. He had fought Hector to a standstill in hand-
to-hand single combat. They had exchanged gifts in mutual admiration. Ajax'
expectation, however, is thwarted. Angered, he resolves to gain his just honor
by killing the entire army which denied him Achilles' armor, with especially
brutal deaths for the leaders, Agamemnon and Menelaus, and Odysseus who
received Achilles' armor in his stead. Athena restrains Ajax (as she had
restrained Achilles in *Iliad* I) by making him mistakenly see the Greek herds
as the army. When Ajax discovers that he has slaughtered domesticated animals
rather than warriors he kills himself. The rest of the play concerns the question
of his burial. Agamemnon and Menelaus want to leave his corpse for the
birds and dogs as punishment, while his half-brother, Teucer, insists on burial.
Odysseus intervenes in this contest to see that his former enemy is buried.
While all of this is superficially clear, the heart of the play is extremely dark—
it is all but closed to us. Its external simplicity hides its internal complexity
from view. The event which would seem to make sense of everything else,
the attempt of Ajax to slaughter the whole Greek army, does not itself make
sense. To understand that event is to understand the peculiar character of the
madness of Ajax. But to understand Ajax we have to look first to Odysseus.

I

The play opens with the word *always* uttered by an invisible goddess.

Always, son of Laertes, have I seen you hunting to snatch some advantage against your enemies. (1–2)[2]

In light of Ajax' later claims about the etymology of his name (430) the first word, *aei*, is suggestive. Ajax, the steady, is always there to defend the Greeks from their enemies. Here, however, the word is systematically ambiguous. It might mean that Athena is always looking at Odysseus, or it might mean that Odysseus is always hunting, trying to snatch some advantage from his enemies. If the latter, Athena would have characterized Odysseus as essentially an enemy, a man *always* at odds with other men. Later Athena and Odysseus together will suggest that to be a man (*anēr*) means to be an enemy.

ATHENA: Was he not a man (*anēr*) before?
ODYSSEUS: Indeed, enemy to this man, and still is.

97 (77–78)

What Odysseus is always doing in general he is here, at the beginning, doing in particular. Odysseus is tracking. The purpose of the tracking seems to be to determine whether Ajax is inside his tent, although it is hard to see why Odysseus does not simply look to determine if Ajax is there. Odysseus either prefers, or is forced, to learn by signs—he reads the event by way of the tracks left by Ajax and the animals (32)—what Athena knows directly.

Tell me for the sake of what you have set out so earnestly, in order that from one who knows [has seen] you may learn. (12–13)

Athena can see not only Odysseus; she can also see Ajax. What Athena "sees" reveals some of the difficulty of "looking" inside the tent. Athena has discerned not only Odysseus' actions, the tracking, but also his intention, his wish to find out whether Ajax is "within or not within." This phrase, *eit 'endon eit' ouk endon*, can also mean that Odysseus is attempting to learn whether Ajax is sane or not, whether he is in his right mind.[3] What Odysseus cannot see and must learn by signs, and what it takes a god to see, is the inside of Ajax.

The action of the *Ajax* is utterly unintelligible without this first scene. Without divine intervention we would never have been sure of Ajax' motives, and without his motives his actions might have appeared simply pathetic, the deeds of a once great man now hopelessly mad. Odysseus, in a similar position, must resort to reading signs to determine whether Ajax is an enemy. Had he looked inside the tent Odysseus would have learned little more. This is confirmed by the account of Tecmessa, the wife of Ajax. She can see what

Odysseus would have seen had he looked (233–44), and she thinks Ajax is mad. Without Athena every attempt to look inside Ajax would have yielded a new outside. To look at the inside of a man is as hard as looking at the inside of a body. Having opened it, its inside has become its outside. One does not learn a man's motives by dissecting his corpse. Knowledge of motives apparently requires indirection, something like tracking. Such knowledge will be imperfect; perfection requires the intervention of a god. Athena will not only tell Odysseus what Ajax' motives for the slaughter were but also stage a conversation in which those motives become clear. By calling Ajax out in such a way that he reveals his inside to Odysseus she will turn him inside out without destroying the character of his inside.

Odysseus can hear but not see Athena, recognizing her from her voice. Later Ajax will be seen by Odysseus, but will not see him, and it is clear that were Odysseus to speak Ajax would have heard him. Athena tells him to "Stand silent in order that you may stay where you are" (87). She puts him in the position of a god with regard to Ajax.

When Tecmessa gives her account of the madness of Ajax she includes her version of his conversation with Athena (301–4). To her it looks as though Ajax is talking with an invisible shadow (*skia*), and she takes that as confirmation of his madness. Odysseus' behavior would look like that as well, were we not privy to the voice of a goddess. Talking to gods looks like madness.

The limits of human sight are emphasized by what Odysseus relates to Athena. Odysseus knows that the herds (and the herdsmen as well) have been slaughtered, and suspects that Ajax did it. But he is puzzled because the deed is so unintelligible, literally invisible (*askopon*, 21). Everyone says that Ajax did it, and there is even a witness who saw Ajax bounding alone across the plain. But Odysseus has doubts which will be confirmed by what Athena tells him. The human *optēr*, or witness, saw what could not have been the case. Odysseus can tell from the confusion of tracks that Ajax did not return "alone," and it is unlikely that he "bounded" (*pedōnta*, 30) across the plain with a herd of sheep and cattle tethered (*desmoisi*, 62) behind him. Odysseus' indirect knowledge turns out to be more reliable than human vision, but it is flawed because it cannot lead to certainty about whether Ajax killed the animals, and if he did, why he did. Athena solves both problems rather quickly. Ajax did it, and he thought he was slaughtering the whole army.

Athena's description of the slaughter is peculiar in two ways. One might overtranslate her remark to Odysseus at 39 to mean that "these deeds of this man are yours." And when Odysseus asks at 38 whether he toils (*ponō*) to some purpose, the *ponō* is soon to be echoed by the *phonō*, murder, used in describing Ajax' action at 43. In a general way, then, it is clear that the whole description of the deed of Ajax is paralleled by the deed, also cut short by Athena, with which the play begins. Both Ajax and Odysseus move against their enemies in stealth. Both are like hounds. Both sneak up on tents and never quite reach the door because Athena steps in. We are led to wonder whether this similarity of the actions of Odysseus and Ajax is mere coincidence. Was Odysseus about to murder Ajax? The play begins with this strange ambiguity. We thought we knew what Odysseus was doing, but what he intends is not at all clear. He may have to rely on signs to know the inside of Ajax, but we are in a similar position with regard to Odysseus. Athena restrains Odysseus with her voice, with speech, while in the *Iliad* (Book I, 197) she had restrained Achilles with a combination of force and speech, pulling him by the hair to prevent him from killing Agamemnon. Ajax apparently cannot be restrained by his inside through speech, but only by a vision, by transforming the outside so that his action is not what he intended it to be.

There is another peculiarity of Athena's account. One can imagine the hatred of Ajax for the Greeks expressed to himself in terms which portray his enemies as less than human, for example, as sheep. Athena simply makes this internal metaphor of anger and enmity real. Was Ajax about to treat the whole Greek army as though they were beasts? Then she will turn the beasts into his enemies. By turning him inside out, Athena makes the anger of Ajax visible to all. When made visible it looks mad, but if invisible it seems understandable. In a way, Athena has simply shown Odysseus that Ajax is really sane. Like Odysseus he was seeking to get the advantage of his enemy. Still, the character of his anger is peculiar. At first, the significance of Athena's action seems to be that she has succeeded in showing the incapacity of Ajax to distinguish between men and beasts. That has something to do with his unwillingness to recognize the gods (758–77). But this unwillingness is rooted in the fact that his own virtue is suspect so long as it depends upon the gods for support.

> Father, with the aid of the gods, even one who is nothing, as well as one mighty, would triumph but I have been persuaded that even without them I will win fame. (766-69)

Of all the Greek heroes Ajax alone scorns the help of the gods. It is this for which he is punished by Athena. At second glance we see that there is something more subtle about the inability of Ajax to distinguish the human from the bestial. Since he slaughters the herdsmen as well as the herds, his madness must involve seeing everything as human. That everything looks human to Ajax means that everything is seen as having purposes or intentions.

One could say that for Ajax the world is fully moral. Wherever he faces opposition of any sort he faces an enemy. As there is no such thing as chance in his world, Ajax never thinks of the possibility of trying again, once his first attempt to kill the army has failed. Having failed once, he has failed simply, for if there is no chance, he can have been defeated only because of his essential inferiority. Now, if all opposition means enmity, then the appropriate response to opposition is anger. The *Ajax* is therefore a play about the absolute character of enmity in a world that is entirely purposive.

All of this sets the stage for the appearance of Ajax himself. Athena says she will show Odysseus the disease of Ajax so as to make it "apparent all around" (*periphanē*, 66), so that having "looked in" (*eisidōn*) he will be able to tell all the Greeks.[4] Later she taunts him with the suggestion that he might be afraid to see a madman all around (*periphanōs . . . idein*, 81). Odysseus never reveals the source of his knowledge to the Greeks, although he tells them its content, allowing them to think that in his usual wily fashion he has deduced the intentions of Ajax. He not only fails to mention Athena; he also suppresses what she emphasizes, the *periphanēs* character of the knowledge she supplies him. That kind of knowledge is supposed to enable Odysseus to laugh at his enemy—the sweetest kind of laughter, according to Athena. Why that should be the case is at first hard to see, but seems linked to the godlike perspective from which Odysseus is to be allowed to view his enemy. To see inside of Ajax and to see him all around while remaining unseen himself, saps Odysseus' enmity of its harshness. Because to be a man (*anēr*) is to be an enemy, Odysseus seems to fear that he will lose himself. That is not a foolish fear, given the subsequent fate of Ajax. It is only because a god contrives to give him a godlike perspective that Odysseus remains to observe Ajax. Otherwise he would wish to be *ektos*, literally outside, or in the context of the *Ajax*, mad. The two alternatives to ordinary enmity seem to be madness and divinity.[5]

Ajax is called away by Athena from torturing the captured animals which he takes to be Odysseus, Menelaus, and Agamemnon. Unlike Odysseus, he apparently both sees and hears her. Everything is visible to Ajax in human form. In torturing the animals he wreaks vengeance on what he takes to be his enemies' bodies, their outsides. Athena, on the other hand, avenges herself through his mind. Ajax cannot be sure that for all his torture those he thinks he is torturing will regret what they have done, while Athena, by getting inside Ajax, can be sure that he will have regrets. Since he has not done what he thought himself to have done, when he regains his sanity he will be doubly ashamed; to become aware of Athena's deception is to become aware that her sort of battle is superior to his, that the mind is stronger than the body.

But if that is so, if the inside is stronger than the outside, then Ajax was rightly denied Achilles' armor. This is the second cause of his shame.

Ajax lost to the wily Odysseus in the contest of arms even though he was by general agreement the stronger fighter. We are not told why Odysseus won, but his superior wisdom consists here in knowing even before Athena demonstrates her power over Ajax, that the gods can do anything (86). Odysseus does not confuse gods with men. He knows the best man does not always win because the invisible gods affect the outcome of human battles, or, what here amounts to the same thing, because chance has its effect in human affairs. Athena, however, indicates the superiority of Ajax by calling him *pronousteros* (119), more wise, prudent, or possessing foresight. Because he is clearly not wise in any ordinary sense, let alone wiser than all others, and because he seems the least likely of the Greek heroes to deserve the epithet *pronousteros*, his superior foresight must have some other meaning.

How are we to understand this peculiar description of Ajax? His steadiness in battle seems to have to do with his failure of imagination. Ajax is most dependable because of all the Greek warriors he comes closest to having no inside. He is least subject to panic and delusion, least inclined to shrink from imagined horrors or, having rashly underestimated the strength of the enemy, to be surprised and then defeated by his enemy's real strength. Similarly, because Ajax cannot be inspired by a god he will never show greater strength than one might have expected. That Ajax is *pronousteros*, then, means that he is least subject to delusion with regard to himself. Athena seems to suggest that if even he has an inside, then having such an inside must be a universal human trait. To say that Ajax is *pronousteros* means that for the gods his is the hardest case: the man who does not recognize the divine.

That he talks to Athena, even calls her an ally, seems to belie this interpretation, but he treats her only a little better than he treats Tecmessa, his captive woman. Although a goddess, Athena is his helper; she is *always* to him *summachos* (117), a word the Athenians use to designate the smaller cities assisting them in their wars. For Ajax to talk to Athena as though she were beneath him is tantamount to denying her divinity. Once again Ajax sees only the human. He sees both beasts and gods as men. He would have perfect foresight in a world as solid and predictable as he. As it is, the epithet given him by Athena is more than a little ironic.

Because Ajax sees only the human, and does not acknowledge the power of chance, he sees only the intentional, the purposive. His world is one in which the best man always wins. That is what it means for him to say that Athena is *always* his ally. Admittedly, Ajax is the best man, as even Odysseus acknowledges without hesitation at the end of the play.

To me this man was the worst enemy in [or, of] the army from the time
when I won the arms of Achilles. But for all that he was such to me, I
would not dishonor him in return by not saying that I see him to be the
best single man save Achilles of all the Argives who came to Troy.

(1336-41)

The world of Ajax is one in which the good prevail. Perfect foresight in such
a world only requires knowing who the good are. He justly considers himself
the best after Achilles, and so does not doubt himself at all. This lack of
doubt is the necessary prerequisite for his lacking an inside. Ajax can be a
superficial man because his is a superficial world, one suited well for sight,
but not at all for speech. It is a world in which there is no difference between
being and seeming. Still, he cannot be closed to the fact that it is a world in
which there are conflicts, and so winners and losers, and conflicts indicate at
least temporary disturbances of that perfect order. Ajax needs the possibility
of such disturbances to justify his initial loss of the armor. But he needs it
more significantly to justify war at all, and so to justify his excellence in war.
His plan to punish the whole Greek army, therefore, is not simply the result
of wounded pride. If there is no punishment beyond the human, then his
punishment of the Greeks is the necessary condition for the morality of the
world. What Athena's trick has allowed us to see is that the substance of the
madness of Ajax is its excessive morality. Ajax treats men as though they
were beasts, not because he is immoral, but because he is too moral. To
justify his anger he must consider his enemies all bad, much as he considers
himself all good. It is almost to make them into a different species. Given
his view of the world, an enemy is someone for whom Ajax could never feel
pity. This is the source of his brutality.

Athena has forced Odysseus to see this brutality in Ajax. That is why the
opening scene ends unexpectedly in Odysseus' expression of pity for his
enemy.

I pity him in his wretchedness, although he is my foe because he is
yoked together with an ill doom, seeing his no more than my own.
(121–24)

He sees his own nature in Ajax, and so concludes that we are nothing but
images or shadows (126). The being of images and shadows consists in their
pointing beyond themselves: they are not what they are. They are not superficial. Odysseus and Ajax are alike, for both are "always hunting to snatch
some advantage against their enemies." The difference between them, however, is that Odysseus sees the fragility of taking one's bearings by enmity.
In various ways the remainder of the play is concerned with understanding

why Ajax takes his bearings by enmity. If we have thus far understood the character of his madness we have yet to understand the necessity for going mad.

II

The world in which the intentional, the moral, reigns supreme is the political world. Whether it be the City of God or the City of Man, a fully purposive world is one understood in essentially political terms. In such a world men are fully responsible for their actions and so are justly held accountable for them. The good are thus thought to be worthy of praise, and not simply fortunate. That Ajax sees only the human means that he sees only the city, the *polis*; but since there is more than the *polis* in the world, whether articulated in terms of chance or of the divine, Ajax' view of the world will be distorted. This distortion will be instructive to us because it is peculiarly political. Because it seems from its own perspective to be self-sufficient, it confuses itself with the natural. The perennial danger of the *polis* is that it will take its view to be all-inclusive (*periphanēs*), and so take itself too seriously, thereby suffering something analogous to the fate of Ajax. It runs the risk of madness and brutality. For Sophocles, the Trojan War means that at the very moment that Greeks come to think of themselves as Greeks, they run the risk of thinking of their enemies as subhuman. All who do not share their language and the way of life of those who speak the language will be enemies— barbarians. It is no accident that in taunting Teucer as the offspring of a non-Greek mother, Menelaus calls him a slave. That non-Greeks are slaves by nature means that they are not really men. They are subhuman. What unifies the Greeks, therefore, threatens to brutalize them. This, the fundamental political problem, is also the problem of Ajax.

Ajax shares the goal of all Homeric heroes, "always to be the best and to be preeminent above others." It is a goal—let us call it virtue—which is intrinsically aristocratic and which the political order must encourage for its own survival. The Trojan War is the story of the dependence of the small on the great, and finally on the greatest of all, Achilles. But Achilles, and Ajax after him, are problematically related to the *polis*. The goal which is collectively set for virtue is that the greatest man is the man who is a law unto himself, autonomous. When Achilles reenters the fighting, he fights for his own purposes and not those of the Greeks.

Ajax is aware of this dependence of the small on the great, but altogether unaware of its corollary, the dependence of the great on the small. The chorus know all about this latter dependence.

Forming such whispered speeches,
Odysseus brings them to the ears of all
and is especially persuasive. For concerning
you now he says things easy to believe.
And each listener rejoices more than the teller,
despising your sorrows. For aiming at great
souls, you will not miss. But someone saying
such things about me would not be persuasive.
For envy creeps up on the powerful.
And yet, the small apart from the great
become a perilous tower of defense
The little with the great would be best,
the great upheld by those smaller.

(148–61)

The chorus look to Ajax for protection, but at the same time are aware that
he is in an awkward position because of the power of rumor. The chorus
imply that since the great alone are always subject to rumor, the "great kings"
(188) Menelaus and Agamemnon are as vulnerable to them as Ajax has proven
to be to the rumors of Odysseus. But rumor is simply the less pleasant
consequence of the honor Ajax demands (98). Far from being autonomous,
Ajax unwittingly depends for what he most values on those whom he despises.
The chorus tacitly identify Ajax as thoughtless by making it clear that it is
the thoughtless who cannot see this mutual dependence (162). Ajax is unaware
of the consequences of a view of virtue essentially comparative. Achilles did
not share the plight of Ajax because he never had to contest his position as
best. Ajax is in the peculiar position of wanting to prove himself the best,
where best means better than all the rest of the Greeks, and of wanting his
own bestness acknowledged. Yet the only way to prove that he is best is to
slaughter the very army on which he depends for the honor he seeks. Ajax
is unaware of the extent to which he depends on the city. His suicide, therefore,
may well be simply a self-aware version of the attempt to slaughter the army.
Without his knowing it, the initial action of Ajax was also a kind of suicide.

Still, he is not entirely to blame. The city itself necessarily encourages a
notion of virtue pointing beyond the political altogether. Accordingly, in his
last speech Ajax traces all his problems back to the *monomachia* with Hector.

For from the time when I received in my hand this gift from Hector, my
greatest foe, no longer have I had any trust from the Argives.

(661–63)

Accepting Hector's sword now replaces the slaying of the animals as the
primary reason for the suicide of Ajax. At first Ajax had fought Hector for
the honor of the Greeks, but the exchange of gifts when neither could defeat

the other represents a crucial change. His admiration for Hector means that Ajax recognized that in some way he shares more with his greatest foe than he does with the Greeks for whom he was fighting. From the perspective of the *polis*, then, the exchange of gifts was the first sign that Ajax was not entirely trustworthy. Accepting Hector's sword is merely a milder version of attempting to slaughter the whole army. Both display an Ajax who fights for his own ends to the exclusion of the common ends. But just as the attempted slaughter represents a kind of suicide, so does having accepted the sword. Having implicitly undermined the order which established Hector as enemy and the Greeks as friends, Ajax confuses the distinction between friend and enemy and therewith his own virtue. Ajax must have friends in order to have enemies. The problem becomes clearest when he makes a direct appeal to Achilles.

> And yet this much I think I know full well. If while alive Achilles were to have judged concerning his arms to whom they belonged in terms of excellence in might, no other would have laid hold of them before me.
>
> (441–44)

Of course if Achilles were alive no one would get his armor. So long as Achilles lived he was a competitor of Ajax. Two cannot be "best and pre-eminent above all others." Only in death can there be a mutuality of interest between Ajax and Achilles.

The confusion of friendship and enmity is in some way the deepest issue of the play. Ajax first addresses the chorus as *philoi*, friends, and then asks them to kill him (349–61). Athena, a goddess particularly dear or friendly to Odysseus (14), holds particular enmity toward Ajax. Tecmessa, who appeals to Ajax on the basis of those who are dear or friendly to him, as his captive woman, was formerly his enemy. Odysseus, for whom Ajax holds the deepest enmity, treats him as a friend at the end of the play. Menelaus, on whose behalf the Greeks came to Troy, and Agamemnon, who leads them, are at first the embodiments of what friendship seems to mean for Ajax (i.e., those for whom one will fight), but end by being almost the greatest of his enemies. His half-brother Teucer and his son Eurysaces are more complicated cases. The other characters point to the instability of friendship and enmity by moving from one to the other. Teucer, in whom Ajax places his principal trust, and Eurysaces, about whom he seems to care the most, are both the offspring of non-Greek women, that is, of women who were once enemies. Teucer and Eurysaces are proofs of the falsity of the view which understands enemies as a different species. Common humanity makes itself visible in the phenomenon of the half-breed. This seems to be why half-breeds are particularly prone to that social ostracism rooted in the city's sense of its own naturalness.

Nowhere is the confusion of friendship and enmity which saturates this play more present than in the speeches of Ajax. His first speech of any length begins with the famous reflection on the etymology of his name, *Aias* in Greek (430–40). He makes a connection between it and *aiai*. It is appropriate that he who suffers so much should be named by the verb which means to bemoan (*aiazō*). Ajax begins with his characteristic mistake, seeing intention where there is only chance. This mistake allows him to collapse the difference between a conventional name and a natural pathos. Collapsing the difference between convention (*nomos*) and nature (*phusis*) is, of course, the necessary condition for seeing one's own *polis* as natural, and so its enemies as natural enemies. However, it brings with it certain difficulties.

> Lift him, lift him here. He will not, I suppose, fear this fresh slaughter if in the things passed through the father he is rightly [justly] mine. But he must at once be broken into the rough customs (*nomois*) of his father and made like his nature. (545–49)

Holding his son, Eurysaces, up to the sight of the just-slain animals is designed by Ajax both as a proof that the boy's nature is like his father's and as a means of habituating him in the customs, laws, or conventions (*nomois*) of his father. That the latter is necessary at all seems to be a sign that nature and *nomos* are not simply the same. The difficulty for Ajax is that he is now the enemy of the gods, hated by the Greek army, and hated (*echthei*) by all Troy (457–59). Ajax is hated by all humans whether understood as divine, human, or bestial. He is therefore an enemy to all men. The consequence of his being *ektos*, outside or mad, is that he is an object of hate (*echthos*). For Ajax, the great defensive fighter, to act virtuously in this situation means for him to fight back. However, he cannot attack the Greeks without aiding the Trojans and he cannot attack the Trojans without aiding the Greeks. Ajax' position is doubly difficult. While one cannot have friends without enemies, apparently it is also impossible to have enemies without friends. What remains for him is to attack the third group of enemies listed in this speech, the gods. Like the circle-men of Aristophanes' speech in the *Symposium*, Ajax is moved to attack the gods for the sake of gaining autonomy. He considers suicide a means to show that it is not possible for the gods to delude him about himself the way Athena deluded him about the Greek army. Suicide cannot be an illusion. Ajax seems to contemplate it as an assertion of friendship to himself. But he has not understood the essential dependency of human beings. The original wholeness of Aristophanes' circle-men was an illusion, the truth of our longing, but no accurate reflection of our primal state. Our original condition is that we long for an original condition; the truth of our natures is political life, where we submit ourselves to the law for essentially rebellious motives. Ajax never understands the necessity of the relation between the great and the small.

That Ajax should despair of the possibility of friends is not surprising. Those most "dear" to him, at least those who can talk, are remarkably self-centered in their reactions to his contemplated and actual suicide. The chorus worry about what will happen to them if he dies. Tecmessa worries about the way she, who has suffered so much as a captive woman (for which Ajax is of course responsible), will suffer again as a captive woman when Ajax is dead. Teucer, after first asking for Eurysaces, worries about what his father, Telemon, will say. In each of these cases, the characters rather naturally tend to do what Odysseus openly avows at the end of the play: they labor for themselves (1367). This is merely the predictable consequence of the view that there is no seeing inside human beings; our motives are necessarily hidden from view. Beings for whom there is no inside cannot have friendship because they lack self-awareness. Beings for whom there is an inside cannot have friendship because they lack awareness of others. Their friendships are necessarily partial.

The suicide of Ajax does not run counter to his nature. It is the only defiance left open to him. He makes that evident in his most famous speech (646–92), a reflection on the power of time in human life. However, it also becomes clear that even this defiance is not really open to him. The speech as a whole is thoroughly ambiguous. The chorus take it to mean that Ajax has changed his mind, that he is one of those beings changed by time, and so they conclude that he does not intend to kill himself. We assume, *after* his suicide of course, that he had decided to kill himself. The only thing which seems initially certain is that Ajax has undergone some sort of change. In fact two things have changed. He has come to pity Tecmessa and he will kill himself outside the tent rather than within it. There is an added ambiguity. Granted that the speech can be read either way, that is, granted that we do not really know what Ajax intends, neither do we know whether he intends the ambiguity. Does he wish to deceive the chorus and Tecmessa, or is the deception unintentional? Because we do not know his intentions we cannot vouch for the truth of Ajax' initial claim that time changes everything. If we do not know and cannot know the inside of Ajax we cannot know whether he has changed. This speech, which has been the source of so much scholarly debate, seems to be intentionally ambiguous, perhaps on the part of Ajax, and certainly on the part of Sophocles; it is an example of the problem which it describes.

As a whole the speech is Ajax' explanation of a change which he has perceived in himself. He is surprised at the change, apparently thinking that

Aias and *aei* belong together. Yet Ajax is most of all unchangeable. Athena can fool him with visions, but that he changes his mind is a shock, and for that reason it is something for which he feels impelled to provide an explanation. The change seems twofold. Ajax has come to pity Tecmessa and Eurysaces. The chorus take this to mean that he will not kill himself. For Ajax it is a revelation about himself. To pity anyone as Odysseus had pitied him (131) means for Ajax to acknowledge that some fates are undeserved, thus undermining his whole understanding of the world as completely human. Ajax has seen the power of chance. The second change has to do with his resolve to kill himself. When Ajax went inside the tent (583), there seemed no doubt about his intention to commit suicide immediately. What he sees there is, of course, the dead bodies of the animals he had slain. He must see, were he to slay himself, that he would be indistinguishable from them, one more piece of carrion. Ajax changes, then, with regard not to his resolve to kill himself, but to the question of how to kill himself. His desire that his death should have some meaning must account for the most shocking of the apparent changes he undergoes in this speech.

> Therefore in the time remaining we will know to yield to the gods, and will learn to revere the Atreidae. (666–67)

Ajax simultaneously discovers chance, his need for the gods (and among them especially Hades—660), and his dependence on Agamemnon and Menelaus (and so on the *polis*). It remains to see how thoroughgoing this change is. Ajax may have decided to revere the Atreidae, but his death speech makes it clear that he hates them still (835–42). He seems only to have realized how limited his alternatives are, not to have forsaken them absolutely. His discovery of chance coincides with his discovery of Hades, or the invisible. Ajax can think of himself as revering the Atreidae only because he has discovered the intimate relation between friendship and enmity. Since he is what he is by virtue of his enemies, he must "love his enemies," but in a sense rather different from our customary understanding. Ajax has learned that he must love to hate. He has learned to speak ambiguously so that he might say but one thing.

Ajax considered the first word of the play, *always*, a fit description of himself until he discovered the way time has of bringing the unexpected, that is the invisible, to light.

> All things long and measureless time both brings forth (*phuei*) from darkness and buries from light, and nothing is unexpected (*aelpton*).
>   (646–48)

But Ajax, who wishes to be always, must therefore hate time, and insofar as he is changeable, hate himself. What he discovers here is that time, and the necessity for change, is itself eternal. That only what is eternal is worthy of love is confirmed by our ordinary experience of love or friendship. When we confide in a friend the tacit assumption (however foolish) is that friendship is lasting and that what is said will therefore be kept *forever* in confidence. But if there is nothing eternal but enmity and hatred then there is nothing to love but enmity and hatred. Ajax' discovery that one must be *sōphrōn*— moderate or *sane*—is therefore merely the truth of which his mad slaughter of the animals is the metaphor. It is the true brutality. Ajax has apparently not changed at all. He remains a man whose morality is the root of his bestiality. He is the same sword with a new edge.

The difficulty with Ajax' final view becomes clear from his last speech. His suicide, in order to be meaningful, has to presuppose more than the indifference of the chance and invisible. The "unexpected" (*aelpton*) must be interpreted as "that which we hope against" (*aelpton*) in order for Ajax to succeed in his last attempt at autonomy. His final speech therefore begins by personifying the sword given him by Hector and the instrument of his death. It becomes the source of all his trouble, and so must be the focus of his enmity. That the last speech of Ajax has to do primarily with the gods and especially with Hades is not accidental. In order to love the eternity of enmity, Ajax must place himself in the position of Homer's Ajax in *Odyssey* XI. He must be a shade in Hades with the possibility for eternally refusing to speak to Odysseus. But that of course requires that there *be* a Hades. In the end, for his own virtue to be possible Ajax is forced to create and turn to the very gods whose assistance at first he scorned. To rectify a world in which there is chance, Ajax must make the chance character of this world intentional. That amounts to inventing a world beyond this one, a world in which chance does not rule. Ajax invents Hades. He who began by acknowledging only the visible, the outside, in the end can commit suicide only because he leaves the dead animals inside and discovers Hades on the outside. And so Ajax, who once saw only the outside, now sees only the inside. But that is to turn the inside into the outside. Ajax has simply rediscovered in Hades the world he had renounced in his speech on time.

III

With the death of Ajax the *polis*, which had been implicitly present since the beginning of the play, comes in with a vengeance. The scholarly dispute that has raged since antiquity about the unity of the *Ajax* unwittingly points to an important problem. The play seems to be a "diptych," divided into two parts which, while related to one another (one part deals with the suicide of Ajax, the other with his burial), do not form the kind of whole one expects from a Sophoclean tragedy.[6] The issue of the second part is the proper way to treat Ajax' body, his outside. By trying to prevent the burial of Ajax, Agamemnon and Menelaus treat his visible part as though it were his invisible part, and so run the risk of repeating the error of Ajax. The second half of the play threatens to repeat the suicide of the first, but this time on the level of the city. The suicide of the city, its pursuing a single principle of morality to the point of self-destruction, seems to be prevented by the fact that it is based on conflicting principles embodied in different men. Requiring the cooperation of the great and the small, the city depends on the coincidence of the noble and the just. Menelaus seems to point to the dependence of the small on the great,

> Moreover, it is the mark of a bad man when a common man deems it his right not to heed those placed over him. (1071–72)

and Agamemnon to the dependence of the great on the small.

> Do the Greeks have no man but this one? Bitter it seems will have been the day when we summoned the Argives to the contest for the arms of Achilles if, however things come to light, we are to be named evil by Teucer, and if you will never be satisfied, even having been defeated by us, to yield to what satisfied the majority of judges. (1238–43)

The city is presented in its ambiguity, but because that ambiguity is not present in one soul it does not lead to self-destruction. The city will be like Ajax in its madness—it demands both the absolute preeminence of the best and their complete submission, but unlike Ajax it will never become aware of its madness. The city therefore runs the risk that its moralism will lead to a brutality of which it never becomes aware. Ajax treated his enemies as though they were beasts. In the name of the city, Agamemnon and Menelaus treat Ajax as though he were a beast. The contest over the body of Ajax is another version of the contest for the armor of Achilles, a contest the ultimate issue of which is the nature of contesting. It is a contest over strife itself (1163).

Teucer's defense of his brother's corpse falls into two parts. He first argues with Menelaus and then with Agamemnon. The two are separated by the reflection of the chorus on the Trojan War (1185–1222). In warning Teucer not to bury Ajax, Menelaus makes it a question of political theory. For the *polis* to exist, rulers must be obeyed. They can only ensure that they will be obeyed if they are feared, and they will not be feared if crimes such as those of Ajax are not punished. Although apparently fearless in life and so beyond rule, even Ajax must die and depend on others to bury him. Menelaus' principle is that the small, because they are dependent upon the great, must obey the great. But if it is the great who are to be obeyed, clearly Ajax surpasses Menelaus. If superior virtue is the criterion for obedience to the great then the great are a law unto themselves. The implication of Menelaus' speech is that the law (*nomos*) by which he is constituted ruler is natural. Like Ajax he is forced to make the conventional and the natural one. Also like Ajax in order for this final fear, fear of not being buried, to have the effect which Menelaus claims it will have, the existence of Hades is presupposed. Menelaus reenacts the problematic relation of Ajax to the gods, needing them to support an argument which otherwise remains fully within the human sphere. He presents the city as though it needed no justification, as having no inside, no invisible part. But his own argument requires the existence of Hades. Menelaus presents the city as an unself-conscious Ajax. The city's law, like Ajax' oath, is its own justification.

Teucer's reply (1093–1117) points to this weakness of Menelaus' argument and at the same time shares that same weakness. According to Teucer, there is no city. Ajax came to Troy for his own reasons. His oath is reason enough. It is not an oath to the Atreidae, but a self-imposed obligation. The manifest superiority of Ajax to Menelaus is sufficient to undermine Menelaus' tacit identification of convention (*nomos*) and nature (*phusis*). The problem with this account is that if it were true Ajax never would have acknowledged the right of Agamemnon and Menelaus to award Achilles' armor; there would have been no slight to his honor, hence no attempt to slaughter the Greek army. Teucer's position is self-contradictory. One cannot deny that the city exists and at the same time covet its honors. Menelaus and Teucer end by exchanging metaphorical insults (1142–58), but not content to leave them as metaphor, they interpret them. When *nomos* and *phusis* perfectly coincide, nothing remains hidden or incomplete. But in this event the city is everything and the city is nothing. When the political becomes everything, the political disappears, for its very being consists in its contrast to the natural. Teucer cannot insist on the autonomy of Ajax and still place him within the city. To live in the city means to be incomplete.

Whereas Teucer had argued against Menelaus that there was no common good, against Agamemnon he now argues that the deeds of Ajax on behalf of the common good deserve gratitude. The change has to do with the change from Menelaus' monarchical principle, that the small depend on the great, to Agamemnon's democratic principle, that the great depend on the small (1243). The city demands not only that men strive to be best, but also that having so striven they be willing to submit to those who are admittedly inferior to them.

But for a city to exist requires that it have some principle of unity. Agamemnon repeatedly emphasizes Teucer's birth. Teucer is not Greek because, being born of a Phrygian mother, he is by nature a slave. Conventional difference has been transformed into natural inferiority. Like his brother, Agamemnon is forced to defend the perspective of the city by exaggerating its scope. The two human events least able to be understood politically are death and birth. Menelaus has politicized the one, Agamemnon the other. Agamemnon's two themes fit together. Being Greek means being born of Greek parents. This alone is enough to make one by nature superior. Greekness is both the lowest common denominator and the limit of human excellence. Ajax in the exchange of gifts with Hector tried to become more than Greek. That the city cannot tolerate. It is able to present equality as a virtue by comparing its citizens to others. With Agamemnon barbarians become natural slaves, but as natural slaves speaking an unintelligible tongue, they cease to be thought of as human. The invention of barbarians, however, runs the risk of making the Greeks themselves barbaric.

These two aspects of the perspective of the *polis* are separated by the third stasimon, where the chorus reflect on the war (1185–1225). They move from lamenting their fate as Greeks in this particular war to lamenting altogether the fate of men who have been shown how to make "common war." The choral ode has a number of peculiarities. As is customary it divides into parts or strophic systems, each containing two parallel subparts—strophe and antistrophe. The first strophe ends with the word, *Hellanōn* (of the Greeks). In the same position metrically in the first antistrophe is the word *anthrōpous* (men). The first antistrophe begins with the following lines:

> Would that he had first sunk into the great heaven or to all common Hades (*polukoinon Haidan*) that man who showed the Greeks the common War (*koinon Arē*) of hateful arms. (1191–96)

In the Greek the comparison of *polukoinon Haidan*, all common Hades, with *koinon Arē*, common war, is powerfully suggested. The stasimon makes Greeks interchangeable with men and opposes common Hades to common war (or Ares). The second strophe shows how much the chorus resent the common war, which is always and unceasing. They have therefore come to think of hatred and enmity as a permanent condition. The result of that permanent war is that *man* and *Greek* have become interchangeable for them. The chorus pave the way for Agamemnon's introduction of the notion of barbarians and his reduction of them to slaves. The chorus therefore point to the fact that Greeks have come to define themselves in terms of what they are not. By defining themselves in terms of what differentiates them from all others they gain unity, but at the expense of perpetual war, for strangers will of necessity be different in a way perceived as essential difference. Agamemnon and Menelaus therefore point to the problem of the city as such. The city is a community of men which discovers its unity in a common war, and so requires the continuation of that war in order to remain a community. Its foundation is enmity. The Trojan War means the death of the dual meaning of *xenos*, stranger and guest-friend. After the theft of Helen, strangers must cease to be guest-friends and become enemies. This is of course the same as the problem of Ajax. Ajax discovers his own dependence on his enemies, and so discovers the priority of enmity. That is also what Odysseus realizes in his claim to labor only for himself.

For whom is it more likely for me to toil than myself? (1367)

The problem then is for the city to avoid the tragedy of Ajax. If the *polis* is allowed to recognize that it is by chance and not by nature, then it will dissolve. If it does *not* recognize this nonnatural character it will become cruel and brutal. If Ajax is buried the city dissolves, and if he is not buried the city is brutalized.

Not to bury Ajax is to say that there is nothing but the *polis*, nothing but the human. If there is nothing but the human there is no such thing as chance. But if there were only chance there would be no intention, no morality, no providence. The solution to this problem, the problem of common war, is common Hades (1193), a realm in which chance does not prevail, but which exists only for the dead. The play began with an invisible goddess, because invisibility is the essential characteristic of the gods. The presence of the gods assures a kind of providence that because it is not fully human will not be fully intelligible or visible to humans. The experience of it will not be so very different from the experience of chance. The gods are therefore necessary within the *polis* to make possible that mixture of providence and chance which prevents the *polis* from sinking into bestiality. The world can be understood as providential as a whole while its parts remain inscrutable, and so contingent.

When Odysseus argues for the burial of Ajax it looks as though he is making the same mistake that Ajax made when he exchanged gifts with Hector.

ODYSSEUS: This man was at one point my enemy, but he was noble.
AGAMEMNON: What ever are you doing? Do you revere a dead enemy thus?
ODYSSEUS: Virtue triumphs with me more than enmity.

(1355–57)

Having come to admire his enemy, he seems to prefer him to his friends. But Odysseus is cleverer than that. He does not argue that the live Ajax should be honored, but rather that the dead Ajax should be buried. In so doing he points to a resolution of the problem of Ajax acceptable to Agamemnon and the city. Agamemnon cannot honor Ajax openly, but he can be persuaded to allow him to be buried. Burial is intended to point to the limits of the political by providing a realm, Hades, in which Ajax and Hector are equally honored. Burial moderates common war by pointing to a realm beyond the city, invisible Hades, which is completely moral in a way that this world is not. The invisibility of this realm and of the gods is crucial; otherwise the claims made on us by this world and by particular cities would be undermined. The existence of Hades is equally crucial, however, in order to prevent the brutality of extreme moralism. Ajax would not have felt the same urgent need to punish his enemies had he thought that they would ultimately be punished in Hades.

Unlike the others, Odysseus seems to know that Hades, too, is a *Greek* god. It is not only the place of the dead, but the name of the god who rules there. Common Hades is, therefore, an illusion of a particular *polis* which serves to protect it against its own particularity. For this reason Odysseus is willing to honor Ajax in death and not simply bury him. If, as he had earlier suggested, we are all shades (126) then Hades *is* realized in this world. The invisible gods are the sign that we know that human beings have insides without knowing what is inside. The awareness that men have insides, like the belief in a general providence, prevents Odysseus from turning into Ajax, whose complete devotion to the human is only a hair's breadth from the attempt to annihilate the human altogether. Because Ajax is like the *polis* in his complete devotion to the human, he is finally not a political man. Political life requires incomplete devotion to the *polis*.

Political life requires the gods, but their presence tends to destroy the *polis*. The gods can be present only indirectly. Their presence, like that of Athena, must be invisible. Hades is therefore the paradigmatic god. It is the limit within the city on the completeness of the city. Rituals of burial are the sign that it is present. But there is another sign within the city of the incompleteness of the political world. The *Ajax* ends with a choral statement of the limits on human foresight.

> Many things are to be known to mortals by being seen; but before seeing, no one is a prophet of the things to come, what he will do. (1418–20)

Ajax was "*pronousternos*" (more wise, prudent, or possessing forethought) because he believed that by doing his duty he would necessarily prevail. His general belief in the triumph of the good allowed him to foresee the future. The chorus end by telling us in general that foresight is unavailable to men.

This of course is itself a general sort of foresight. In general it is prudent not to trust too strongly in one's predictive powers.

If the *Ajax* is a play about the limits of human sight, about our inability to see the inside, it is also about a certain way by which we *can* see the inside. The play is itself an attempt to show us the limits of our vision by showing us the inside of Ajax. It begins with a scene setting in which Athena uses the word *skēnais* (tents) to refer to the tents of Ajax (3). But the word has another meaning as well. It may refer to the backdrop for a stage.[7] By setting the stage Sophocles enables us to see inside Ajax. He makes it possible for us to do the impossible in order for us to learn that it is impossible. Of course, to do that it is necessary for him to reproduce the error of Ajax. Everything in the world of tragedy is significant; it is wholly a moral world. This is a necessary dramatic fiction. The *Ajax* therefore points to tragedy as the vehicle for revealing the incompleteness of the city to itself. Tragedy can do that only by being like Hades. Because it is a fully purposive world it can reveal the inside by the outside, but it does so in such a way that we are not tempted to reproduce its tragic fiction in our own lives. The *Ajax* ends by pointing to the fact that what seems necessary in retrospect is always contingent in prospect. It is this fact to which tragedy points that makes politics both necessary and possible.

3
The Origin of Modern Science:
Descartes' Discourse on Method *I-III*

And you shall bring out of Hades a dead man restored to strength.

—Empedocles, Fragment III

T HE *AJAX* IS A tragic play about the nature of tragedy itself. Insofar as tragedy is a solution to the problem of the presence of certain dangerous moral passions in the political community, the *Ajax* is a play about the solution to the problem of politics, and so is not simply tragic. This may account for why that action from which all others develop in the play, the slaying of the animals, is almost a caricature of tragic action. Were the consequences slightly less severe the play could be a comedy. That Ajax cannot quite rise to the level of Achilles and that his nature runs parallel to the nature of the city point to the moral of the play: it is best for the second best not to try to be best.

To understand, however, that one is second best seems to entail some understanding of what is best. If the *Ajax* points to the necessarily imperfect character of political life it forces us to wonder about the possibility of a transpolitical solution to the problem of the human longing for autonomy. It is by no means at first obvious that René Descartes is concerned with politics or with the tragedy of the perfectly political. His central concerns seem to be Christian metaphysics and the establishing of a new science. That these two concerns are compatible is not clear. What they seem at first to share is their nonpolitical character. At first glance, Christianity seems transpolitical, science apolitical. The one seems to postpone the solution to the problem of human autonomy until the next life, the other to be altogether indifferent to its resolution. It is necessary, however, to take a second look. Throughout his writing, but especially in the *Discourse on Method*, Descartes' preoccupation with Christian metaphysics and mathematical science conceals a deeper reflection on the human desire for autonomy, and on the necessarily transpolitical character of any satisfaction of such a desire. Understanding this deeper reflection involves first turning to the question of Descartes' peculiar rhetoric.

The mark of Descartes' success as an author is that his rhetoric is so noticeable and yet so little noticed. The following remarks occur in the fifth, seventh, and eighth paragraphs of part I of the *Discourse*:

> But considering this writing only as a history, or if you prefer, only as a fable, in which among some examples that one can imitate, one will perhaps also find several others that one will have reason not to follow, I hope that it will be useful to some without being harmful to any, and that all will thank me for my frankness. (I.5)

> I knew . . . that the prettiness of fables awakens the spirit; that the memorable actions of histories elevate it, and that being read with discretion, they aid in forming judgement. (I.7)

> Besides, fables make us imagine many events as possible which are not so at all; and even the most faithful histories, if they neither change nor augment the value of things in order to render them more worthy of being read, at least they nearly always omit in them the basest and least illustrious circumstances; from which it follows that the rest does not seem such as it is, and that those who regulate their morals by the examples which they draw from it are subject to the extravagances of the knights of our romance, and to conceive plans which pass their powers. (I.8)

If the *Discourse* is a "history or fable" then it "awakens" and "elevates" the spirit. But it must be read with "discretion," for otherwise it will lead us to think "many events as possible which are not so at all," and to see our world "not such as it is." Descartes takes great pains to inform us that his book must be read with discretion, especially that part devoted to "the rules of morality which he has drawn from this method" (Synopsis). It is here that we are particularly prone to knightly extravagances and heroic virtue. Descartes means to make the rhetorical character of the *Discourse* clear, and to warn us of its dangers. The primary danger of moral rhetoric seems to be that we will try to regulate our lives on the basis of standards quite impossible to fulfill. At the same time, we must realize that Descartes himself calls attention to the fact that the *Discourse* is a history or fable (it is striking that the difference between fact and fiction is so casually slurred). He calls attention to his own use of moral rhetoric. However, if his use of rhetoric is clear his reasons for using it are not. The question we are forced to ask at the outset about the form of the *Discourse* will prove to be the key to understanding it as a whole: Why does a man famous for the celebration of clarity and distinctness write in such an obscure and involved way? And what does this manner of writing have to do with the question of human autonomy?

I

The full title of Descartes' book is *Discours de la méthode pour bien Conduire sa Raison et Chercher la Vérité dans les Sciences*: it is a discourse on the method for conducting one's reason well and for seeking truth in the sciences. The title alerts us to the underlying assumption of the book. Reason is weak. It is not by itself sufficient to conduct itself.[1] The title also suggests that reason is always attached to a person. It is always "*sa raison*" and never simply "*la raison*." Reason is weak and reason is always found in persons. It is necessary to see how these two are connected to understand Descartes' mode of writing and his motive for writing.

The *Discourse* proper is preceded by a synopsis where Descartes indicates that the book may be too long to read in one sitting. For our convenience he has divided it into six sections and further subdivided each of the sections. One is very grateful for help of this sort with the *Phenemenology of Mind* or the *Critique of Pure Reason*. Here it is nice but appears less necessary. The *Discourse* is after all only about one hundred pages long. Because it is not so obviously necessary, the synopsis calls attention to itself and so to the structure of the book as a whole. Its most general purpose is to unify perhaps discrepant parts, to unify a plurality. If the length of the book prevents its being taken in all at once, the synopsis provides a solution to this weakness of human reason. It gives us a whole prior to the examination of the parts which makes the diversity of the parts manageable. Reason appears to be weak because as *someone's* reason it is always limited by time. It cannot grasp wholes all at once. Hence one always begins looking at things in a partial way, which is to say, in a distorted way.

The rhetorical character of the *Discourse* is nowhere clearer than in its first sentence, Descartes' famous claim for the equality of reason:

> Good sense is of the things in the world the best apportioned; because everyone thinks himself to be so well provided with it that even those who are the most difficult to satisfy in every other thing are not at all accustomed to desire more of it than they have. (I:1)

The argument is surely ironic. That we are all satisfied with what we have indicates rather our self-satisfaction than our rationality. Descartes, aware of the humor of his beginning, proceeds to deprecate his own intellectual gifts (I:2–3), thereby indicating that reason is not equally distributed in all men. Cartesian "rationalism," therefore, begins not with a statement of the equality of reason, but with a hint of the inclination all men have to value themselves as highly as they can. It is not reason that is equally apportioned but natural egoism.[2] Still, why begin with an ironic claim? By seducing us into accepting the equality of reason Descartes himself appeals to what is truly equal, our natural egoism. By doing so he points to what it is about *sa raison* which prevents it from being pure, that is, *la raison*.

Even were we to take Descartes at his word and accept the claim about the equality of reason, we would still need an account to explain the diversity of opinions in the world. If reason is equal, why don't people believe the same things? Descartes suggests that this plurality of opinions is owing to the diverse ways in which we conduct our thoughts and the different things we consider (I:1). In other words, reason is always connected to the particulars of our lives. It is always someone's reason. What then accounts for this corruption of reason? While reason is equal in all men, mind or spirit (*l'esprit*) can be good (and therefore, since it can be present to a greater or lesser degree, bad). What holds of *l'esprit* also holds of soul. Souls can be not only good but great (I:1). There is then something decidedly unequal in human beings which constitutes our potential for great virtue or great vice. The source of this inequality is *l'esprit*.

There is a connection between *l'esprit* and what makes Descartes Descartes. (The second paragraph of part 1 begins with an emphatic *pour moi*.) It is not accidental that this word, which points to what makes us individual men, will be used in part 5 in the plural to refer to "animal spirits," the very tiny bodies that account for movement in our bodies. Both *l'esprit* and *les esprits* seem to be givens of our natures. They are what we begin with and do not have complete control over. Descartes claims that he never presumed to judge his *esprit* to be more perfect than that of common men, and that he even longed to have his thought, memory, and imagination as good as others (I:2). *L'esprit*, then, consists of some combination of the faculties of quickness of thought, imagination, and memory. Reason is what makes men men; they must therefore have all of it or none of it. But what individuates men is *l'esprit*. However, as quickness of thought, accuracy and distinctness of imagination, and retentiveness and amplitude of memory are accidental qualities, the differences among men must be accidental—which is of course not to say that they are unimportant.

It is therefore not accidental that Descartes attributes his own intellectual successes to good fortune (I:3). (*Beaucoup d'heur* could almost be rendered "much time.") He was, as we would say, a "gifted child." What he is depends very much on what he has been given, which of the cards he has been dealt. From his youth Descartes "encountered" or ran into (*rencontré*) many things which "conducted" him to some considerations and maxims from which he formed *one* method. He had the good fortune to run into a plurality that allowed itself to be forged into a one. He was limited only by the mediocrity of his *esprit* and the shortness of his life, limitations essentially the same. Had he possessed an *esprit* which was quicker he could have gone farther, but the same goal would have been achieved by a longer life. While *l'esprit* may be an accidental quality, given our mortality, it turns out to be the critical element in Descartes' success and in the limitations thus far on his success. If the manner in which Descartes is limited is meant to stand as a paradigm for human limitation then overcoming human limitation would either mean making thought quicker or life longer.

These two problems, shortness of life and slowness of thought, point back to the problem of fortune, of the given. The method of Descartes is meant to lead to the mastery of nature or fortune. This temporal problem, short life and slow thought, stands as the major obstacle to that project. In this sense mastery of nature means mastery of time for Descartes. He wishes not simply to lengthen life. The science of medicine will accomplish that end, but the tacit claims of part 6 that the method will lead to immortality seem to be among those parts of this fable that lead one to imagine things possible which really surpass one's powers. Instead, the method will "lengthen life" by making it possible for different men to do parts of the same enterprise. For that to be possible, the enterprise would have to be uniform. Uniformity would require the imposition of an overall structure, even if arbitrary. Given something like a uniform method for all science, the mediocrity of mind (which is only the other side of shortness of life or mortality) would cease to be a problem. Autonomy may, as the *Ajax* indicates, be a tragic goal for a political community. Perhaps it will not be tragic for a scientific community.

The method is not so much for the direct mastery of nature as for the mastery of human nature so that humans can, in turn, master nature. It is a means of overcoming death by making all the various parts of science potentially whole. This is the deeper level of his suggestion that good sense or reason is equally apportioned among men, his emphasis on the common in men to the exclusion of the special. The problem of the *Discourse on Method* is therefore the same as the problem of the synopsis. If the *Discourse* as a whole, or the world as a whole, is too long to be read in one sitting, or in one life, what is required is a general plan of the whole. The synopsis is therefore to the *Discourse* as the *Discourse* is to nature. The *Discourse on Method* begins with a parallel between itself and nature, and so between mastery of it and mastery of nature. Descartes writes as he does so that learning to read him we will have learned to read the "great book of the world." The problem of rhetoric with which we began is an image of the problem of science.

If the first four paragraphs of the *Discourse* point to the problem of rhetoric, they also point to the problem of a world in which rhetoric is necessary. There were, of course, entirely practical reasons for Descartes' rhetoric. He has constantly before him the fate of Galileo (VI:1). Still, there is more to the question of rhetoric than mere personal caution. Writing as he does, Descartes wishes to gain acceptance for the method before its implications are fully understood. He therefore presents the method as an image or fable to appeal to men without their understanding why. The fact that it is possible to appeal to men in this way is both the reason why Descartes can write as he does and that about which he is writing. It is because he knows "how subject we are to deceive ourselves in what touches us" that it is necessary for Descartes to found the method. Reason's weakness is natural egoism. At the same time this very weakness makes it possible for him to found a new method. Natural egoism is the principle behind all persuasive rhetoric. It is also the reason for the defective character of all previous science.

All of this sheds a great deal of light on the self-deprecatory character of the *Discourse* thus far. On one level this humility is heavily ironic; on another, it is meant quite seriously, thus compounding the irony. The discovery of the power of natural egoism, that is, the discovery of the weakness of reason, means the humbling of the species. At the same time, discovery of the principle of human ignorance is a kind of knowledge and brings with it its own peculiar pride. This mixture of humility and pride, characteristic of the book as a whole, points to the peculiar structure of the method. It will involve a self-doubt that is so thoroughgoing as to presuppose some rather extraordinary abilities. The man who institutionalizes humility can take great pride in his achievement.

While the insight into the power of natural egoism and its connection to rhetoric is the concern of the very beginning of the *Discourse*, the major portion of part I is devoted to careful examination of Descartes' course of studies. The connection between the two issues is clear. Descartes will find his education wanting in utility; science will be measured by the standard of natural egoism. The list of studies is revealing in a variety of ways. As Richard Kennington has pointed out, mathematics stands at its center and is the only science given unequivocal praise.[3] The first part of the list is made up of language, fables, histories, eloquence, and poetry. The second part of the list after mathematics is made up of morals, theology, philosophy, jurisprudence, and medicine. Histories and fables, as we have seen, arouse the spirit and elevate it. The *Discourse*, as a history or fable, is therefore an appeal to *l'esprit* and not to reason. As fables and histories are not methodical, it is not methodical. It is an appeal to what is by nature unequal in men for the purpose of doing away with its necessity. The book is a history or fable written in such a way as to rouse us and raise our spirits by means of images of grandeur, a fabular attempt to make fables unnecessary. In describing the *Discourse*, Descartes says he will present his life as a "*tableau*"; histories and fables depend on such image making. Indeed, the whole of the first part of Descartes' list of studies seems to be dependent on images in a way not typical of the second part of the list. The first part of the list is, broadly speaking, poetic. While the members of the second part of the list may use images, it seems possible to imagine them as purged of images. All of this has something to do with the fact that the second part of the list can be understood to be practical, its goal, the good understood as the useful. However, the first part of the list, the poetic part, is not so susceptible to this utilitarian principle. That has something to do with the connection between poetry and the beautiful.

About the distinction between what is image-dependent and what is not, and about the connection of the image-dependent to the beautiful, Descartes has the following to say in *The Passions of the Soul* (II:85, "Of Delight and Horror"):

> And I find one distinction alone notable which is similar between the one and the other. It consists in the fact that the objects as much of love as of hate can be represented to the soul by the external senses, or by the internal and by its own reason. For we commonly call good or bad what our internal senses or our reason makes us judge fitting to our nature or the contrary; but we call beautiful or ugly what is thus represented to us by our external senses, principally that of sight, which alone is more of note than all the others. From which is born the two species of love, to wit, that which one has for the good things and that which one has for the beautiful, to which one may give the name delight in order not to confound it with the other, nor again with desire to which one often attributes the name love. And from thence also are born in the same fashion two species of hate, of which the one is related to bad things, the other to those which are ugly. And this last may be called horror or aversion in order to distinguish it. But what is most remarkable here is that these passions of delight and horror are usually more violent than the other species of love and hate, because what comes to the soul by the senses touches it more strongly than what is represented to it by its reason, and that, even though they ordinarily have less truth. So that of all the passions these are the ones which deceive most, and from which one must guard oneself most carefully.

Descartes' list of studies is so composed as to suggest the difference between the beautiful and the good. Insofar as sciences are image-related, that is, insofar as they are related to the beautiful rather than the good, they will be deceptive. That deceptiveness is rooted in the more violent character of the passions attached to the beautiful. But these are the very passions which constitute our natural egoism, make us what we are, make our reason impure, and make rhetoric both possible and necessary. The good may be what our reason and internal sense tells us to love, but the beautiful is what we do love, and passionately. It is our own sense of our own good. The impurity that self-interest brings to reason—the fact that *la raison* is always *sa raison*— is directly proportional to the image-dependent character of thinking.

With all of this in mind it is easier to understand the foundational role that Descartes will make mathematics play in the new science. Mathematics is much the most solid of the sciences because it is in a way the least solid. To the extent to which it is not image-dependent it is perspectiveless and contains no concealed interest. It is closer to *la raison* than the other sciences. Consequently, the grounds for differences of opinion in mathematics are minimal. It is clearest on the level of mathematics that good sense or reason would be equal, given an unlimited amount of time. For this reason Descartes has in mind using mathematics, which because it is not image-dependent does not arouse the passions, to lay the foundation for a science that will ultimately provide knowledge of all that is useful in life.

It is therefore no accident that Descartes' attack on the ancients comes in the form of an attack on their teaching about virtue (I:10). The ancients make a direct appeal to what *seems* good. And yet they fail to realize that the beautiful is always contaminated by "good sense"—that is, by natural egoism. The good as sensed is always imageable; it is always the beautiful—although it is not self-evident that the ancient teaching of virtue was as blind to the tension between the beautiful and the good as Descartes suggests. The expression *kalos te kai agathos* means something like "gentleman" in ancient Greek, and is meant to indicate what it means to be a gentleman, that is, both *kalos*, beautiful or noble, and *agathos*, good. That both terms are needed suggests that they are not simply thought to be the same. Still, Descartes' point might be put in the following way. The ancients put together two things that do not mix so easily, the beautiful and the good. This mistake is elevated to a principle in the formula *kalos te kai agathos*, an expression betraying the unfounded optimisim that the beautiful and the good go naturally together, that what seems attractive to us is in some way good for us. A theodicy of this sort is antithetical to Descartes' understanding of the natural deceptiveness of the beautiful.[4]

If the beautiful and the good are not naturally together, our desire is to understand a way in which they can be brought together. We wish to avoid tragedy. Descartes indicates the ancients' failure to do so by pointing out that what they thought to be virtue was really parricide (I:10). The alternative to this tragic split between what appears good, the beautiful, and what is good is heaven. If what seems noble or beautiful to us can *in the end* be good for us there will be no final discrepancy between the beautiful and the good, and so between morality and happiness. Descartes speaks of this possibility in a curious way. The revealed ʻruths of religion "conduct" us to heaven (*et que les vérités révélées, qui y conduisent*—I:11). The language here parallels the way he speaks of the method. In fact throughout the *Discourse*, the structure of Descartes' project, and so frequently the language used to describe it, parallels the structure and language of Christianity. This accounts for the fact that a book devoted to elaborating a means for overcoming our "fallen" condition through our own efforts and in this life, a book, therefore, at its core hostile to Christianity, can so successfully present itself as essentially Christian. And it accounts for Descartes' presentation of his project in the guise of Christian metaphysics when he might have circumvented altogether the need to discuss theological issues. The *Discourse on Method* uses a Christian mode of presentation because Descartes' central problem is understood by him to be essentially the same as the central problem of Christianity. That images are deceptive, that the good and the beautiful are at odds, the equal apportionment of "good sense," the possibility of and need for rhetoric— these problems are really one problem, the fallen nature of man. The difference is important, however. The Christian solution is heaven. The way to heaven is described in the revealed word of God, but that word is not to be understood unless one is "more than man" (I:11). Descartes, on the other hand, had settled the question of his occupation by choosing the one best "for men purely men" (I:3). The Grace of God is no solution to the rule of fortune because, from the perspective of men purely men, it is indistinguishable from fortune.

   This reflection on theology points to the problem which occupies Descartes for the last section of part 1. When he turns to a discussion of philosophy (I:12), Descartes begins by pointing out that it has been cultivated by *les plus excellents esprits*, the most excellent minds, to have lived during several centuries. Descartes does not have the *présomption* to hope he will *rencontrer* better there than others have. This coupling of *présomption* and *rencontrer*, of presumption and encountering or running into, points back to their previous coupling (I:3). It points again to Descartes' peculiar modesty. Here he claims to *know* that the conflicting opinions among the learned show that all of their teachings are dubious. This claim is surely hyperbolic. Any one of the opinions might easily be true. But Descartes' hyperbole might be justified as itself the means to overcoming the chaotic diversity of opinion among the learned. What Descartes knows is not that all previous philosophers have been wrong, but rather that it is necessary to proceed as though they were all wrong. His knowledge is not of the content of his hyperbolic claim so much as of the necessity for hyperbole, a species of rhetoric.

Descartes had said (I:4) that he would set forth his life as a *tableau*, a picture. He means to reproduce in the *Discourse* the sort of attraction that the world has for us. He means to reproduce the attraction of the beautiful, but now for the purpose of wooing us from the world, that is, from images and from the beautiful. That would place the *Discourse on Method* among the first group in the list of his studies, the poetic "sciences." Part 1 of the *Discourse* prepares the way for the project of the book as a whole, to overcome through images the power that images have over us. It is a premethodical appeal for method which, if successful, would result in a science which promises success by undermining the need for brilliance, that is for *les esprits forts*, *bons*, or *excellents*. However, this project turns out to be possible only given the most *excellent* of *esprits*. Descartes has composed an autobiography of sorts because he is the deepest problem his project confronts. The method is to be our hope for "mastery of nature" (VI:2), our hope for ceasing to be buffeted by fortune, for autonomy. But this method owes its origin to Descartes' excellence, and he owes his fortune, his excellence, to the Grace of God (I:13), that is, to what has been given him. The emphasis in part 1 on the rhetorical or image-dependent character of the *Discourse on Method* is a sign of the serious difficulty for any attempt to become autonomous. It must come from within. If our mode of experiencing the world is image-dependent, then freedom from the image must be won from within that mode. Mastery of nature must be a kind of self-transformation.

Descartes raises this issue himself in the final two paragraphs of part 1 by emphasizing what he owes to fortune. Fortune has placed him in a position where he can have *rencontres* with diverse situations. This good fortune, like his fortune, understood as wealth, is given him by the Grace of God (I:13). But it is clear that from the perspective of "men purely men" (I:11) it is impossible to distinguish between the Grace of God and accident. While Descartes profits from seeing all this variety, as yet all he has is an experience of variety. He is still in some sense chained by the given. He is not autonomous.

The problem is still more serious than it appears at first. Ordinary men are said to "read the world" by means of the pain they suffer when they err in assessing their interests. However, in philosophers natural egoism has become a kind of pure vanity. They have removed themselves from the sphere of what they actually sense where their speculations could be punished for lack of "good sense." The problem for Descartes will be to avoid this difficulty which he attributes to the philosphers. What will punish him if he fails to judge correctly? The difficulty is only compounded when Descartes refers to his "extreme desire to learn to distinguish the true from the false" (*un extrême désir d'apprendre à distinguer le vrai d'avec le faux*—I:14). The phrase "extreme desire" has occurred before in conjunction with learning (*j'avais un extrême désir de les apprendre*—I.6). It implies something more than truth-seeking. It is easy to see how the very passion of the desire for truth might interfere with finding truth. Seeking to be a god tends to get in the way of being a god.

Descartes ends the first part by returning to the problem of plurality (I:15). It is a problem connected to the question of natural egoism and to the violence of the passions which attach to images. Plurality of opinion seems rooted in our diverse "interests." None of us has a synoptic view. Part 1, therefore, leads us to wonder how it is possible to acquire such a view. We are confronted in the world with variety. In the *Discourse*, whether the variety consists of philosophical views (I:12) or of the customs of men (I:15) or of the various pluralities present in the synopsis, there is in each case a demand for unity. But the unification seems in turn to depend upon Descartes' peculiar talents, talents for which he is not responsible. Part 1 then points to the origin of Descartes' method out of the accidental experience of variety plus the will or resolution to study himself and employ all the force of his mind (*l'esprit*) to choose the way he must follow. But this second element, the will, thus far seems something of an accident, a given. It is therefore appropriate that part 2 of the *Discourse on Method* should begin with Descartes' reflections on the passion for unity, that is, on mastery, for the question part 1 has given rise to is this: What does it mean that the mastery of nature or chance is rooted in the chance character of Descartes' nature?

II

In part 1 Descartes made an issue of his own origins in order to make an issue of the problem of origins for men generally. Autonomy or freedom would mean not to be bound by the given. At the same time, the given is all one has to work with. How, then, is one to prevent being enslaved to one's origins? Most of all, the method is meant to solve this problem. At the beginning of part 2 the question of autonomy is introduced in general by way of the question of mastery, and in particular by way of the question of war. Parts 2 and 3 of the *Discourse* comprise a unit. As Kennington has pointed out, part 2 begins with a reference to the Thirty Years War and part 3 ends with a reference to the same war. The discussion of the rules of the method and of the rules of morality "drawn from them" is enveloped by references to war.

It is not such a surprise that Descartes will use war as the context for his discussion of autonomy and mastery. The most brutal result of the conflict of human passions, of that natural egoism with which part I was concerned, is war. And yet there is more to it than that. We do not go to war simply because our passions are naturally at odds with each other. Not natural passion but fables make many things seem possible which are really beyond reach. Knights errant are not so much moved by natural passion as by passion transfigured by convention. The Thirty Years War is a religious war between Christian sects.[5] The problem is then twofold. Passions contradict each other both among and within men, but convention makes those conflicts rigid. The account of mastery, therefore, will be of necessity an account of the mastery not only of nature but also of conventions. In a way, the purpose of part I is simply to point out the implications of the fact that it is human nature to be governed by conventions. That is what the rule of fables and images means. Descartes, therefore, says that it is his good fortune to find himself in a situation where he is untroubled by cares or passions and, he adds, conversation (II:1). The addition makes all the difference. Conversation is a different sort of trouble from hunger and cold. In "giving voice" to passions it changes them, and in so doing creates the real obstacle to mastery.

The analysis of mastery in the first paragraph of part 2 takes the form of a list of examples. The list points to the principles underlying Descartes' understanding of perfection, as mastery seems to mean something like the perfecting of what one masters.[6] Perfection appears to have to do with unity as opposed to plurality, and unity in turn seems to be better ensured by one master than by many. The first example of this principle is the single architect of a building. The sign of his superior perfection is that the building he builds is "more beautiful and better ordered." Beauty and order seem to have to do with the fit between the thing made and the purpose for which it was made, with final causes as they relate to an artisan's making. In ancient philosophy final causes or purposes were thought to be made visible in the world in beautiful things.[7] Beauty is the visible manifestation of the existence of things which are for their own sakes, are ends in themselves, and therefore provide ends for everything else. But if, as we have seen, Cartesian philosophy must be understood to begin with as an attack on the power which images have over us, and if the beautiful differs from the good in being linked to external perceptions or images, then Descartes' attack on images constitutes an attack on the role of the beautiful in human life. Cartesian philosophy and the science it gives rise to are founded on the view that beauty in nature is an illusion, and the most powerful illusion for men. At the same time, it is clear from the very first example of mastery that any human understanding of perfection will require some consideration of purposes. For mastery to have any meaning something like final causality, and so beauty, will be necessary. The fabular form of the *Discourse* is the sign of the provisional character of Descartes' attack on final causes. The attack on the beautiful results in a most beautiful book.

Kennington has made clear that Descartes' examples at the beginning of part 2 ascend from smaller to larger objects of mastery.[8] The list begins with the single architect, and then moves to the single city planner who is concerned not only with houses taken individually but with how they are related to one another, and then from the city understood as a collection of buildings to the city understood as a collection of people. That is, Descartes moves to the issue of legislation. His examples are first the general case of the single prudent legislator, then God as legislator, and finally the legislator for Sparta, Lycurgus, who goes unnamed. This might seem an exception to the generally ascending character of the list. Yet the context of the whole section, religious war, suggests an imperfection in God's legislation. It may treat the object of the greatest magnitude, the world, but it seems to be defective in terms of the unity of its design. The legislation of Sparta on the other hand is singled out as having tended toward one end. The tension between God and Lycurgus therefore merely points to the problematic peak toward which the list as a whole is ascending: to secure the greatest possible unity in mastering the objective of the greatest magnitude. The ultimate goal, mastery of nature, would require combination in the single prudent legislator of two criteria, unity and magnitude, but the two have not been combined and perhaps cannot be combined in a political sense. That seems the reason why the examples of mastery abruptly change their character. Descartes moves from legislation to the simple reasonings of a man of good sense, and then to a final hypothetical example of mastery, a human being born with the full use of his reason, a being for whom need does not precede power. The list of examples as a whole, then, is as follows:

1. single architect
2. single city planner
3. single prudent legislator
4. God
5. Lycurgus
6. man of good sense
7. one born with the full use of reason

The necessity for this shift away from legislation becomes somewhat clearer when one considers the other list embedded in the first paragraph of part 2. Descartes' examples of mastery are always presented as alternatives to more conventional approaches. Single architects are opposed to those who remodel houses, cities which are planned by a single planner to those which grow out of villages, and prudent legislation to the customs of societies which grow out of more savage situations. The simple reasonings of a man of good sense are in turn opposed to the gradual accumulation of sciences in books. All of these more conventional alternatives are defective. They are always responses to particular necessities and specific problems. When forced to fix a leak in the roof during a rainstorm one has no time to redesign the whole roof. It has to be fixed with whatever material is available and in whatever way is possible. Necessity is the mother of only limited inventions. However, if the goal is perfection, one must do something more radical than re-form something already having a form of its own. Perfection means overcoming the very notion of necessity; it means overcoming the given. Descartes therefore understands that perfection is necessarily at odds with re-formation and not the least with political reformation.

The final example in the ascending list is hypothetical and is never actually called a species of mastery. The virtue of the penultimate example, the simple reasonings of a man of good sense, over the sciences of books is that it is more unified. Like the Spartan legislator, the man of good sense is consistent. His consistency has its root in his natural egoism since on the whole the configuration of our passions remains fairly constant. We tend to be pleased and pained by the same things; we have "personalities." But this virtue of the man of good sense is also his vice. We may be predictable but we are not the source of our own predictability. Men of good sense are not really masters but slaves of what is given to them. Our peculiar and idiosyncratic needs always precede our reason. We are all born children before becoming men. (The only two human beings to escape this difficulty were, of course, born in paradise.) That our passions precede our reason means that we never begin from scratch. We begin by seeing things as already serving our purposes and filling our needs. That apples are classified as fruit and fruit as food is a classification rooted in our needs. To look at the world as though it were purposive or teleological is therefore an error, but a natural error. We are naturally enslaved by the given. Because we are born dependent we must regard the world as providing what we need. We are therefore precluded from regarding the world as possibly not beneficent. It is only chance or fortune which places Descartes in a warm room and protects him from the cold winter and ravages of war.

> I was then in Germany, where the occasion of the wars which have not ended there, had called me; and as I returned to the army from the coronation of the Emperor, the beginning of winter stopped me in a

quarter where, not finding any conversation to divert me, and having moreover through good fortune neither cares nor passions to trouble me, I remained the whole day shut up alone in a stove-heated room where I was entirely at leisure to entertain my own thoughts. (II.1)

It is therefore only chance which enables Descartes to begin to consider the nonpurposive character of nature. To be born with the full use of reason from birth would mean to be born without any tendency to classify anything on the basis of our needs and passions. Mastery of nature requires something less idiosyncratic than "good sense."

Descartes' understanding of the deficiencies of good sense is connected to his subsequent rejection of political reform.

These great bodies [public bodies] are too difficult to raise again, having been knocked down, or even to secure them when shaken, and their falls can only be very violent. (II.2)

This is why I can in no way approve of those mischief-making and restless temperaments, who being called neither by their birth nor by their fortune to the management of public affairs, do not fail always to have in mind (*en idée*) some new reformation. (II.3)

Legislation was central in the account of mastery because politics is the most natural response to our awareness of our vulnerability in the world. As natural, it is, of course, suspect. Descartes seems at first quite adamant that he is not concerned with political reform. He makes himself quite clear, as clear as he had made himself with regard to the equal apportionment of good sense in part 1—and to the same effect. In part 1 "good sense or reason" was first claimed to be equal in all men. We were subsequently encouraged to see that this equality was rather implausible. Yet the very way in which we were led to reject the surface argument, the equality of reason, by means of the obvious inequality of mind, of *l'esprit*, led us back to a sense in which the surface could be said to be true. Something remarkably similar happens here, and, indeed, proves to be typical of the structure of Cartesian rhetoric altogether. Here, although Descartes first denies it, it is in some sense obvious that he is a political reformer. He publishes a popular work in fabular form and in French. He does say that not everyone should follow his lead, but stipulating who should not follow his example is also a way of stipulating who should.[9] Still, in another way we are meant to see that Descartes is in earnest. What Descartes is specifically not concerned with is political reform which always involves a spirit of righteousness, of which the ultimate expression is war. The *Discourse on Method* is meant to provide an alternative to the necessity for war.

The ordinary response to the realization that the unimpeded pursuit of what seems good leads to no good is that we attempt to control ourselves. Virtue is the cure for letting the passions run wild. However, we pay a price for this self-mastery. To master oneself means to think of part of oneself as worthy of being enslaved. Virtue, therefore, tends to involve a sense of anger at what one is. The complete cure for what ails us would therefore require the purging of this anger. As political reform always involves something like anger, it cannot be the means for curing men. It will always leave behind a residue of self-hatred. The dilemma seems quite clear. In following the passions we are deceived and so still dissatisfied. In resisting them we will also be dissatisfied. To begin to understand Descartes' solution to this dilemma we will have to understand more clearly his view of the passions. That will require a digression to another of his books, *The Passions of the Soul*.

Descartes follows his criticism of political reform in the *Discourse* with a denial that he wishes to be imitated (II:3); his reason is human inequality. There are those to whom "God has better apportioned his graces." Becoming more specific, Descartes suggests that the world all but divides into two sorts of *esprits* who should not follow his example. In two ways, then, human inequality is grounded in the given. By stipulating who should imitate him, Descartes is simply identifying which natures are "gifted" enough to do what he has done. He cannot teach them; he can only provide an image or fable that will either arouse the appropriate passion or not. This is what it means to say that the passion for mastery of chance is aroused by chance. By writing as he does, Descartes simply imitates what happened to him in the warm room; he imitates nature.

Still, that cannot be the whole story if his goal is the conquest of chance. As it stands, it looks as though the freedom or autonomy which is the result of mastery is simply equivalent to following one's dominant passion. That leaves us on the level of the simple reasonings of a man of good sense, the man with a "personality," but it sheds no light on what Descartes might mean by the hypothetical case of a man born with the full use of his reason. Yet suppose that all passions turned out ultimately to point to one passion. Under such conditions, to follow one's dominant passion *truly* would lead to this master passion. The plausibility of this suggestion is supported by Descartes' analysis in *The Passions of the Soul* where he lists six principal passions out of which all others are generated: wonder (*l'admiration*), love (*l'amour*), hate (*la haine*), desire (*le désir*), joy (*la joie*), and sadness (*la tristesse*).[10] Love is our attitude toward an object perceived as good in relation to us, hate our attitude toward an object perceived as bad in relation to us. Joy and sadness are considerations of present goods or bads respectively. Desire, on the other hand, is future-oriented. We desire to acquire what we perceive as good relative to us and to avoid what we perceive as bad. Wonder is a condition of neutrality toward objects which we have not yet determined to be either good or bad. Taken together, the six certainly confirm the importance of natural egoism for Descartes. Human beings are naturally disposed to perceive the world as either good or bad for themselves. What is added here is that since this goodness or badness comes to light in time, the structure of natural egoism involves more than being attracted to the good and repelled by the bad. Still, with the possible exception of wonder, to which we will return, the basic passions are all intelligible as the various ways in which a temporal being is related to a world in which he perceives everything in terms of his own good. Desire is still a bit more complicated, however, and wants special attention.

It seems likely that what we desire is always to be in the presence of things which appear good relative to us.[11] But then we do not want to be without them. This explains why it is that for Descartes desire is the only one of the five principal passions dealing with good and bad which has no opposite. It needs no opposite because it is itself both good and bad. All desire contains within itself the desire not to desire, and so is necessarily a form of self-hatred. We want and that means that we are wanting. Desire is a hatred of the passions and their structure in relation to the perception of the good and the bad in time. This self-hatred is on a deeper level dependent on self-love. It is only because we wish the best for ourselves that we resent the fact that our natures are so constituted as to make the best unavailable to us. In part 3 of the *Passions* (Article 199) Descartes describes anger as "desire joined to the love that one has for oneself." Desire become self-aware is anger.

This desire not to desire, which is the truth of all desire, is the most difficult obstacle to human autonomy. If Descartes' method is meant to enable us to be masters without this underlying feeling of self-hatred it must make a purer form of mastery possible. The sixth of the principal passions, wonder, seems to supply the possibility for purified mastery. When we first meet upon things we do not know yet whether they are good or bad. Nevertheless we have an interest in them because we know that eventually they will prove either good or bad for us. Descartes seems to have in mind contriving a method which will make it possible for us to wonder again. The most famous part of the method, the hyperbolic doubt of everything that we do not know to be certain, is a means to induce an artificial ignorance. The method is to be rooted in wonder to enable one to master nature without feeling the need for mastery. It is meant to make possible a contentment untainted with pain. If the goal of the method is artificial wonder, and if such wonder means a provisional suspension of our knowledge of what is good and bad for us, and if that in turn means the suspension of desire, then the goal of the method is to make possible the joy from the consideration of a present good without the desire from anticipating its presence. Self-love would remain as it must, but by neutralizing desire, Descartes would have undermined anger.

The parallel to Christianity should be clear. The problem is how to combine knowledge of good and evil with the innocence of man before the Fall. For Descartes makes a certain return to innocence possible, but it is an innocence which is understood as a means to a further end—not as an end in itself. One might say that although Descartes follows the Book of Genesis in its suspicion of cities and of the political life, he nevertheless has in mind a "political" use of his apolitical method. In the context of the discussion of political reform in part 2, Descartes' project could be characterized as an attempt to found a method with the design of taking the anger out of war. It is a war to end all war. As long as there is anger in war, the victors will be ruled to a large extent by what they conquer. Their victory will be tainted by what Nietzsche will come to call the "spirit of revenge." But if it could be arranged that victory were perceived as the almost accidental result of a passionless method, that is, if we could be freed momentarily from the rule of desire while at the same time we were led to "encounter" or happen upon something which satisfied our desires, we would then be made aware of our ability to satisfy our desires simultaneously with our being made aware of the desires themselves. Feeling no antecedent lack, we would feel joy without desire, or we would feel desire only in its satisfaction. We would therefore be aware of ourselves not primarily as slaves, as needy, but as masters able to satisfy our own needs, and so as autonomous.

The *Discourse on Method* as a whole is so structured as to seduce its readers into solving problems before they are aware of them as problems. Descartes' true innovation is the substitution of the method for politics or war. The virtue of a general method for solving problems is that it is not, nor can it be, preoccupied with a single problem. The final example of the first paragraph of part 2 is therefore not explicitly called mastery because it discovers itself as mastery only in its act of mastering. Descartes does not have political reform in mind because it is always necessarily a reformulation, and so is linked irrevocably to the past. This problem is made clear in a quite beautiful manner by his remark that he cannot approve of those turbulent "*humeurs*" called neither by birth nor fortune who nevertheless embark on a program of reform (II:3). One need only reflect for a moment to see how peculiar this claim is.[12] What is the sign that one is called by birth or by fortune? It does seem as though the only way one could know would be if one succeeded.

Descartes is hardly so moderate, then, in his attitude toward political reform as at first he seems, a fact especially clear when one notices that part 2 begins with his claim to have been "called" (*appelées*) by the occasion of the wars. And yet, to be called by fortune is in its way precisely the solution that Descartes has in mind. One ought not to long for success because the longing gets in the way of the success. Success should be happened upon. One knows one is called at the moment one succeeds.

Given this very elaborate preface to the statement of the method that will accomplish these ends, one cannot help being a little startled by the exceedingly modest character of the rules which Descartes enumerates in the remainder of part 2. A glance at Descartes' earliest work, a work he never finished or published, *Rules for the Direction of the Mind* (*Regulae ad directionem ingenii*), is sufficient to show that the "rules of the method" proposed there are considerably more detailed than what we see here. (Rules IV–VII correspond roughly to the four rules articulated in *Discourse* part 2.) Nevertheless, the *Discourse* is the deeper of the two books. It differs from the *Rules for the Direction of the Mind* in being throughout concerned with the question of the origin of the method. How is it possible for reason understood as weak to be the source of the method which will deliver it from the effects of its own weakness? From the beginning the *Rules for the Direction of the Mind* are radically incomplete, and so perhaps were left uncompleted, because they do not contain a reflection on their own possibility.[13] The turn from this first unfinished book to the *Discourse* is Descartes' version of the turn from pre-Socratic to Socratic philosophy. It is his second sailing.[14]

In a letter to Mersenne (March 1637) Descartes himself acknowledges the thinness of the rules of the *Discourse*. "I did not write *Treatise on Method*, but *Discourse on Method*, which is the same as *Preface*, or *Announcement Concerning Method* to show that it was not my plan to teach it, but only talk of it. For as one can see from what I have said it consists more of practice than of theory." The second half of part 2 is therefore not a full statement of Descartes' method. It remains to be seen what it is and how it is connected to the treatment of mastery which immediately precedes it.

Descartes presents his method as a synthesis of logic, geometrical analysis, and algebra (II:6). But each of these elements is flawed and therefore must be purified. Logic before Descartes, Aristotle's logic, is categorical.[15] In treating particulars as members of classes it presupposes that all things fall naturally into classes. That may be fine, Descartes suggests, for presenting what one already knows in an orderly way, but it is not a logic for discovering what one does not already know. The classes into which it groups things are bound up with our naturally selfish way of regarding the world. Descartes' opposition to Aristotle's logic, then, is rooted in his opposition to the final causality which he understands it tacitly to presuppose. Geometry is impure because of its dependence on figures or images. It forces one always to deal with a particular, even as one is supposed to be concerned with something essentially nonparticular. On the other hand algebra, precisely because it contains no images, is extremely difficult to hold on to. Its formulas lead to confusion. Once again the problem is how to unify a plurality. The images of geometry make possible the unification of a number of cases of, say, triangle. But like Lycurgus' laws which were "even contrary to good morals" the unity is defective because particular and idiosyncratic. On the other hand, without images unification of a plurality seems impossible. Descartes' goal seems to be to establish a method for discovery which gives one a whole without giving one a particular. We need to look at the particular rules he presents in order to see how.

The first of the rules is a statement of Cartesian doubt:

> The first was never to accept anything as true that I did not know evidently to be such; that is to say to avoid precipitousness and prejudice; and to include in my judgments nothing more than what presented itself so clearly and so distinctly to my mind (*esprit*) that I could have no occasion to place it in doubt. (II:7)

Now, to reject everything that is not so clear and distinct as to be absolutely certain is not simply rational.[16] Still, it does free one from the particular which is being doubted. Because the doubt is programmatic we are not required to find special reasons for doubting everything which we doubt. We are moved to doubt in a rather mechanical way, and so are not moved to doubt by particular passions. It is not because we hate or desire that we doubt. Programmatic doubt allows us to doubt without any hard feelings because it is so utterly detached from the world being doubted. Precisely because the world always presents itself to us as particulars, a general doubt does not enslave us to the world which is being doubted. Of course there is a difficulty hidden here. Since it is not natural to doubt, we must have a motive for doubting. The doubt, as rooted in our will (II:6) is rooted in a perceived sense of lack. Something must be desired in order to instigate the doubt which is designed to neutralize the effects of desire. Still, the general character of the doubt has the effect of obscuring its origin and rendering the doubt neutral to the effects of "good sense."

The second of the rules is as follows:

> to divide each of the difficulties that I examined into as many parts as should be possible and as should be required for the best results. (II:8)

Once again, these divisions are not governed by the nature of that which is to be divided, but by our wish to resolve the difficulty which it represents for us. Analysis is here subordinated to will. The third rule prescribes an order for our thoughts:

> The third, to conduct my thoughts in an orderly way, beginning with the simplest objects and the most easy to know in order to rise little by little, as by degrees, to knowledge of the most complex, and even supposing an order among those which do not at all follow naturally the one from the other. (II:9)

In Rule VI of the *Rules for the Direction of the Mind* Descartes makes the import of this procedure quite clear:

> Although this proposition seems to teach nothing very new, it contains, nevertheless, the chief secret of the method, and none in the whole of this treatise is of greater utility. For it tells us that all facts can be arranged in certain series, not indeed in the sense of being referred to some ontological genus such as the categories employed by philosophers in their classification, but so far as certain truths can be known from others: and thus, whenever a difficulty occurs we are able at once to perceive whether it will be profitable to examine certain others first, and which, and in what order.

Somewhat later Descartes gives an example of what he has in mind. Providing an order where we find none in nature means something like assigning geometrical patterns to colors.

> For it is certain that the infinitude of figures suffices to express all the differences in sensible things. (Rule XII)

If the object of our inquiry is like the color continuum, and so does not easily admit of division into simples, then we have to assign simples. Color must be made to be measurable. A quantitative measure has been allowed to stand for something that resists being measured quantitatively. Thus far what the rules of the method share is a dependence on the will of the inquirer. Thinking has been transformed into construction, into making. It has become theory building, and as such it is less difficult to see the connection between the method and the various examples of mastery with which Descartes began part 2. The order being sought is not exactly an order in things; it is rather an order which facilitates movement from the simples which we "know" to the composites of which they become the parts. It is a way of ordering our knowing which has as its goal the making of a certain kind of whole.

For that reason the fourth rule, which seems especially innocuous, points to the real problem which the method is meant to address.

And the last, to make in all cases enumerations so complete and reviews so general that I was assured of omitting nothing. (II:10)

In the *Rules for the Direction of the Mind* Descartes cites the weakness of memory as the reason for the necessity of repreated enumeration (Rule VII). The problem then is time. We do not grasp composites as simultaneous wholes with our reason. For that we require imagination. But images are untrustworthy because so thoroughly under the influence of passion. If he could combine the virtue of geometry, its use of images as an aid to memory, with the virtue of algebra, its ability to deal with the general relations among things apart from the idiosyncratic and particular, Descartes would have discovered a method to substitute for an ability to grasp complete wholes all at once. The fourth rule is therefore important because beyond the simples into which things are divided, the first three rules produce no whole. Yet, the problem with the procedure of the fourth rule, enumeration, is that this overcoming of time requires time (II:5). The method as a whole might be characterized as an attempt to make it possible to do in time what looks as though it can only be done atemporally. It is an effort to give us a whole which is not tainted by the admitted necessity of apprehending the whole serially through its parts. The method is therefore an attempt to make available to "men purely men" what has hitherto been the preserve of God alone.

Descartes intends that analytic geometry provide something of a paradigm for the method. If we are concerned with the proportions among things we must first reduce those proportions to the least distracting of images, to lines; we graph them. That in itself neutralizes them. The result is a little like a sales chart; it is altogether indifferent to what is being sold. Next we reduce the lines to formulas or ciphers representing the proportions that the lines are meant to express. We may then perform various operations with these formulas without being distracted by the things whose relations these proportions are meant to express. One can determine what must be done to one variable in order to increase the slope of a line. But the variable remains just that, a variable. One is conveniently insulated from the real consequences of an increase in slope. The increase might well involve the number of mortgage foreclosures made by a bank. The formula leaves no room for worrying about widows and orphans. The method allows one to think dispassionately by removing objects of passion from view, but not from thought. The general scheme is that one abstracts from the concrete particular in order to remove from view those images that arouse the passions of love and hate, joy and sadness, and desire. One then develops problems within this abstraction, problems which might otherwise not even come to sight. Then one returns to apply what has been done to the concrete particulars, foreclosures, for example. By means of an act of will, the initial abstraction, an artificial neutrality is induced to make an artificial wonder possible. A condition is created wherein we do not yet know whether what we are looking at is good or bad for us. This general scheme, which follows the model of analytic geometry, has a familiar sound. It points us back to the problem of part 1 of the *Discourse*. What was needed then was a method to neutralize the intellectual differences among men, a method to eliminate the idiosyncracies of brilliance. The method outlined in part 2 is meant to make possible formulations of problems which, because they do not rely on those idiosyncracies, are transferable from one person to another. In this way, by making reason equal among all men, nature can be progressively mastered.[17] Equalizing reason will of course mean minimizing the importance of *l'esprit* (Rule VIII and I:12). But the motive for minimizing the importance of *l'esprit* is like everything else, rooted in our natural egoism. The neutrality achieved by the method is temporary and provisional. In the terms in which the *Discourse on Method* begins, men are willing to say that reason is equal only because they think they are better. Part 2 has made clear that the method depends at its deepest level on an act of will; however, it is not yet clear what moves the will. Descartes turns to that problem in part 3. The "provisional morality" presented there is more important to the argument than it first appears.

III

That parts 2 and 3 are intimately connected is clear from the synopsis:

In the third, some [rules] of morality that he has drawn from this method.

Two things are striking. The rules of morality are drawn from the method, and they are not said to be provisional. Yet the connection between the rules of the method and the rules of morality is initially quite dark, and throughout part 3 the morality is said to be provisional. These are the puzzles at the heart of part 3.

While Descartes begins as though he were redesigning a house, in fact he is redesigning his own soul. As he is both architect and material he will not be able to reside elsewhere while the work is being done. Living in a house while rebuilding it is always a messy affair. But that is our lot, since unlike God we never begin from nothing. Descartes is in the position of having to mix the irresolution characteristic of his doubt in the first rule of the method with the resolution which is requisite for action of any kind, and especially requisite for the hyperbolic doubt in which Descartes is engaged. The morality "*par provision*" is designed to make this mixture possible. As provisional *morality*, it acknowledges the necessities of action. As *provisional* morality it acknowledges the necessities of thought. The problem remains how one can function with a morality one knows to be provisional. Provisional morality means suspending judgment about what finally is good and bad. It is the moral counterpart of wonder. But "if our will inclines us neither to follow nor to flee from anything except as our understanding represents it to it as either good or bad" (III:5), any suspension of judgment will be at odds with the activity of will. The natural result of doubt is paralysis, or, for a being who must act as though it knows in order to live, doubt will be painful. And Descartes wishes to live "as happily as possible." It is not yet clear how the provisional morality will serve that end.

While the substance of the rules of morality seems to be moderation itself, a more careful examination discloses that they are not nearly so moderate as they at first appear.[18]

> The first (rule) was to obey the laws and customs of my country, holding constantly to the religion in which by the Grace of God I had been instructed from my childhood, and governing myself in everything else by following those opinions most moderate and furthest from excess which were commonly received in practice by the most sensible of those with whom I would have to live. (III:2)

Now Descartes has already told us of his doubts concerning his childhood beliefs (I:6, II:1). Here he warns us to pay attention to what people do and not to what they say. In the context of a book, what an author does is his arguments, that is what he says, and what he says is what he claims to have said or argued.[19] Descartes claims to behave moderately, but he redefines moderation altogether by first opposing it to excess and then defining excess as "all the promises by which one limits something of one's freedom," that is, all laws, customs, and religion. His argument comes to a head in a sentence phrased in the strangely negative way that will prove typical of part 3.

> Not that I disapprove of laws, which in order to remedy the inconstancy of weak minds (*des esprits faibles*) permit, when one has some good plan, or even for security in commerce, some plan which is only indif-ferent, that one makes vows which obligate one in order to preserve it. (III:2)

When untangled, this sentence appears to mean that Descartes does not dis-approve of laws which permit the weak to obligate themselves—scarcely a ringing endorsement of law-abidingness.

The apparent meaning of each of the rules of the provisional morality will be similarly undercut by Descartes' "deeds." In this case "Be moderate!" has been transformed into "Don't limit your freedom!" If the structure of the rhetoric in the *Discourse* thus far is to serve as a model, we would expect that what is first asserted and then undermined will forthwith be reasserted as being in an odd way true. It is this third level at which the provisional morality will prove to have some positive content. In the assertion of the first rule Descartes seems to introduce gratuitously a distinction between what we believe and what we know that we believe:

> Because the act of thought by which one believes a thing being different from that by which one knows that one believes it, one often exists without the other. (III:1)

Now, because each can exist without the other, the fact that human beings do not act in accordance with what they think they believe to be good means that it is possible to reform what they think without affecting what they do. Descartes' conduct might therefore appear to alter very little as a result of adopting the provisional morality of part 3. His behavior might appear perfectly lawful, conventional, and pious while his reasons for behaving as he does might be fundamentally revolutionary. If that is so, then the method will be as concerned with rebuilding our sense of why we do things as it will with changing what we do.

That Descartes' advocacy of moderation in the first rule is not to be taken at face value is clear from the second rule.

> My second maxim was to be the most firm and the most resolute in my actions that I could be, not following the most doubtful opinions less constantly once I should have determined them than if they had been the most assured. (III:3)

Descartes likens his fate to being lost in a forest. Choosing a direction—any direction—and sticking to it is one's best course of action.

> And thus, the actions of life often not allowing any delay, it is a truth very certain that, when it is not in our power to discern the most true opinions we ought to follow the most probable. (III:3)

Startlingly enough, before the famous "I think, therefore I am," we are presented with a "truth very certain." The argument seems to be that we do not know very much, but we do know that we end up better off if we act as though we knew. For practical purposes, therefore, we ought to assume that the probable, even less than probable, once chosen, is true.

The second rule looks as though it contradicts not only Descartes' advocacy of moderation, but the first rule of the method, the doubt. Actually, it is possible only because of the doubt. When lost in a forest, one must first acknowledge that one is lost before having the presence of mind to pick out a tall tree at random and move toward it. The crucial step in the argument thus far was the separation of belief and knowledge of belief. Put somewhat differently, the problem is not so much what we know as it is what we expect ourselves to know.

> And this was henceforward capable of delivering me from all the repentance and remorse which are accustomed to agitate the conscience of those weak and vacillating minds who inconstantly let themselves go to practice as good the things they afterwards judge to be bad. (III:3)

The problem, then, is guilt. Weak minds (*les esprits faibles*) feel it because they do not realize that mistakes owing to necessary ignorance are not moral defects. However, if they are not responsible for their lack of knowledge of good and evil then they cannot sin. The second rule seems to be an attack on the power that guilt has over human beings. It therefore points us back to the beginning of part 2, Descartes' reflection on mastery. Guilt is what we do not like because what we do like is feeling responsible, that is, mastery. The first step toward that end is to keep us from feeling responsible for inevitable failures.

It is no surprise then that the third of the rules of the provisional morality is concerned with that for which we can take responsibility because it *is* within our power.

> My third maxim was to try always rather to conquer myself than fortune, and to change my desires rather than the order of the world; and generally to accustom myself to believe that there is nothing which is entirely within our power but our thoughts. (III:4)

This, of course, sounds very little like mastery of nature. But it is worth wondering whether Descartes' attempt at stoicism might not be an example of one of those things in the second rule which he resolves to treat as though they were true. It would then be a necessary stage in the mastery of nature rather than an accommodation to the present situation. This suspicion is supported by the way in which Descartes points to the principle of his stoicism so as to point also to the problem with the principle. It may be that

> our will only induces us naturally to desire what our understanding represents to it as in some way possible, (III:4)

but this principle is undercut by the example ostensibly meant to support it, namely that

> we will no more desire to be healthy being sick or to be free being in prison, than we do now to have bodies of a material as little corruptible as diamonds or wings in order to fly like the birds. (III:4)

Of course we do want such things. It is not so strange to want to fly, that is, to be quicker, nor to desire to be incorruptible, that is, not to die. Given that we desire these things we must also desire the others, to be healthy when sick and free when in prison. And the latter must therefore be presented by our understanding as in some way possible. Descartes has not so much provided an argument in favor of stoicism by showing that certain things are in fact beyond our power as he has given an example of the way in which the understanding can be brought to bear to regulate our passions. While we cannot compel ourselves to have certain passions, we do seem to be able to control those we have, to diminish them, if we can call into question the possibility of their objects. This is what it means to make a virtue out of a necessity. The same act of will that lies behind the doubt of the method also lies behind Descartes' stoicism. Our passions are attached to things that seem real. Destroy the belief in reality and the passions too are destroyed. Neutralizing the desires by an act of will gives men "some reason" (III:4) to esteem themselves more highly than others, but only some reason. By implication there is something for which self-esteem is still more justifiable. Descartes praises the Stoics, but his stoicism, fundamentally different from theirs, is marked by its provisional character.

The first three rules of the morality are all provisional and all impossible unless understood as provisional. Moderation is possible only because of the distinction that Descartes has made between believing and knowing that we believe. Only because we do not know the principles which really govern our actions can we be content to accept the appearance of holding conventional opinions. But that knowledge suggests the need to resolve the difference between what we believe and what we know we believe. The resolution characteristic of the second rule is only possible because of a prior awareness of how little we know. We can only escape guilt because we are aware of the provisional character of our situation and of our attempt to overcome it. Finally, Descartes' "stoicism" is possible only because he is *not* renouncing the world forever; his stoicism makes sense only as a means to an end. It begins, therefore, to look as though the provisional morality is moral not despite the fact that it is provisional but because of it.

The three rules thus point to the fourth, where the meaning of provisionality is spelled out. Descartes had introduced part 3 by referring to the "three or four maxims" which would provide him with moral housing during his self-rebuilding. Given the emphasis in the *Discourse* on precision, this indeterminateness is sufficient to point to the peculiarity of the fourth maxim. The fourth rule of the method had called for enumerations for the purpose of bringing parts together into a whole. Here Descartes resolves to make a review of the diverse occupations available to men in order to choose the best. This decision is never explicitly called a rule or maxim, and it is never referred to as provisional. It is distinguished from the three rules preceding it by retrospectively providing a purpose for them; they are provisional in terms of it. In particular the contentment of realizing one's own limits (the most one could hope for from the stoicism of the third rule) is here supplanted by an extreme and innocent contentment.

> I had experienced such extreme contentment since I had begun to use this method that I did not believe that one could receive any more sweet or innocent in this life; and discovering every day by means of it some truths which seemed to me sufficiently important, but commonly unknown by other men, the satisfaction that I had so filled my mind (*esprit*) that all the rest did not touch me at all. (III:5)

What is the source of this extreme and innocent satisfaction?

> Besides, the three preceding maxims were founded only on the plan I had of continuing to instruct myself; because, God having given to each of us some light to discern the true from the false, I should not have believed that I ought to be content with the opinions of others for a single moment if I had not proposed to use my own judgment to examine them when there was time. And I should not have known how to exempt myself from scruple in following them if I had not hoped to lose for all that any chance to find better ones in case there were any. And finally I should not have known how to limit my desires nor to be content if I had not followed a way by which, thinking to be assured of the acquisition of all the knowledge of which I was capable, I thought by the same means to acquire all the true goods which should ever be in my power. For inasmuch as our will does not incline us to follow or to flee anything except as our understanding represents it to it as good or bad, it suffices to judge well in order to do well, and to judge the best that one can in order also to do one's very best, that is to say, to acquire all the virtues, and with them all the other goods that one can acquire. And when one is certain that that is the case, one cannot [knows not how to] fail to be content. (III:5)

Descartes' contentment derives from his view of the life which the method has made possible for him. That life is more praiseworthy than the life of the stoic because far from limiting one's power, it extends it as far as possible. Descartes suppresses his own judgment only as a means to its liberation; he follows the opinions of others without scruple only because he has resolved to follow them as a means to the discovery of his own opinions; and he limits his desires only as a means to their extension. He does all of this as a means to the best of possible lives, and the most deserving of praise. By describing this life as so choiceworthy Descartes presents himself as responsible for having chosen it. And as responsible for its choice, he would have been equally responsible had he not chosen it. The price he pays for taking credit for the choice is the possibility of guilt. We must therefore take Descartes quite seriously when he informs us that

> he should not have known how to exempt [himself] from scruple in following them [the opinions of others] if [he] had not hoped not to lose, for all that, any chance to find better ones. (III:5)

When the web of negation is unravelled here, Descartes seems to be saying that there is one thing only for which he would be unable to avoid a feeling of guilt, namely, not trying on every occasion to discover true opinions. Only the refusal to philosophize legitimately inspires guilt. This fourth rule is not called provisional because it points to the final character of the morality which Descartes has articulated in part 3.

In general, it is the goal of part 3 to overcome the problem of guilt. Descartes must establish that "in the corruption of our morals" few of us wish to say or can say what we believe. Or, "the act of thought by which one believes a thing, being different from that by which one knows that one believes it, one often exists without the other" (III:2). This distinction between what we believe as that which really leads to our actions as opposed to what we think we believe splits the soul of a moral being in such a way as to make guilt possible. Judging well may be sufficient for acting well, but that we feel guilty means that we accept responsibility for our judging even when we are mistaken. Without this split in us between what we think we are doing and what we are really doing, between what we think we believe and what we really believe, it would not be possible to do something which we later wanted to take back. Every action would be an infallible expression of the passions of the moment, and we would know those passions infallibly.

The problem with which part 3 is so concerned is really only another version of the problem of rhetoric presented in part 1 and the problem of mastery presented in part 2. Rhetoric requires the possibility of seeming to mean one thing and really meaning another. A soul in which rhetoric can have appeal is susceptible to the way things seem; it is a soul in which the thing which is not can seem to be. That is the condition of a soul that knows about the truth but does not know what the truth is. The situation is analogous to the soul that knows about perfection but does not know what perfection is. Mastery, or autonomy, can only be the goal of a being who lacks autonomy. The discovery that one is not what one had hoped oneself to be is the precondition for guilt. The problem of part 3 is what to do about guilt. For it to be overcome it would seem to be necessary to close the gap between what one believes and what one knows oneself to believe. Either one must arrange things so as never to do anything shameful (one must be virtuous, making what one believes really conform to what one thinks oneself to believe), or one must understand oneself as not being responsible for errors (one must make what one thinks oneself to believe correspond to what one believes in fact). Descartes seems to have chosen the second of the two possibilities. His "one truth very certain" implied that we were not responsible for our lack of knowledge of good and evil (III:3). If, however, we are not responsible for our mistakes, how can we be responsible for our successes? To do away with guilt seems to do away with mastery as well. Part 3 is Descartes' attempt to dispense with guilt without sacrificing mastery. Toward that end the morality of part 3, like stoicism, seeks to make us content, but only provisionally. It must do that in order to avoid rooting the mastery of nature in an awareness of our own lack. If the satisfaction of mastery is to be "sweet and innocent" it must be the result of the activity of one who is already content. The goal of Descartes' provisional stoicism, then, is to create a situation in which you discover your needs only as you discover their satisfaction.

That is why the provisional morality has a structure drawn (*tirée*) from the method. The power of the method is that it abstracts from the passions and from their power to deceive. The difficulty is that in doing so it also abstracts from purposes. A man born with the full use of his reason has perhaps no reason to use his reason. But this example was only hypothetical because, since one must act in order to live (III:1), it is never really possible to abstract from purposes. On the one hand then it seems as though all reasoning is necessarily distorted reasoning. Natural egoism is the precondition for the use of reason, and at the same time the cause of its imperfect use. On the other hand, when you act you are never really content unless you feel that you know what you are doing. The truth of the passions is a passion to be in control—mastery. The result of not knowing what one is doing is guilt. Descartes' provisional morality substitutes knowledge (the one truth very certain) that it is necessary to act as though one knew for knowledge proper. It substitutes knowledge of the need for knowledge for knowledge itself. Or, it substitutes methodology for metaphysics. The result is that it becomes possible both to act resolutely and to doubt, and, rather ironically, it becomes possible to act more resolutely (i.e., without guilt) because one doubts. This possibility is revealed to us in "the corruption of our morals." We see that it is possible and even customary to believe one thing and "know" we believe something else. Descartes' great experiment is to turn this capacity to fool ourselves, a capacity rooted in our imagination and in our passion, on itself, and literally to make " virtue of necessity" (III:4). Had he completely removed the possibility of guilt he would have completely removed the possibility of responsibility, and so of mastery. Men would have been automata. What he leaves, the possibility of feeling guilty for passing up any chance at really knowing, gives Descartes' actions some purpose in general while not wedding him to any of their specific purposes. Aristotelian teleology is to be replaced by a general notion of teleology that applies to no particular instance. The provisional character of Descartes' morality releases him from guilt and frees him to enjoy what he does discover rather than worrying about what he does not know. The provisional morality is rather like impersonal self-confidence. It is drawn from the method in the sense that the method, as artificial worry, does not bother you as much as real worry. There is nothing personal about scientific doubt. And so, there is no mention in the synopsis that the morality is provisional because it is precisely this provisional character which makes it possible for the morality to be final. Cartesian philosophy is open-endedness in its final form. Its child is a science with such self-confidence in its own finality that it can, without guilt, change its fundamental opinions regularly every generation and pride itself on that fact.

4

The End of Modern Science: *Descartes'* Discourse on Method *IV-VI*

If there were gods, how could I bear it not to be a god! Thus there are no gods.

—Nietzsche, *Thus Spoke Zarathustra*, part 2

I

T HE PROVISIONAL MORALITY OF part 3 of the *Discourse on Method* lays the foundation for replacing traditional morality with the morality of science. The need to replace the former by the latter has been at issue since the beginning of the book. That "good sense" is not good enough suggests that there is an alternative to it. Such an alternative would, of course, have to overcome the problem of the distorting effect of the passions on judgment; it would have to overcome the problem of natural egoism. That, in turn, would seem to require a mode of judgment independent of images, one that protects us from the most natural of errors, mistaking the beautiful for the good. If part 1 is an attempt to articulate the problem of natural egoism, part 2 is an attempt to point to the method as the means for solving the problem. All of that would be fine if Descartes' goal were simply to replace traditional morality by science, but it is not. He has in mind rather the introduction of a new morality based on science. Part 3 points to the goal of this morality: to achieve a sense of mastery without guilt. That is the formula for autonomy.

The difficulty with the account thus far is that its two goals seem at odds with one another. On the one hand, the method is meant to ensure neutrality toward the things of the world; its goal is to establish something like artificial wonder. On the other hand, there is always a motive for artifice; artificial wonder is not really neutral. It can be maintained only by telling oneself that one's neutrality is provisional, that it is for the benefit of a subsequent gratification of the passions, of natural egoism. Scientific morality remains morality, and Descartes knows it. He must, therefore, give an account of the connection between the epistemic neutrality of his science and the purposiveness of his science.

Descartes is also aware that his problem is not altogether a new one. It has a great deal in common with older questions about the connection between the true and the good. For this reason, it is not accidental that he chooses to conduct his account of the connection between the doubt and purposiveness under the guise of a proof for the existence of God and for the immortality of the soul. God represents, for Christian metaphysics, the resolution of the tension between the true and the good. God is the image of perfect autonomy. Part 4 will attempt to dismantle that image in order to replace it with the science of part 5 as the image of autonomy. Descartes has purged the beautiful from human experience in parts 1 and 2 only to reintroduce it here for his own purposes.

By his own claim, part 4 deals with Descartes' metaphysics. It is generally accepted that the metaphysics of part 4 provide the foundation for the physics of part 5.[1] Part 4 seems to move from programmatic and hyperbolic doubt to Descartes' new understanding of the soul as a thinking thing, to a proof for the existence of God, and finally to the consequences of that proof for those matters originally doubted. This structure is also generally recognized. Disagreements about this text and about its parallels in other Cartesian writings tend to focus more on precisely how the arguments in it are wrong than on whether they are wrong. In fact, the arguments for the existence of God and for the independence of soul from body are not very persuasive. But here, as elsewhere in Descartes, widespread recognition of the defects in his arguments ought to incline us rather to reexamine what we think his arguments are about than to reject them out of hand. In the *Discourse* we have already some precedent for undertaking such a reexamination. Descartes characterizes his intention in part 4 rather curiously in the synopsis.

> In the fourth, the reasons by which he proves the existence of God and of the soul, which are the foundations of his metaphysics.

Now, if God and the human soul form the foundation of this metaphysics, and if the proofs for them are suspect, then suspicion is cast on the whole of the metaphysics. However, the synopsis is nicely ambiguous about what exactly it is which forms the foundation of the metaphysics. It might be God and the soul, but it might be "the reasons" by which Descartes proves their existence. Those reasons need not be suspect merely because the proofs built on them are not convincing. Understanding the metaphysics of part 4 and therewith the physics of part 5 would seem to require that we identify these reasons.

Descartes begins part 4 by expressing some doubt about whether he ought to reveal his metaphysics at all. His meditations (in the warm room) were, he says, so metaphysical and so unusual that they would not be to the taste of everyone. However, he is "in some fashion constrained to speak of them" (IV:1) in order to make it possible to judge the firmness of his foundations. The fashion in which he chooses to speak does not necessarily require a full and open disclosure of his meditations. This introductory section has a further peculiarity.

> I had noticed for a long time that for morals it is necessary to follow opinions which one knows to be very uncertain just the same as if they were indubitable, as was said above. (IV:1)

In thus reminding us of what he earlier had called a "truth very certain" (III:3) at the very moment when he is about to doubt that anything is very certain, Descartes calls our attention to the difference between moral doubt and epistemic doubt. He is about to doubt the truth of all that he had previously held to be true, but, as we have noted, he is doing that for a purpose, and the purpose is never called into question. Far from doubting the rules of the provisional morality of part 3, the doubt of part 4 is an instance of the second rule of the provisional morality. By resolving to doubt everything even though he *knows* it to be extremely doubtful that everything deserves to be doubted, Descartes is about to "follow [an opinion] which [he] knows to be very uncertain" (IV:1). In this way the epistemic doubt of part 4 is subsequent to and founded upon the moral certitude expressed in the provisional morality.

The derivative character of the doubt is emphasized by the language used to introduce it.

> But because I now desired to devote myself solely to the search for truth, I thought that it was necessary that I do quite the contrary, and that I reject as absolutely false everything in which I could imagine the least doubt in order to see if there remained after that anything in my belief which was entirely indubitable. (IV:1)

Everything having to do with images is about to be called into question. It thus seems ironic that the doubt is itself a product of the imagination. And yet, if the imagination is what provides us with purposes, founding the doubt in imagination means acknowledging that the doubt is for a purpose. This allows us to pose the question of part 4: What is the image providing the purpose for the doubt?

That the doubt is not universal in the *Meditations on First Philosophy* and elsewhere has been shown persuasively by Richard Kennington.[2] What is true in the *Meditations* is equally true of this present meditation. The doubt has three parts here.

> Thus because our senses sometimes deceive us I wished to suppose that there was not anything which was such as they made us imagine it. And because there are men who make mistakes in reasoning, even touching the most simple matters of geometry, and make paralogisms with regard to it, judging that I was as subject to fail as any other, I rejected as false all the reasons that I had formerly taken as demonstrations. And finally, considering that all the same thoughts we have while awake can also come to us when we sleep, without there being any at that time which are true, I resolved to feign that everything that had ever entered into my mind was no more true than the illusions of my dreams. (IV:1)

Were Descartes really to doubt the truths of demonstration all reasoning would cease, and the argument of the *Discourse on Method* with it. Were he really to doubt that there existed anything in the external world that corresponded to the objects presented to him in images, then he could scarcely doubt that his images of the world correspond to the real world. Descartes' doubt of what Kennington calls the "existence thesis" is at odds with his doubt of what Kennington calls the "similarity thesis." The doubt is not universal; it is limited to doubt of the similarity thesis. Descartes doubts that the real world is such as it appears to us in our images of it. By doing so he lays the groundwork for the separation of the everyday world of ordinary phenomena from the world as described for us by modern mathematical physics.

Descartes can doubt that his images of the world are correct, but he cannot doubt that he has images of the world. That is the meaning of "I think, therefore I am."

> And remarking that this truth, I think, therefore I am, was so firm and so assured that all the most extravagant suppositions of the sceptics were not capable of shaking it, I judged that I could receive it without scruple as the first principle of the philosophy which I sought. (IV:1)

It is because the very act of doubting is an act of thinking that Descartes cannot doubt his thinking. He can, therefore, accept it without scruple, that is to say without fear of guilt. The power of this first principle derives from the fact that it is rendered certain in the very act which is designed to render all else uncertain. It makes virtue out of necessity.

The argument of the first paragraph of part 4 is apparently a preparation for a proof for the immortality of the soul in the second paragraph, one proceeding roughly as follows. It is possible for Descartes to doubt even his own body, that is, to doubt the truth of his images of himself. Consequently, he knows only that he is a thinking thing. But since this knowledge of himself as thinking does not depend on whether he is a body, Descartes' essence as thinking is independent of whether he is a body. Therefore, his soul is entirely distinct from his body, and so there is some reason to think that he may be immortal, or at least that his soul does not perish with his body. The problem with the argument is acknowledged elsewhere by Descartes himself.[3] The argument moves from the order in which we know things to the order of their being. It is rather like arguing that since my knowledge of myself as having been born is independent of my knowledge of where I was born I was therefore not born anywhere. Kennington has pointed out that the first sentence of the third paragraph indicates how wobbly the argument of the second paragraph is. Descartes claims to know what is required for a proposition to be true and certain because he has just discovered *one* proposition to be true. But that is surely the "I think, therefore I am," of the first paragraph. If that is the case, then is the second paragraph simply prudential, a precaution necessary if one is to write about metaphysical issues in Descartes' day? It may be that, but if Cartesian rhetoric runs true to form it should be more. There should be a level at which Descartes is quite serious about the surface of his argument. The whole argument depends on the movement from the order of knowing to the order of being. The meaning of that movement seems to be that for Descartes, the being or essence of something *means* whatever one can know of it independent of knowledge of anything else. This is the "reason" which is used to prove the independent existence of the soul, and so this reason is meant to be one of the two pillars of the foundation of Cartesian metaphysics. Put differently, the first sentence of paragraph 3, that Descartes has discovered one truth, could be true only if the truth of the first paragraph, "I think, therefore I am," were the same as the truth of the second paragraph, "I am a substance or nature the whole essence of which is to think." The significance of the two sentences is that Descartes and we are beings capable of thinking of ourselves as thinking apart from thinking of ourselves as being anything in particular.

The ambiguity of the first two paragraphs of part 4 is underscored by the third paragraph, where Descartes announces that since he has found one proposition he knows to be true and certain, he ought now to know what is required for propositions in general to be true and certain. While there is some truth to this argument, there is also a danger that in moving from a particular truth to truth in general we will mistake the peculiarities of this particular truth for attributes of all truths. In fact, Descartes' double characterization of the requirements for a proposition to be true suggests that he is aware of the difficulty. To be true, a proposition must be clear and distinct.[4] "I think, therefore I am," is clear to Descartes, but he does not indicate that it is distinct. However, in the second paragraph he purports to show that the soul is "entirely distinct from the body." At first we naturally take this to mean that the soul is independent in its being from the body. But if we assume that Descartes means to have shown in the second paragraph only that the soul can be known independently of knowledge of the body—that its distinctness is altogether cognitive—then the fact that Descartes claims at the beginning of the third paragraph to have discovered *one* true proposition makes a good deal more sense. In the first paragraph Descartes discovers with clarity that he is a thinking thing; in the second he discovers with distinctness that he is a thinking thing. That is, in the second paragraph Descartes begins to understand how the clear truth of the first paragraph is related to other things that he knows, and so he begins to understand how it is different from them. The irony of the section is that Descartes presents us with what at first seem to be two truths. They seem to be two only because all we understand of either is that neither can be false. As yet we do not understand the relation between the two. In discovering their relation we discover that they are not two but one. All of this is a reminder of the way Cartesian rhetoric works in the *Discourse*. Descartes consciously imitates the way in which truths disclose themselves to us in the world. He first makes an assertion which upon examination proves to mean quite the opposite of what it appeared to mean. Further reflection discloses that in a peculiar way the two opposing assertions are the same. It is probably not accidental that we are reminded of this feature of Cartesian writing just before his proof for the existence of God.

The argument for the existence of God may be briefly summarized as follows. It is more perfect to know than doubt. That seems to be implied by the structure of doubt itself; it is a tacit desire to know. Because Descartes doubts he knows that he is not perfect. Nevertheless, he has an idea of perfection. Without such an idea, doubting would not be possible. Where then does the idea of perfection come from? It must come from something more perfect than Descartes. That cannot be the external world since the brunt of the argument of the first paragraph was to show that his sole contact with the external world came through images, and, true or false, they depend on him. The idea of perfection cannot come from Descartes, for it is not possible for him to be more perfect than himself. It cannot come from nothing since nothing comes from nothing. Consequently, there must be a being who possesses all the perfections of which Descartes is aware.

Now there are difficulties galore with this proof. At most it proves the existence of some being more perfect than Descartes. That hardly justifies the conclusion that there is a being possessing all of the perfections of which Descartes is aware. And even accepting this conclusion, it is not at all clear why one being must possess all of these perfections. Descartes certainly does not argue for the compatibility of the various perfections ordinarily attributed to God. But that is only to say that Descartes seems to assume a clear and distinct idea of God at the very moment he points out to us that he has lapsed into the language of scholasticism, the language he had previously (I:12–13) criticized as obscure and involved.

If the proof is so obviously flawed, perhaps we should attempt to understand it in a different way. If it was not the soul but the reason used to prove its distinctness which was meant to constitute one half of the foundation of Cartesian metaphysics, perhaps it is also not God but the reason used to prove God's existence which is meant to constitute the other half. Descartes articulates this reason at the beginning of the fourth paragraph.

> Following which, reflecting on the fact that I doubted, and that consequently my being was not all perfect, because I saw clearly that it was a greater perfection to know than to doubt, I thought to seek from where I had learned to think of something more perfect than I was. (IV:4)

The reason behind the proof is Descartes' awareness of his own imperfection which is rooted in his awareness of himself as a doubter. Why did Descartes see clearly but not distinctly that it was a greater perfection to know than to doubt? He calls our attention to the problem himself at the end of the preceding paragraph, where he takes it as a general rule that whatever he conceives clearly and distinctly is true

> but that there is only some difficulty in ascertaining well which are those which we conceive distinctly. (IV:3)

Descartes knows that he doubts, and knows it clearly. He knows, therefore, that his condition is defective. But that does not mean being aware of the alternative to doubting, namely knowing, in any but a general way. Descartes does not know where his idea of perfection comes from. But this perfection or being like a god is simply another word for the autonomy which has been the concern of the *Discourse* from the beginning. Descartes, therefore, does not know the source of autonomy. Earlier (II:1) he had identified perfection with order and beauty. By turning to *The Passions of the Soul* we discovered the connection between images and purposes. The difficulty underlying the entire analysis thus far is that perfection has proven to be the goal of the moral argument and of the epistemic argument. As moral it must be imageable, that is, purposive or capable of arousing desire. As epistemic it must be independent of the image.

All of this changes rather drastically the way in which one must read the proof for the existence of God. The question of God has become the question of perfection. The question of how we have an idea of God has therefore become the question of how we have an idea of perfection. Where does that idea come from? It could not have come from the world because we are connected to the world only through images. And images are always partial and particular while perfection is finally complete and universal. Therefore, my idea of perfection must come from me. It is simply the reverse side of my desire for mastery. Put differently, if the will wills only what the understanding presents to it as possible, then the idea of perfection is the necessary condition for the existence of the passion of mastery. But the idea is not itself clear and distinct. That is, there is no positive idea of perfection; there is only a general sense of lack which does not translate into a general desire. The paradox is that the idea of perfection, or God, is the necessary condition for the passion of mastery and so for happiness, while on the other hand, it is necessarily an obstacle to mastery and so to happiness. It makes us and it mars us. That Descartes has such an idea is therefore the origin both of the possibility of guilt and of the possibility of mastery. Part 4 of the *Discourse on Method* is Descartes' reflection on where he got the idea of perfect satisfaction. Nothing outside of him can give him perfect satisfaction since the desire to be satisfied is complete and universal while the things of the world are always partial and particular. The question then is what sort of object in the world could a desire for complete mastery ever attain which would satisfy it.

The specific function of God in the second half of part 4 is to provide a means for making certain what has been doubted. Descartes needs a lever to move the world. This lever must work on the level of the doubt and also on a deeper level. To doubt our images of the world means to doubt natural purposiveness. But that nature is not purposive means finally that there is nothing within nature which can really satisfy our deepest longing. In forcing us to reject the teleology of Aristotelian physics, Descartes wishes to cast doubt on the possibility of satisfying our deepest longing. Yet he wishes to do so in such a way as to satisfy our deepest longing. The doubt is instrumental both morally and epistemically. It is meant to make possible a kind of mastery that will release men from guilt by cutting them free from the fable of complete contentment. To release men from that fable would mean to free them to take complete contentment in the successive mastery of the parts of nature. Descartes means to make possible from the inside and in time what was hitherto understood as possible only for a creator god outside of nature and outside of time (part 4 alone of the parts of the *Discourse* does not contain the word *temps*.) Descartes has in mind changing the world so that it is possible for us to live up to our expectations of ourselves.

Part 4 is *the* treatment of God in the *Discourse*. By pointing explicitly to the connection between his proof for the distinct soul and his proof for a perfect God, Descartes also points tacitly to the connection between the self which is sure of itself as a maker of images, that is, of purposes, and God as the ultimate image of purposiveness within the world. God is the ultimate illusion of "good sense," the perfect answer to the human problem. He is the image of autonomy. The difficulty is that God turns out to be like a chimera or a golden mountain, a composite solution generated out of diverse particular desires. For that reason the perfection of God is unavailable to human beings and at the same time serves as the one thing most needful for them. God is the origin of human guilt and unhappiness. One could therefore say that the foundation of Descartes' metaphysics is not really God and the soul; it is rather what these two are images of—the idea of perfection and metaphysical neutrality. Both are meant to teach us that the only way to master the whole is via the parts. Consequently, Descartes moves from what has proven to be a problematic metaphysics in part 4 to the account of his physics in part 5. The physics will be meant not simply to provide an "infinity of artifices" (VI:2) but also to provide an alternative to the understanding of human autonomy which the Christian God both represents and forecloses.

II

As the synopsis indicates, part 5 divides into three sections.

In the fifth, the order of the questions of physics that he sought, and particularly the explanation of the movement of the heart and of some other difficulties which pertain to medicine, as well as the difference which exists between our soul and that of beasts.

In the first section (V:1–4) Descartes seems to be concerned with the order of nature, of external things. However, as the French of the synopsis makes quite clear, the order that Descartes seeks is an order of questions (*l'ordre des questions de physique qu'il a cherchées*). He will be concerned not so much with the world as with questions about the world. That is, he will be concerned not with the world, but with his suppressed treatise, *The World*.

Once again Descartes begins with the question of rhetoric.

I would be very glad to proceed and to make visible here the whole chain of other truths which I deduced from these first ones. But because for this purpose (*à cause que pour cet effet*) it would be necessary now that I speak of several questions which are in controversy among the learned, with whom I do not at all desire to embroil myself, I believe that it will be better that I abstain, and that I say only in a general way what they are, so that it be left to the more wise to judge if it would be useful that the public be more particularly informed. (V:1)

One motive for this reticence is obviously prudence. The learned are the Christian learned, and Descartes does not wish to get into trouble with them. He goes on to say that "some considerations" prevented him from publishing his treatise, *The World* (V:2). In part 6 he will make clear that he is referring to the fate of Galileo (VI:1). Descartes therefore suggests early in part 5 that the contents of *The World* are at odds with the contents of the world according to Christianity. There is reason for prudence here.

At the same time Descartes goes deeper. We are not reading the world, or even *The World*, but rather a summary of *The World*. Descartes uses this occasion on which he must summarize to give an account of what it means to summarize and the deeper reasons for having to do so. This account will prove to be the heart of his physics. The question of summary has been present tacitly since the very beginning of the *Discourse*, in the synopsis. It was introduced there to alert us to a parallel between the manner of Descartes' writing and what he was writing about, i.e. the deceptive character of nature. Having learned to read Descartes, we must now return to nature.

About the treatise he did not publish, Descartes tells us the following:

> I had planned to include in it everything that I thought I knew, before writing it, touching the nature of material things. But in just the same way as painters not being able to represent equally well in a flat painting (*tableau*) all the diverse surfaces of a solid body, in choosing one of the principal ones which alone they put toward the light, and shading the others make them appear only insofar as one can see them in looking at it, thus, believing myself unable to put in my discourse everything that I had in thought, I undertook to expose there very fully what I understood of light. (V:2)

We sometimes think while writing, but Descartes has been at great pains to distinguish between thinking and writing here. Given his previous distinction between the act of thought by which we believe a thing and the act of thought by which we know we believe a thing (III:2), it seems fair to assume that, as Descartes presents it here, the act of writing involves an awareness that one knows and not simply a knowing. By putting one's thoughts on a page, one makes an object of them. In parts 5 and 6, Descartes' reflections on what it means to write will all have something to do with he question of self-awareness.

In describing *The World* Descartes likens it to a *tableau*. The word appears only one other time in the *Discourse*, in part 1 (I:4) where it is used to describe the *Discourse* as a *tableau* of Descartes' life. We now learn the significance of that description. What is true of *The World*, that it was a view from a particular perspective, will be even truer of the *Discourse on Method*, which is a summary of a summary. Even had we gotten the whole of *The World* we would not have gotten the whole of the world. This is confirmed by the opening sentence of part 5, where Descartes describes his willingness to make *visible* the whole chain of truths to have come from his principal truths. To try to make them visible means to confront once again the problem of the image. It is not possible to see the whole of the world all at once while one is in it. To see it at all, therefore, means to adopt a perspective, or to pick a problem and see how everything else relates to it. This is the problem of Descartes' physics and at the same time of being autonomous while immersed within the given.

Descartes is aware of this problem, as is clear from the perspective on the world he chooses in *The World*, namely, light. With the proper light and shading, he will make light visible. But since this amounts to placing light in the proper perspective, and the problem of shading has served as a metaphor for the problem of perspective, it is fair to say that Descartes' project in *The World* was to provide a perspective on perspective. He did not publish that attempt for other reasons besides his fear of suffering the fate of Galileo. He also worried about putting into his *discours* everything he had in thought. By referring here to his discourse and not to his treatise he suggests two things: a tacit reference to the most common meaning of *discourse*, that is, speech, and at the same time that what was true of *The World* is at least equally true of *the* discourse. The *Discourse on Method* can be understood as a perspective on the necessity of perspective. The heart of part 5 is this problem of speech. *The World* can never quite give us the world. The *Discourse*, where Descartes gives an account of how he turned to "the great book of the world," is a reflection of this problem. Insofar as part 5 is concerned with speech as the distinguishing feature of man, and with the necessary incompleteness of speech, it will prove to be a reflection on the necessary incompleteness of man. Of course it purports to give a complete account of this incompleteness.

What was contained in *The World*? After mentioning light, Descartes adds the sun and the fixed stars as the causes of light, the heavens as the transmitter of light, the planets, comets, and earth as the reflectors of light, bodies on the earth as either transparent, luminous, or colored, and finally man as the spectator of all of this. It is worth noting in passing that since *The World* was to have been an account of all Descartes knew concerning material things, he seems to have included men in the category of material things. Conspicuously absent in Descartes' list is any reference to motion.

After giving an account of what is contained in *The World*, an account organized around light as its privileged question, Descartes proceeds to give an account of what is contained in the world.

> For this very reason, in order to shade all these things a little, and to be able to say more freely what I judged of them without being obliged either to follow or to refute the opinions which are received among the

learned, I resolved to leave all this world here to their disputes, and to
speak only of what would happen in a new one if God now created
somewhere in imaginary spaces enough matter to compose it and if he
agitated diversely and without order the various parts of this matter, so
that he made of it a chaos as confused as the poets could feign it, and
that afterward he did nothing else than lend his ordinary agreement to
nature and let it act following the laws which he had established. (V:2)

But this plan is for purposes other than avoiding controversy. By ignoring
the account in Genesis Descartes declares himself unconcerned with the question of how the world was in fact made. The distinction between "could have
been made" and "was made" becomes irrelevant.

Immediately following this declaration of his procedure Descartes gives
another list. Had God simply created a chaos and the laws of nature, the order
of creation would have been first matter, then the heavens (including the earth,
planets, comets, sun, and fixed stars), light (and the movement of the heavens
now sensible because of light), mixed bodies on the earth (including gravity,
tides, winds, mountains, oceans, rivers, metals, and plants), fire (as capable
of transforming matter), and finally men and animals. This list is spread out
somewhat more than the first. Directly after it (V:3) Descartes disclaims any
intention to replace God's order with his own. By doing so he reminds us of
God's order in which light was created first, then the heavens, then the earth,
sea and plants, then the heavenly bodies, then fish and fowl, and finally
animals and man. All three of these lists fall into six parts, as shown in figure
4.1.

God	Descartes 1	Descartes 2
1. light	light	matter
2. heaven	sun and fixed stars	heavens
3. earth/sea and plants	heavens	light
4. heavenly bodies	planets/comets/earth	mixed bodies on earth (including plants)
5. fish and fowl	bodies on earth	fire
6. animals and men	man (spectator)	men and animals

Fig. 4.1. Creation according to Genesis and Descartes.

There are a number of interesting discrepancies. Descartes includes plants
with such things as metals in his second list, implying that they have no
special status for him; they are not ensouled. He singles out fire for treatment
in the second list. This seems to have to do with the role of fire in explaining
animate life (V:4–5). But perhaps the most interesting problem with the three

lists is the traditional difficulty of the order of creation of light, plants, and sun. In Genesis, light and plants are created before the creation of the sun. Descartes' two lists seem to avoid that problem. In the first list, light precedes the sun because the order in question is an order of knowing. It makes no pretence to be an order of being. Light is Descartes' chosen perspective; the account of the sun must come next as being the cause of light. In his second list Descartes means by the heavens the heavenly bodies, and so the source of light precedes light. He needs two lists because they are doing two quite different things. The first is analytic, the second, causal. That the two are always kept separate is the genuine "Cartesian dualism."

The biblical account, on the other hand, attempts to do both things at once. Roughly speaking, the first three days are an analysis of the kind-character of things independent of the question of motion, whereas the second group of three days is an attempt to give an account of motion. The Bible seeks to combine an account of the intelligibility of things with an account of the goodness or desirability of things.[5] If it contradicts itself it does so because of its attempt to reflect these two perspectives at once. The innovation of Descartes is to separate the two perspectives and to claim that they do not have to be brought together. That is the real significance behind his claim that we can both accept the view of the creation set forth in Genesis and at the same time accept the fact that the world is much easier to understand when we see it being generated little by little. What God can do all at once humans must do little by little while keeping in mind the all at once.

Descartes' two ways of looking at the world, his analytical list and his synthetical, causal list, seem at first to provide a model for looking at everything else. In fact, however, his treatment of the heart in the second section of part 5 shows that this is not quite the case. The real tension between the account of motion in the second list and the account of the order of knowing in the first list is reflected in their final members. In the first, man is treated as a spectator, and he occupies the final position alone. In the second, he shares his position with animals. Descartes' dual way of looking at the world is rooted in his dual way of looking at man. This dualism begins to become clear in the treatment of the heart and becomes the explicit problem of the last section of part 5. The first step is to make the movement of the heart paradigmatic.

But in order that it may be seen in what way I treated this matter I want to place here the explanation of the movement of the heart and of the arteries, which being the first and most general that one observes in animals, one will easily judge from it what should be thought of all the others. (V:5)

The matter in question is the Cartesian treatment of man in connection with his nature as animal.

> From the description of inanimate bodies and of plants I passed to those of animals and particularly to that of men. But because I had not yet enough knowledge to speak of them in the same style as of the rest, that is to say by demonstrating the effects through the causes, and making visible from what seeds and in what fashion nature must produce them, I contented myself with supposing that God formed the body of man entirely similar to one of ours, as much in the external figure of its members as in the internal conformation of its organs without composing it of any matter other than what I have described, and without putting in it at the beginning any rational soul or anything else to serve as a vegetative or sensitive soul, except that he excited in the heart one of those fires without light. (V:4)

Descartes has "not yet" succeeded in reducing man to matter plus spontaneous combustion, but that is the goal. He aims to describe all motion in men, and one supposes that to include the motion of thought, in the same way in which he is about to describe the principal motion, the movement of the heart. Such as account would, of course, undermine the traditional account of the soul as principle of both cognition and of motion or life.[6] The account here parallels the account of the world. In both cases the ancient error was to attempt to combine two perspectives. Beginning with a confused togetherness, the ancients were never able to gain a sufficiently distinct object of inquiry so as to achieve clarity. Descartes achieves clarity, but at the expense of the separation of man the spectator, that is, the order of knowing, from man the animal, that is, the order of being. And yet he is aware that the two are in fact one. The thinking of man the spectator is possible only given the motion of man the animal. This is nothing but the inseparability of "good sense" and natural egoism in part 1 and of morality and epistemology in parts 3 and 4.

Descartes agrees with modern accounts of the heart and of the circulatory system and with the account of William Harvey as to the shape of that system at rest or even insofar as he describes the movement within the circulatory system. It is with regard to the cause of the motion of the heart and of the blood that Descartes differs. Harvey, who saw that the heart was a muscle, and that its contraction was the cause of the movement of the blood, understood the heart as a pump. He called the heart a "household divinity" and identified it as the mysterious source of the heat, movement and nutrient quality of the blood. Descartes on the other hand understands the heart to be like a furnace, and the movement of the blood to be very much like a steam-heat system. The unknown in Descartes' account is what makes the heart to be hot, although this lacuna does not trouble him.[7]

For the rest, in order that those who do not know the force of mathematical demonstrations, and are not accustomed to distinguish true reasons from probable will not hazard to deny all of this without examination, I wish to inform them that this movement which I have just explained follows as necessarily solely from the disposition of the organs that one can see in the heart with the eye and from the heat that one can sense with the fingers and from the nature of the blood that one can know by experience, as does that of a clock from the force, from the situation and from the form of its counterweights and of its wheels. (V:6)

All of this follows according to "the rules of mechanics which are the same as those of nature" (V:8).

The world, or the heart, can therefore be explained given the laws of nature, mechanics, and someone to wind the clock, or warm the heart. But this winder/ heater need only be presupposed, not understood. Our experience of the heat in the heart and of the existence of the world is our sign that we are already *in* the world, and therefore have a warrant for our presupposition. Men can be understood in the same fashion as material things, that is mechanistically, once motion is presupposed. And the fact that we are looking for a cause of motion is in itself a motion. Reflecting on that fact, making a virtue out of a necessity, allows us the presupposition we need. From that point on it is useful to think of ourselves mechanistically. Descartes leaves no doubt that mechanism is meant to extend to the very motions we are aware of prior to our mechanistic theory, and which are necessary to justify mechanism. That is, he leaves no doubt that he intends to give an account of thinking as a motion caused in its turn by the motion of animal spirits which are like "a very subtle wind, or rather like a very pure and lively (*vive*) flame" (V:8).

This account clearly runs more or less parallel to Descartes' second list, his causal or synthetical account of the creation. It is subsequent to the first list which justifies the order of questioning altogether. Just as Descartes had made it clear that we could think of the world as coming to be little by little and still accept the creation all at once by God, here he makes clear that we can think of ourselves as coming to be little by little, and still accept the view that we were made all at once, whole, by God. In both cases God points to the need to think of ourselves as whole so that we can have some notion of the way our parts add up. Once again, God functions like the idea of perfection. God is the necessary condition for the parts to be parts; he is also the sign that the parts taken together are not simply the whole. That is not at all to say that there is any possibility of knowledge other than by way of parts.

The last section of part 5 deals with what can and cannot be understood mechanistically. Descartes considers light, sound, smell, taste, heat, and all other qualities of external objects, hunger, thirst, and interior passions, and finally the common sense, memory, and fancy. All of these can be understood as caused by the movements of animal spirits, that is, bodies. Therefore the actions which are born of them can be regarded as the movements of automata. Given the breadth of the range of things that can be understood mechanistically, Descartes is under some obligation to explain precisely what the difference is between men and complicated machines. He gives two reasons for our not thinking of ourselves as machines and hints at a third.

> Of which the first is that they would never be able to use words, nor any other signs in composing them, as we do in order to declare our thoughts to others. (V:10)

But if the fancy can be explained mechanistically, and it is responsible for changing ideas in divers ways, and even composing new ones (V:9), then why should there be any difficulty in explaining such novel formulations as are present in speech in the same way? Descartes himself points to this difficulty in the version of this first reason which he uses to distinguish men from animals.

> But by these same two means one can also know the difference between men and beasts. Because it is a very remarkable thing that there are no men so depraved and stupid without excepting even the insane that they are not able to arrange together divers words, and compose from them a *discourse* [emphasis mine] through which they may make their thoughts understood; and on the other hand there is no other animal at all as perfect and as happily born as it may be which can do the same. (V:11)

And somewhat later in the paragraph:

> And when one notices the inequality among animals of even one species, as well as among men, and when one notices that some are more easy to train than others, it is not believable that a monkey or a parrot, which was of the most perfect of its species would equal in that a child from the most stupid [of its species], or at least a child who had a troubled brain, if their soul was not of a nature completely different from ours. (V:11)

Descartes surely knows that "*un enfant*" understood as an infant can do none of the things which he here asserts all members of the species are able to do, not to mention those men so mentally retarded as not to be able to speak. His argument is therefore persuasive neither in its claim that speech is something proper to all men nor in its claim that speech is something proper only to men. And yet the two claims are by themselves not implausible. Descartes had made them seem implausible by using weak arguments to support them, arguments both unpersuasive in themselves and very much at odds with what Descartes had previously claimed about the range of things that can be explained mechanistically.[8]

He offers a second reason why we ought not to consider ourselves machines.

> And the second is that, while there are many things they do as well or perhaps better than any of us, they are infallibly lacking in some others, by which one discovers that they did not act by knowledge, but only by the disposition of their organs. (V:10)

Because machines can do some things better than we, but fall short of what we can do in others, we conclude that they act only from a disposition of their parts when they do better and not spontaneously as we do. Yet, as Kennington has pointed out, if we assume that the argument works, then it can also be turned around. Because we can do some things, but not all things, better than machines, in those things we do better can we be seen to be acting out of a disposition of our parts? Does that mean that machines have a "universal instrument?" Once again the argument, which was to have established a distinction between men and machines, has served only to render them alike. Descartes uses a similar argument in the following paragraph concerning animals, and indeed, concludes it with the suggestion that animals are essentially machines.

> but rather that they have none [mind or *l'esprit*] at all and that it is nature which acts in them according to the disposition of their organs, just as one sees that a clock which is composed only of wheels and weights can count the hours and measure time more exactly than we with all our prudence. (V:11)

The weakness of these two arguments meant to distinguish men from animals and machines is tacitly acknowledged by Descartes' claim that it would be "morally impossible" for a machine to respond to situations in life in the same way that our reason allows us to respond (V:10). One is compelled to ask what this moral possibility means. Does "not moral" mean "not true"? Descartes has previously used the notion of "moral assurance" to speak somewhat disparagingly of our confidence in the existence of the external world (IV:7). Moral possibility seems on the one hand an admission by Descartes that his argument is a failure, while on the other hand it invites speculation that the real difference between men and animals is on an altogether different plane.

Descartes' rhetoric here takes a form by now quite familiar. At first, the argument seems designed to show the difference between men and animals, and machines. However, the very way in which the argument is weak points toward the underlying sameness of men, animals, and machines. All act out of a disposition of parts; the rules of nature are the rules of mechanics. We expect, however, to be shown that in a peculiar way the initial claim is indeed

true. To see how that is the case it is helpful to take our bearings by Descartes'
own conclusion to part 5. The last paragraph is concerned with the soul as
the distinguishing feature of men.

> In conclusion, I have extended myself here a little on the subject of the
> soul because it is the most important. Because after the error of those
> who deny God, which I think I have sufficiently refuted above, there is
> nothing at all which more quickly alienates weak minds from the straight
> path of virtue than to imagine that the soul of beasts is of the same nature
> as ours and that consequently we have nothing to fear or to hope after
> this life, any more than the flies and ants. (V:12)

It is only necessary to remember what Descartes had said previously about
"weak minds" to realize the limits of the claim he makes here.[9] At the same
time, to discover the third level of his rhetoric would mean to take seriously
"moral possibility" and speech as the distinguishing features of the species.
When those two are put together the result is something like the rational soul.

We need to ask what is really at issue in Descartes' examples of what
machines can do as opposed to what we can do. By themselves machines can
do certain things well, and they can do certain things not at all. In a way,
then, what distinguishes human beings is that they are able to do some things
badly. Descartes provides his example when he states that humans "speak"
even when their instruments of speech are defective (V:11). Clocks, on the
other hand, do not tell time without hands. That is what it means to say that
human beings have an adaptability greater than any other animal "however
perfect or happily born" (V:11). It looks as though it is our imperfection
which distinguishes us and our awareness of that imperfection which constitutes self-awareness. We begin to see why doubt is the beginning-point for
Descartes. Doubt is possible only for a being who does things imperfectly.
It is *l'esprit* in all of its gradations and not reason which is the distinguishing
feature of men.

Moral possibility has to do with the fact that men, and not machines or
animals, have an idea of perfection. Descartes places only the denial of God,
or the idea of perfection, above the denial of the difference between men and
beasts in importance. The idea of perfection had been linked previously not
so much with thinking as with doubting as the most fundamental form of
thinking. Doubt is the sign of the specifically human soul. Making a machine
in all regards like a man but without a soul (V:9–10) would be making a man
without doubt. Such a man, unaware of his own imperfection, would be
"happily born," and would lack knowledge of good and evil. Descartes'
automaton would be man in the Garden of Eden.

What does all of this have to do with speech and the ability to speak? Part

5 began with a reflection on the distinction between *The World* and the world. Writing a perspective on perspective meant thinking about thinking. Or,

> the act of thought by which one believes a thing, being different from that by which one knows that one believes it, one often exists without the other. (III:2)

Doubting does not mean not believing so much as it does knowing that one does not believe. The capacity for speech is what makes this perceiving of one's perceiving possible. It is, therefore, this capacity which makes it possible to reply to the sense of what is said even when one responds *wrongly*. Otherwise our responses would simply be predictable reactions to external stimuli. But knowing that we believe something means knowing that we might believe otherwise; it means possibly doubting. The externalizing of our belief in speech, and especially in writing, means exposing our belief to ourselves, and that means exposing it as potentially different from what it is. In a way, then, the most interesting thing about self-awareness is its being grounded in unhappiness (we are not happily born) and imperfection. For that reason one suspects, with Leibniz, that Descartes' God could not be self-aware.

Descartes seems to suggest that the human capacity to understand is rooted in the human capacity to misunderstand and not vice versa. He first points to what he has to explain—the world. He then presents his hypothetical theory which he claims, correctly, is not a description of the real world. *The World* is not the world, and part 5 is yet a further step removed; it is an account of *The World*. The very reason this hypothetical theory can work, that is, explain the world, is that it claims not to. Recognizing the need for finality, Descartes attempts to institutionalize provisionality. This is the real liberation effected by science. Part 5 as a whole is Descartes' reflection on the fact that human beings are what they are by virtue of their capacity to have a perspective on their perspectives. It is not method but discourse or speech about method that distinguishes men. Speech makes possible a general sense of oneself as lacking, and therefore a general desire, a passion arising out of the perception of the various passions in their incompleteness. In this way the perspectival character of human understanding, far from serving simply as an obstacle to human autonomy, is a necessary precondition for its realization. The *Discourse on Method* recognizes and celebrates this fact.

III

There is something disarming about ending a book with a reflection on whether it ought to be published. It is like a mystery in which we are already privy to the conclusion. By preserving both the mystery and the finality

Descartes gives the *Discourse* an end which is at the same time a beginning. In a certain sense he refuses to finish the book; in a certain sense he does finish it. He thereby gives us provisionality in its final form. By reflecting on what we are doing, reading his book, we already know Descartes' decision. Just as our doubt of the existence of the world led us to a recognition of our having already affirmed the world, our doubts about whether *The World* should be published are the sign that the *Discourse on Method* has been published. We are not so much being asked to undertake to decide whether it is to be published as we are being asked to understand the reasons why it has been.

Once again, the synopsis points the way toward the unraveling of part 6.

> And in the last, what things he believes to be required in order to go further forward in the research into nature than he has been, and what reasons have made him write.

Part 6 is the only place in Descartes' writings where he reflects at length on the goals and purposes of his philosophy.[10] On the other hand, the goals and purposes of his philosophy are not simply identical with the results of his research into nature. He plans to go further into his researches, but the goals of the inquiry need to have been established from the outset. They are what makes further research possible. The continuous progress of science must be supported by principles in some way final and in some way known. But they cannot be the same principles which are understood to be the goal of the progress of science. The *Discourse on Method* does not end by completing a description of the world; it ends rather by explaining why such a description, *The World*, had to be replaced by a discourse on method. Descartes' only extended account of philosophy as a whole serves, not accidentally, as a preface to a collection of treatises devoted to specific sciences: optics, geometry, and meteorology.[11]

To understand why part 6, which seems to belong at the beginning of the *Discourse*, is placed at the end, it is helpful to note what Descartes says in a different context about the proofs in the *Dioptrics* and *Meteors*.

> For it seems to me that the reasons follow from one another in such a way that as the last are demonstrated by the first which are their causes, the first are demonstrated, and reciprocally, by the last which are their effects. And one ought not to imagine that I commit here the fault which the logicians name a circle; because experience, rendering these effects for the most part very certain, the causes from which I deduce them do not serve so much to prove them as to explain them. But, quite the contrary, it is they that are proved by them. (VI:10)

It is experience which is crucial for this alleged "rationalist." Science is not deductive in the sense that one can arrive at the end of an argument simply by following the rules of logic without having known where one was going, or where one wanted to go. Indeed, under such circumstances one would have no way of recognizing the end when one reached it. Any stage in the deduction would be as good a place to stop as any other. Were it possible, a purely deductive science would be the science of a purely innocent being. It would be a manifestation of autonomy and not a tool to achieve it. In Descartes' earlier indictment of the logic of the schools as a logic of explaining what one already knows rather than what it should be, a logic of discovery, the implied criticism was that while Aristotle recognizes the distinction between what is first to us and what is first by nature, he does not in any final way account for the way we are to move from the former to the latter. He presents no systematic resolution of the tension between being and seeming.

In the present case, Descartes presents the issue as a question of whether he will publish. But it must necessarily take the form of providing reasons for the fact that he has published already. This fact of publication is the experience that "proves" its causes rather in the way the success of a reformer renders his reform legitimate. Descartes presents his deliberation about whether he should publish as though the reasons for publishing were causes for publishing, as though they were elements in an order of being. In fact, since his deliberation is really a reflection on something he has already done, the act of writing his reasons down makes them part of an order of knowing meant to explain what has already happened. Similarly, while parts 1–5 of the *Discourse* are clearly in some way the cause of part 6, that is, the discovery of the physics is the cause of the consequences of the physics, in another way part 6 proves parts 1–5 by making their purpose clear. At first, it looks as though the uses of the physics are simply deduced from the physics itself, as though knowledge of what to do with physics were of the same order as physics. In fact, knowledge of what to do with the physics is one of those things rendered sure by experience. Descartes' explanation of physics as a form of mastery of nature in parts 1–5 would be worth very little as an explanation were it not "proved" by something given in human nature, the desire to be autonomous.

Put somewhat more simply, part 5 of the *Discourse* is an outline of a mechanistic physics. The criterion of truth for that physics has been present since part 1; it is "the useful for life." Because mechanistic physics must be silent about what is finally useful, it is not surprising that Descartes should turn to the question of whether to publish. To say why he publishes is to say what he expects from his physics, what its purpose is prescientifically, and so postscientifically. It is in this way both the beginning and the end of the book and as close as Descartes comes in the *Discourse* to an account of whatever is left of final causality in his philosophy.

There is another reason why part 6 follows part 5. If, as part 5 had suggested, any attempt to grasp the world as a whole is doomed from the outset to be perspectival, why should one make the attempt? The answer, hinted at in part 5, has to do with the human capacity for speech as grounded in the capacity to misunderstand, doubt, and err. In other words, speech is possible because of the distinction between the act of thought by which we believe and the act of thought by which we know we believe. What we believe and what we "know" we believe are not always the same. Or, the principles by which we act are not always known to us. It is for this reason that part 6 can be the cause of parts 1–5 while being discovered to be so only after the fact. Indeed, the difference between *The World* and the *Discourse* indicates that Descartes discovered his physics before having discovered its cause. But this is simply another way of describing what it is about us which makes us susceptible to the deceptive powers of nature. It is what makes us simultaneously more and less than merely cameras.

The awareness of our own defective nature accounts for our wish to be flawless. In the present context, that would mean closing the gap between what we believe and what we "know" we believe. Otherwise we would be placed in the predicament of thinking we want something only to discover repeatedly that getting it will not make us happy because it is not what we really wanted. Contentment would seem to require closing the gap between thinking and acting. In a way this tension has proven to be the central issue of the *Discourse on Method*. In part 6 it emerges once again as the problem of rhetoric. That rhetoric is necessary and possible in the world means that the goals of thinking and acting do not automatically coincide. Rhetoric always appeals to the split between belief and what Descartes calls knowledge of belief either by appealing to what we believe but do not know we believe or to what we think we believe but do not really believe. This distinction, which has again and again proved so important to the *Discourse* is, to be sure, a curious one. One is first inclined to think that the distinction between believing and knowing that one believes makes no sense. A belief is, after all, an act of a cognitive being. One tends, therefore, to think that what Descartes means is that when we are moved by passions we are only sometimes aware of the fact. This makes sense, but it does not explain why he persists in calling this being moved by the passions a belief. Only when one realizes that Descartes means us to see that the apparently natural passions which move us without our being aware of what moves us are not simply natural, but are formed rather by all sorts of conventional expectations, do we see that the act of thought by which we believe a thing is really Descartes' way of speaking about the way all of our actions are informed by conventional opinion. For human beings to act at all is to believe. Descartes' reflection on whether to publish is therefore also a reflection on the relation between philosophy and society, and so on what can and ought to be said publicly. It is consequently also a reflection on the relation between thinking and acting. Publication is an action in the deepest sense in that it will affect the conventions and beliefs that human beings have, do not necessarily know that they have, but which necessarily affect all that they do. In part 6, the tension between acting and thinking goes deeper than one at first suspects. It is not only the case that there is a tension between what we want and what we think we want; it is also the case that were there no such tension, we would not think we wanted anything. Descartes' analysis thus far makes it appear that a reflective being's actions will never seem adequate. We need to ask what sort of contentment will be possible for such a being.

Part 6 divides into four sections. In the first (VI:1) he tells the reader why he did not publish *The World*. In the second (VI:2–3) he tells why he had wanted to publish it. In the third (VI:4–7) he says why he resolved nevertheless not to publish. And in the last section (VI:8–12) he gives reasons for his final decision to publish the *Discourse on Method*.

The obvious reason for not publishing is the fate of Galileo.

> It is now three years since I arrived at the end of the treatise which contained all these things, and since I began to review it for the purpose of putting it in the hands of a printer when I learned that some people to whom I defer, and whose authority can be scarcely less over my actions than my own reason over my thoughts, had disapproved of an opinion in physics published a little before by someone else, which I do not want to say I held, but rather that I had remarked nothing in it before their censure that I could imagine to be prejudicial either to religion or the the state, nor consequently which would have prevented me from writing it if reason had persuaded me of it. And that made me fear that there might all the same be found some opinion among mine in which I was mistaken, notwithstanding the great care that I have always taken to receive nothing at all of which I had not demonstrations very certain, and to write nothing at all which could tend to the disadvantage of anyone. (VI.1)

Why has Descartes suddenly become so deferential? It is clear than on some level he cannot be entirely serious. This is the same Descartes who previously had said he would never trust anything but the evidence of his reason (IV:8). On the other hand, his newfound deference is important for having introduced the clear distinction between thought and action. His thoughts are governed by reason alone. He claims that his actions are governed by the authorities, the Church, and the state. The elements are all in place for the emergence of guilt. Descartes fears he is wrong despite having taken so many precautions. Now, previously he had acknowledged only one thing about which it is still possible for him to feel guilt, failing to try to replace provisionally accepted opinions by better ones. But why might publishing get in the way of such an attempt? Publishing means running the risk of inflexibility. It forces one to defend views as established doctrines. Descartes wishes to avoid the immobilizing effect of declaring doctrines. The danger is that he will have to defend himself just as the Church has had to defend itself against Galileo. That amounts to renouncing reason. In its first paragraph, then, part 6 points to the conflict between theory and action. The danger to be feared is something like the "sedimentation of the tradition." The very power by which a new view becomes accepted and taken seriously makes it inevitable that the view will be repeated. The more it is repeated the more obvious it will seem, the less the difficulty of winning it from the world will be understood and consequently the less it will be understood. In writing *The World* Descartes knows that he has adopted a particular perspective but no one else will know that. As a result, he is sure to be systematically misunderstood. Descartes' final decision to publish the *Discourse on Method* means that he thinks he has found a way to overcome this problem. Publishing *The World* would have been somewhat like trying to stand outside of the whole in order to describe the whole. It would have been pre-Socratic in character. The form of the *Discourse* suggests the possibility of observing the whole from a perspective inside the whole. It is Descartes' equivalent of Socrates' "second sailing."[12]

Descartes claims to have had "very strong" reasons for publishing. It is clear at least that his desire to publish meant that he did not think that what he had written "could turn to the disadvantage of anyone." And yet, his "inclination" has "always made him hate the trade of making books." Later in part 6 Descartes makes a point of telling us that he hates something else.

> For although I do not love glory to excess, or even, if I dare say it, I hate it as much as I judge it contrary to the repose which I esteem above all things. (VI:8)

Do the passages go together? That is, does Descartes hate the trade of making books because it is contrary to the repose which he so values? Descartes says he is inclined to hate making books. The word *inclination* occurs only three times in the *Discourse*, and all three instances are in part 6. In the very last paragraph of the book Descartes says that he is particularly inclined against all plans which would be useful to some while harming others. The phrase, of course, reminds us of his initial description of the goal of this "history or fable" (I:5). Writing books inevitably leads to harm as well as good, and so Descartes is inclined to hate it. Writing books will turn out to be a great deal like waging war. Both require that one hold a position. Descartes wishes to avoid that. His reasons are fairly clear by now.

> And I think I can say without vanity that if there is someone who is capable of it [completing his experiments] it must rather be myself than any other, not that there may not be in the world several minds incomparably better than mine, but because one cannot so well conceive a thing and make it one's own when one has learned it from another as when one invents it oneself. The truth of the matter is that I have often explained some of my opinions to people of very good mind who, while I talk to them, seem to understand these opinions very distinctly, and yet when they repeated them I noticed that they nearly always changed them in such a way that I could no longer acknowledge them as mine. On account of which I am glad here to beg our descendants never to believe that the things that will be said to them come from me when I have not divulged them at all. (VI:6)

Elsewhere, Descartes warns against those who will seek to "build some extravagant philosophy on what they believe to be [his] principles" (VI:10).

Nevertheless, Descartes did desire to publish. Neither the advances in science made possible by the method nor its use in regulating Descartes' own morals account for why he is under an obligation to write. Both are idiosyncratic, rooted in the particular passions of a particular man. In morals, everyone is so confident of his own sense that there are as "many reformers as there are heads," and although Descartes' speculations please him, others no doubt have their own which please them more. There is then nothing sufficiently general generated by the method to warrant publication. Apparently writing requires something like universality,

> as without doubt one always looks more closely at what one believes ought to be seen by many than at that which one does only for oneself, and often things which seemed true when I began to conceive them have seemed false to me when I wanted to put them on paper. (VI:4)

What, then, changed which made Descartes feel obliged to write?

> But as soon as I had acquired some general notions touching physics, and beginning to test them in various particular difficulties, I noticed how far they might conduct us, and how much they differ from the principles which have been used up until the present, I believed that I could not hold them hidden without greatly sinning against the law which obliges us to procure as much as is in us the good of all men. (VI:2)

This is the only place in all of Descartes' writing where such a categorical obligation is asserted.[13] It is important that Descartes emphasizes the *general* notions he has acquired and the *general* good of men. On the surface it seems as though what has changed to move him to write is this combination of the two. The physics provides the general means for benefiting men in general, the categorical obligation describes the end to which this means is to be applied. The result is perhaps the most famous passage in the *Discourse on Method*.

> Because they have made me see that it is possible to attain knowledge (*connaissances*) which is very useful to life, and that in place of that speculative philosophy which is taught in the schools one could find a practical philosophy, by which, knowing the force and actions of fire, air, stars, heavens, and all the other bodies which surround us as distinctly as we now know the various trades of our artisans, we could employ them in the same fashion in all the uses for which they are fit, and thus render ourselves like masters and possessors of nature, which is not only desirable for the invention of an infinity of artifices which would enable one to enjoy without pain the fruits of the earth and all the conveniences which are to be found there, but also principally for the conservation of health, which is without doubt the first good and the foundation of all other goods in this life. Because even the mind depends so much on the temperament and disposition of the body that, if it is possible to find some means which commonly renders men wiser and more able than they have been until now, I believe that it is in medicine that one must search for it . . . and that one could exempt oneself from an infinity of maladies, as much of the body as of the mind, and even also perhaps of the enfeeblement of old age, if one had enough knowledge of their causes and of all the remedies with which nature has provided us. (VI:2)

It looks as though the end in question is the mastery of nature. Physics offers us release from labor and hope of overcoming death. It offers us a kind of redemption from our fallen nature. Through our own efforts we will cancel the curse laid upon men in the expulsion from Eden. We will no longer labor or die. Descartes presents his physics as making possible a collective self-sufficiency or autonomy. This possibility is presented as the unforseen by-product of inquiries which originally had nothing to do with the mastery of nature. Descartes suddenly discovers that what satisfies him has the potentiality to satisfy mankind at large. This discovery is the source of his decision to write.

Still, one must wonder how possible this mastery is, and how possible Descartes believes it to be. For science to be able to make life qualitatively different and not simply a good deal more comfortable, mastery would have to mean more than an increase in the level of technology. It would have to be total. The problem of human mortality is not solved by increasing the average age at which men die by a few years, or a few dozen years. Descartes does not say, of course, that we will be masters of nature; he says rather that we will be *like* masters and possessors of nature. That the mastery cannot be total in any ordinary sense is clear from the way Descartes uses the word *infinite* in part 6. In the second paragraph he speaks of "an infinity of artifices" which will assist in the curing of "an infinity of maladies." In the third paragraph he speaks of the need for the science to be experimental rather than deductive because he

> did not believe it was possible for the human mind to distinguish the forms or species of bodies that are on the Earth from an *infinity* [italics mine] of others which could have been there. (VI:4)

And finally, in the eighth paragraph Descartes speaks of his need for others to provide him with an "infinity of experiments." If one needs an infinity of experiments to know an infinity of causes of an infinity of maladies in order to develop an infinity of cures for the human condition, it seems clear that mastery of nature is not a finite task. It requires unending invention, and is therefore unfinishable. This alone should make it clear why Descartes cannot publish anything approximating a list of solutions. An infinite task does not admit of that sort of dogma.

Nevertheless, the *Discourse on Method* is meant to be a cure for the human condition. If science cannot finish the task of mastering nature, perhaps it can provide a uniform method with which to approach all problems. The mastery of nature would then be a constant activity, not a task to be finished. The desire to master nature is the desire to be autonomous, the desire to be perfect. Since God is the image of that perfection for men, it is now clear why Descartes earlier (V:3) appealed to the commonly held theological view that the activity whereby God creates the world is the same as the activity whereby he conserves it. Mastering nature, like creating it, is a full-time job.

The remainder of part 6 deals in one way or another with our finite lives in relation to the infinity of the task we have set ourselves. The infinite is the reason why *The World* had to be replaced by the *Discourse on Method*. For mortal beings, the only way to be satisfied by the mastery of nature is to understand mastery as an on-going process in which we are constantly getting the better of nature. The method must be a method for "conducting" and "seeking" and only incidentally for finding. Human life can only be redeemed by means of a method which makes what is provisional final.

With all of this, of course, comes a problem. The on-going process of mastering nature is fine for Descartes, who experiences it. It may also be advantageous, if not perfectly redemptive, for future generations who reap its benefits. But what about the present generation of natural egoists to whom the *Discourse on Method* is addressed? Why should they make sacrifices for a method which will be of no benefit to them? We begin to see why Descartes must introduce the categorical obligation of benevolence even though there seems to be absolutely no foundation for it in his previous psychology. Descartes has acknowledged this difficulty from the beginning of the *Discourse*. He uses a fable to undermine the need for fables. He uses rhetoric to hold out the goal of immortality and perfection although knowing full well that living forever without pain is simply another form of the illusion of "good sense." It is one of those things that fables make seem possible that are not really possible at all (I:8). Descartes enlists the ordinary man's longing for a kind of autonomy not possible on behalf of a kind of autonomy which is possible. The question will be how he can still understand his behavior as being "useful to some without being harmful to any." How can he expect "all to thank [him] for his frankness?"

The problem can be put in a still different way. This section of the *Discourse* is peculiar in the way it moves freely back and forth between the first person singular pronoun *je* and the impersonal pronoun *on*. The science Descartes wishes to promote requires collective action, which is the only possible response to an infinite threat. But collective immortality does not satisfy individual desire. Descartes' use of the impersonal pronoun makes it seem as though the experience of various ones are one experience. When he restates the obligation to be benevolent hypothetically rather than categorically (VI:5), he forces us to ask why one should will the general good of mankind. The problem of Cartesian science has slowly turned itself into the problem of justice. It is not an accident that later in this part (VI:6) Descartes will make oblique references to Plato's *Republic*.

In a way the question of justice is taken up in the treatment of Descartes' need for the experiments of others. He needs help because of the shortness of life and the infinity of the task. The two are really the same; he is a finite being with a longing to accomplish an infinite task. The ambiguity of the French *expérience* is useful to him here; it can mean both experience and experiment. The narrowness of Descartes' experience requires that he share experiments. Since his experience is restricted to those objects which have been present to his senses, he needs to borrow the senses of others if his science is to have the necessary universality. But that means that Descartes needs experiences which are collective and not idiosyncratic. They cannot be colored by the particular genius of a particular *esprit*. An experiment is something like an experience that can be generalized, a sort of scientific version of Rousseau's general will. An experiment points to what anyone would see under identical circumstances. In that sense it is an appeal to what all men have in common, *la raison*, and not to what distinguishes them, *l'esprit*. This generalizing of experience in experiments is really the heart of the method. Mastery of nature is possible from the inside so to speak by artificially making perspectives regular. And so Descartes needs experiments; and yet

> I see also that they are such and of so great a number that neither my hands nor my income, although I were to have a thousand times more than I have, would be able to suffice for everything. (VI:3)

Consequently, he must publish in order to seek assistance. The argument thus far concerns whether he should publish *The World*. In the third section of part 6 he discovers new reasons why he should not do so. Overcoming these reasons will lead him to publish not *The World*, but the *Discourse on Method*.

Descartes' reflection on his own finitude had led him to conclude that he needed help, but his reflection on the nature of the help likely to be forthcoming led him to reject his plan to ask for it. His book would immerse him in controversy. Others would attack it not so much because they doubted what was in it as because what was in it was not theirs. Still, Descartes indicates that he will continue to write. While writing is not identical to publishing, there is a connection. He writes because writing is like the experimental method. In writing, one necessarily writes for others. In this way writing is more like rethinking than thinking. But things written for others in the abstract may have benefit for others in reality. Descartes therefore resolves to let his writings be published after he is dead, when they may do others some good but will do him no harm.

> For although it may be true that each man is obliged to procure so much as is in him the good of others, and that properly speaking to be useful to no one is to be worthless, all the same, it is also true that our cares ought to be extended beyond the present time, and that it is good to omit things which might perhaps bring some profit to those who live when the plan is to do others which would bring more advantage to our descendants. (VI:4)

In part 3, Descartes' "provisional morality" had left him with only one source of guilt, that of not attempting to replace his present opinions with others more true. Here he indicates that to be useful to no one is to be worthless. The two claims do not seem to fit well together. The one is selfish, the other apparently self-forgetting. However, being useful to others and trying to think are connected in a quite accidental way. For entirely selfish motives Descartes wishes to understand nature in a way that is also available to other men, a way not rooted in his idiosyncracies. The real meaning of beginning with the equality of good sense or reason in all men is that even the best minds are forced to think in a mode which would be reproducible, at least theoretically, for another. Given that, it is clear why future generations have such a hold on Descartes. The future is the test of the universality of his concerns. Immortal glory would be the appropriate result of thought truly without idiosyncracy.

The criticisms of others are not useful to Descartes because they originate in vanity, in the desire to win arguments. Descartes is better able to play the role of critic himself. His own objections are more methodical than those which others would make. He may be vain, but his vanity is purer than that of others. On the other hand, neither would his experiments be of use to others.

> As for the usefulness that others would receive from the communication of my thoughts, it would also not be very great, inasmuch as I have not yet conducted them so far that they are not in need of adding many things before applying them to practice. (VI:6)

What is being conducted here? The *them* is ambiguous. It might apply to the experiments, and it might apply to the others. If the latter, then the passage suggests that it is useless for Descartes to publish his experiments until he has conducted or led men further. Like the "chief of an army" who "conducts" his forces (VI:4), Descartes would need to teach the method before experiments could be useful to him, since otherwise they would lack the uniformity necessary for them to be exchangeable. This is the perennial difficulty of the relation of philosophy to society. It is the difficulty of Socrates who cannot defend himself against the political order without defending philosophy, who would not have to defend himself if the political order were philosophic, and who cannot defend himself unless it is. It is the problem expressed by Plato in the image of a cave.[14] Men are like prisoners bound in a cave, who unable to turn their heads, see only shadows on the wall in front of them, images of things which they take to be the things themselves. Men in the cave think they see, but do not. Out of vanity they are unwilling to confess that they do not see; they are unwilling to acknowledge their ignorance. And so, on the one hand, Descartes requires experiments to broaden his experience, while on the other hand the fact that he needs them, and that others are like him, signifies why he cannot trust their experience.

Descartes needs some way to overcome the problem of "good sense" on a large scale. The natural egoism of men taints their experience and so their experiments. Wanting to succeed, they manipulate the data. Volunteers want to be paid for their help in conversation; they, too, need to be assured of their worth. What Descartes really needs is something like foundation grants. With money he could pay men to help him (VI:7), and so be sure that they would do what he wanted them to do. The whole enterprise would be under the direction of one mind. These remarks on the sort of help he could use, in addition to being advertising, are a perfect image of the relation between Descartes and Cartesian philosophy on the one hand, and society at large on the other. Because it is always possible to count on the natural egoism of men, on their passions, all one needs to do is to find an artificial way, like money, to enlist the general desire for gain in the service of the desire for objectivity. The irony is that objectivity is available only when it is not perceived as the goal. Descartes had to do to those who work for him what the method in its way does for him, but without their realizing it. The result is a relationship in which Descartes gets the satisfaction of mastering nature, while his helpers, the society from which he is asking help, also gain something. To forge this alliance, however, Descartes must find a way to present his philosophy to the public. This way is the *Discourse on Method*, and the remainder of part 6 is devoted to explaining why this book, and not *The World*, is the appropriate means to introduce the world to Cartesian philosophy.

Two reasons, neither one of them a categorical obligation to be benevolent, finally decide Descartes to publish. The first is that were he not to do so, those who knew that he had intended to publish would conclude that he could not do what he had set out to do. Not publishing appears to be not doing anything. Descartes may hate glory in excess, but since he must have some sort of reputation he wants a good one. He is trapped in a world in which even his act of not publishing is a public act. His second reason for changing his mind is his need once again for experiments. He is not convinced that they will do much good, but he does not want future generations to accuse him of failing to do as much as he might have done to further such an important project as the mastery of nature. Both of these reasons, when pressed, reduce to his concern for his own reputation. On the initial level of the argument Descartes claims that he is unconcerned with glory and reputation. We have just discovered that in fact he does care. Is there a third level on which his unconcern for glory is genuine? This third level points to the conclusion of the book as a whole.

The last paragraph of the *Discourse* contains Descartes' criticism of a certain kind of glory.

> My inclination distances me so greatly from every other sort of plan, principally from those which can only be useful to some while harming others, that if some occasions had constrained me to use them I do not believe at all that I would have been capable of succeeding. Accordingly,

I make a declaration here that I know well can not serve to render me considerable in the world, but neither have I any longing to be so. And I will always hold myself more oblilgated to those by whose favor I enjoy my leisure without hindrance than I would be to those who would offer me the most honorable employment on earth. (VI:12)

In preferring freedom to rule, Descartes points to the problem of all previous rule or mastery. Mastery of some has always meant slavery for others. Where there are winners there are losers. The battle imagery of part 6, however, suggests a species of war in which winning does not imply losing. If one is engaged in a battle with something nonhuman and inexhaustible as in the continuing attempt to master nature, then there need be no slavery. Descartes' repeatedly stated goal is to be useful to some without being harmful to any. He wishes to be perfectly just, and realizes what Socrates forces Polemarchus to realize in the first book of Plato's *Republic*. The ordinary understanding of justice as helping friends and harming enemies must give way to the philosophical understanding of justice as helping friends and harming no one. However, in the *Republic*, not to mention what we have seen in the *Ajax*, justice understood in this way proves unrealizable. Helping friends always seems to generate enemies. Helping is inseparable from harming, even if the harm means only to be excluded from those privileged few who are being helped. Where there are Greeks there are barbarians and where there is a chosen people there are neglected peoples. The solution for Descartes is in a very peculiar way like the solution of the *Republic*; it is the rule of philosophy. However, in the *Republic* the solution proves so radical as to make us see that the problem is not solvable. Here Descartes has in mind a different kind of philosophy and a different kind of rule. Cartesian mastery is a project to replace politics as the human response to dependence and neediness. That is necessary because politics, including the City of God as well as the city of man, always carries with it the necessity to harm those whom one is not helping, even if only by depriving them of the possibility of mastery and so of autonomy.

This necessity of harming is owing to the necessarily local or perspectival character of political life. Ajax and Hector may share a common nature, but what they share ultimately divides them. The *polis* requires that common humanity be overlooked. In this regard there is a parallel between the city and man, between the perspectival character of political society and the perspectival character of the reflective soul. Both are, in a way, signs of the imperfection of the creation. Descartes concludes the *Discourse on Method* with a consideration of writing because writing underlines that imperfection. Reading *The World*, we would be inclined to take our perspective from within the whole as final. But to do that is to live in the cave. Descartes' alternative is to refuse this finality and accept the provisionality of our condition. He therefore invents a method which will allow men to feel the flush of victory, of being the masters who conduct nature, without the need to harm. Descartes' project for the mastery of nature is meant to liberate us from politics and in that way purify the exercise of the human will. Previously, the condition for the expression of the will has been the distortion of the will. Willing is the most complete expression of ourselves as free autonomous beings, and yet in real willing, in being righteously indignant, we inevitably treat a part as the whole. We fail to see the perspectival character of our own vision. The Cartesian project is to direct the will, that is, to direct anger, equally and indifferently, toward each part of the whole so that there is no longer anything personal or idiosyncratic in it. He means to replace righteous indignation by the controlled experiment.

The *Discourse on Method* is therefore an attempt to overcome that tragedy of the perfectly political which was the tragedy of Sophocles' Ajax. Descartes seeks to find a way to affirm the wholehearted devotion to the partial, while still acknowledging the partial as partial, and so still acknowledging the fate of man to be locked within the whole. It is an attempt that shares much with Socrates' famous "second sailing," but that in the end is not content with the idiosyncratic and accidental character of Socrates' second sailing. It is in the end an attempt to make the second sailing, Socrates' second best way, into a first sailing, a completely adequate solution to the problem of the human longing for autonomy. It is an attempt to provide a method which will take the pain out of holding things in abeyance and so take the fear and guilt out of doubt. We can rule the whole from the inside only if we can make ourselves indifferent to the partiality of the parts. The question is what the hidden costs will be of this indifference. Will it be possible to make men perfectly happy by means of the knowledge of the structure of their unhappiness and imperfection? Is it possible to turn a second sailing, an analysis, into a first sailing, a causal or synthetic account? This is the problem with which Plato's *Meno* is concerned: What is the connection between knowing what virtue is and becoming virtuous? Descartes saw the need to make virtue out of necessity, but that need is in the end itself governed by necessity. The third level of Descartes' rhetoric and the first level may in the end be still closer than they were meant to be. In the end the philosophic life remains a human life.

5

The Limit of Autonomy: Plato's Meno

I have never yet written concerning these things, and there is no
writing of Plato, nor will there be any, but those now said to be
belong to Socrates become beautiful and young.

—Plato, *Second Letter*

AJAX' ATTEMPT TO TAKE what he saw as the whole led to his inability to
distinguish men from beasts. Odysseus is saved from the same plight by the
help of a goddess. Athena lets him see Ajax as a god would see him, but
unless we are prepared to accept Athena's intervention at face value we are
forced to wonder whether in fact it is possible for Odysseus to be spared the
tragedy of Ajax. This question becomes doubly pressing when we realize that
Sophocles has given us the sort of vision that Athena gave Odysseus. The
most puzzling question in the play is the status of the gods. Upon reflection,
this question turns into another: How is it possible for the poet himself to see
what he claims to see? With only a bit of poetic license this question may be
understood to be an attempt to disclose the nature of the *esprit* of Sophocles.
The question of the gods is inevitably paired with the question of the nature
of men. Descartes saw that. The *Discourse on Method* takes the question of
God most seriously. But Descartes' project is not a theodicy so much as it
is an explanation of the centrality of the question of God for any understanding
of human beings. It involves an articulation of the structure of the human
longing for autonomy. By showing what God means to *les esprits faibles*
Descartes has in mind to show the real significance of their longing. God
becomes the crucial image or fable. But Descartes does not mean to leave it
at that. He has in mind to substitute a new fable for the old, so transforming
the fables that guide men that they will no longer have need of gods. The
new fable offers its own version of immortality and bliss. It is meant to be
a testament to human autonomy. Descartes has it in mind to make methodical
the process by which he glories in the successful working of his own *esprit*.

By so doing he will provide a new model for the exercise of the human will, one in principle available to all, which retains the lure of the satisfaction of conquest while removing the need to inflict pain and suffering on those conquered. In seeking to be useful to some while being harmful to none, Descartes seeks to solve the dilemma of Ajax. In his motive for action Descartes is as proud and willful as Ajax, but in the universality and charity of his goal he imitates Christianity.

This version of complete human virtue requires the transformation of what we understand by mastery, and so politics. Avoiding holy wars means removing the aura of holiness from public life. On the other hand, this version of complete human virtue requires the transformation of what we mean by thought, and so philosophy. The public stock of philosophy, or science, is to be raised considerably under Descartes' new order. In fact, the aura which once attached to political life is to be transferred to the life of science. Descartes knew before the fact that enlightenment did not really mean that all human beings would be equally knowledgeable, not to say equally possessing good sense or reason. He knew that the rhetoric of the equality of reason, when managed in a certain way, could lead to the celebration of reason, of science, and so of scientists. Because the whole of his project depends on these transformations it is well to spend some time considering their possibility. The celebration of philosophy as science and the corresponding denigration of the importance of politics will leave neither philosophy nor politics untouched. It is for that reason helpful to turn to a thinker who understood very well the intimate but problematic connection between philosophy and politics and to dwell at some length on a writing where he examines this connection.

I

Among Plato's dialogues the *Meno* is the only one explicitly to raise the question "What is virtue?" By the conclusion of the dialogue the question is answered. Virtue is true opinion, and it is acquired through divine dispensation. This answer is not particularly enlightening. Socrates' pretense that it is enlightening borders on comedy. It leads him to ask Meno to attempt to persuade Anytus, whom Socrates has just bitterly and deeply offended, of this doctrine of divine dispensation which has just persuaded him. The rather queer suggestion is that Meno will thereby make Anytus more virtuous. If virtue is acquired by divine dispensation, and Meno is here dispensing virtue, then it looks as though Meno must be a god. This puzzling consequence leads us to wonder about the man for whom this dialogue is named. Who is Meno, and why has he been chosen as *the* interlocutor in *the* Platonic dialogue on virtue?

The question is more complicated than it seems, which becomes clear when we take stock of what we know about Meno in a gossipy sort of way. We know that he comes from Thessaly, the semibarbaric north, and that he comes from a good family. He is the guest-friend of Anytus, and his family is traditionally associated with the Great King of Persia. Meno has studied with the famous rhetorician Gorgias, who is said to have argued that virtue cannot be taught. Meno is young and handsome (*kalos*); he is the beloved of Aristippus, a man from one of the leading Thessalian families. Socrates twice calls Meno *panourgos* (80b,81e).[1] The word means something like "rogue," but its etymology suggests "one who does everything," almost "one who will stop at nothing." This sounds a little extreme until we notice that for all of his interest in how virtue comes to be, Meno seems rather unconcerned with what one might call "conventional virtue." Socrates has to remind him repeatedly about justice, and although Meno is not so bold as to refuse to acknowledge it, he does not seem to attach much importance to it. In fact, Meno commits at least one injustice in the dialogue itself. When Socrates presses him for a definition of figure (75b) Meno says peremptorily "No, but you speak, Socrates." To this Socrates responds that he will speak if Meno will agree to follow him with an answer about virtue. Meno emphatically agrees. Two pages later he reneges; he demands a definition of color as well. There seems as well to be a certain greediness about Meno. When asked at 78c whether he means by goods things such as health and wealth, he says,

and I say to possess gold and silver and honors and offices in the city.

And when Socrates asks if Meno considers anything other than these things good, Meno says no. Goods are apparently things to be possessed.

As yet these are merely hints about Meno's character, but they are particularly revealing when coupled with what is likely to have been the contemporary opinion of him. Meno is described rather unflatteringly by Xenophon at the end of *Anabasis* II.[2]

Meno the Thessalian was greatly desirous of being wealthy, desirous of ruling in order to get more, and desirous of being honored in order to gain more. And he wanted to be a friend to those with the greatest power in order that, doing injustice, he would not have to pay the penalty. And to accomplish whatever he desired he thought the shortest way to be through perjury and falsehood and deception, but simplicity and truth he thought to be the same as folly. He manifestly felt affection for no one, but when he claimed to be a friend of anyone it became clear that this was the one against whom he was plotting. He ridiculed none of the enemy, but in conversation he always ridiculed his associates. And he would not scheme for the possessions of his enemies, for he thought it difficult to take from those on their guard. But he thought he was alone in knowing that it was easiest to take the things of friends, as they were unguarded. And whomever he would perceive as perjurers and unjust, he would fear as being well armed. But he would try to make use of those who were holy and practiced truth, since they were unmanly. And just as one prides oneself on piety and truthfulness and justice, Meno prided himself on being able to deceive, fabricating lies and mocking friends. But he always held one who was not a rogue (*panourgos*) to be among the uneducated. And with regard to those with whom he tried to be first in friendship, he thought it necessary to win them by slandering those already first with them. And he accomplished making the army obedient by sharing their wrong-doing with them. He thought himself worthy of being honored and attended because he showed himself especially able and willing to do injustice, and he counted it a good deed, when someone broke off with him, that when dealing with him he [Meno] had not destroyed him.

Meno was not a nice man. There are quite a few flawed characters in Platonic dialogues, but as a villain Meno is unsurpassed. All of this serves to underline our original question: Why is *the* Platonic dialogue on virtue conducted with and named after a man like Meno?[3]

The problem becomes still more puzzling with a glance at the very beginning of the dialogue. Meno abruptly asks Socrates the following question.

Can you tell me, Socrates, whether virtue is teachable, or not teachable, but acquired by practice, or neither acquired by practice nor learnable, but comes to be among men by nature, or in some other way?

Now the commonsense answer to Meno's question is that virtue requires all three: practice, teaching, and nature. Aristotle, for example, in response to the very same question, makes it clear that all three must be involved.[4] In the same context he emphasizes that if there is a single condition most important for the acquisition of virtue, it is to be raised under good laws. This possibility is of course not unknown to Plato. In the *Apology* (24e) it is precisely this answer, the laws or *nomoi*, which Socrates' accuser, Meletus, gives in response to the question "Who makes the young better?" And we are inclined to be reminded of the *Apology* here because another of Socrates' accusers will make a threatening appearance later in the dialogue. Given that the conventional answer to Meno's question is law, it is all the more startling that the word for law, *nomos*, and the verb connected with it, *nomizō*, to hold or believe, nowhere appear in the *Meno*.[5] Nor do any words cognate with them.[6] For some reason this dialogue which is concerned with virtue abstracts from the law. Put somewhat more boldly, the *Meno* is a dialogue in which two future criminals, Socrates and Meno, have a conversation about virtue. There is a connection between virtue and criminality. To see what it is we will have to begin again.

The beginning is peculiar in a number of ways. Meno's question is almost comically abrupt; it is of the sort one might expect more from Socrates than from his interlocutor. The center of the question forms a chiasmus, a rhetorical figure favored by Gorgias. But the figure is not quite perfect. Meno does not say "or not teachable but acquired by practice, or neither acquired by practice nor teachable." His chiasmus limps because of the substitution of *learnable* where one would have expected the second *teachable*. Meno treats the two as one, an assumption which is allowed to stand throughout the dialogue although it is to say the least doubtful. The difference between teaching and learning is a difference of perspective; it is a difference between what something looks like from the outside and what it looks like from the inside. Meno's limping chiasmus suggests that this difference is one to which he is indifferent.

Meno's question has yet another peculiarity. Its form is something like the following: Can you say if V is X, or not X but Y, or neither Y nor X, but Z or W? The form itself discourages looking for an answer which is some combination of these elements. However, if virtue means something like excellence of soul, Meno's very question encourages one to think of the soul as something simple. Meno suggests that men can be understood either as acquiring virtue through teaching or learning, that is to say, as rational, or as acquiring virtue through practice or training, that is to say, as animal, or as having virtue by nature, that is to say, as simply alive, but not as all three. Aristotle's solution has been rejected out of hand. One wonders why.

If Meno's question is peculiar, Socrates' immediate response is utterly bewildering. Instead of an answer we get an account of the way Meno has probably come to ask the question. Socrates is about to transform Meno's question about the coming to be, or *genesis*, of virtue into a question about the essence, or *eidos* of virtue. He is about to attempt to transform the question "How does virtue come to be?" into the question "What is virtue?" But preliminary to that he gives an account of the *genesis* of Meno's question. The question "How does virtue come to be?" is replaced by the question "How does the question 'How does virtue come to be?' come to be?" The two questions would seem to be the same only when one understands virtue to be asking what virtue is.[7] But in that case virtue could not be virtue as conventionally understood, although it would presuppose some conventional notion of virtue to initiate inquiry. Socrates goes on to indicate that the question of virtue does depend in some way on virtue as conventionally understood. He remarks that the Thessalians were previously in good repute (*eudokimoi*) among the Greeks for horseback riding and wealth, but now they are also apparently to be known for their wisdom. It would seem that they have perfected not only the desiring and spirited parts of their soul but also the rational part.[8] The cause of this change is said to be Gorgias, who arrived in Thessaly and made the Thessalians "lovers for the sake of wisdom" (*erastas epi sophia*). It is a strange phrase, but seems to mean that Gorgias made the leading men of Thessaly love him, with the result that they ended by loving wisdom. As a consequence they acquired a habit (*ethos*) of fearlessly and magnificently (*megalaprepōs*) answering any who ask "just like those who know." That is, they copy Gorgias, who claims to have an answer for every question (*Gorgias* 447c–448a).

In the dialogue which does not mention law or convention (*nomos*) Socrates' first speech is a description of how habits are engendered in men so as to specify them as distinct peoples. It is a description of how conventional virtue originates. The Thessalians wish not so much to be wise as to emulate Gorgias, a very impressive man who "himself offers up himself" to answer any question. He performs the function which in its way any *nomos* performs. Gorgias does openly what every *nomos* does tacitly; he claims to be able to answer any question. It is no accident that in pointing out what the Thessalians are now reputed for (*eudokimon*) Socrates foreshadows the claim at the very end of the dialogue that virtue will mean to trace the origin of that good opinion which enables men to answer "just like those who know" (70c) even though they do not know. It will mean to ask after the origin of *nomos*.[9]

So that we will not make the mistake of thinking that it is ever really the case that the *nomos* so utterly forms a man as to account entirely for what he is, Socrates proceeds to make the ironic claim that Athens is entirely responsible for what he is. He intimates that something like knowledge of ignorance is the prevailing *nomos* in Athens. Athenians, he says, do not even know what virtue is, let alone how it is acquired. And they are so aware of this ignorance that they think anyone who did know would be one of the blessed. Now this is clearly an enormous exaggeration. Anytus, the democratic leader who is brought into the discussion later in the dialogue (89e–95a), seems a far more typical Athenian than Socrates, and he will prove very confident of his knowledge of how to acquire virtue. He will also find nothing to laugh at in Socrates' claim to be ignorant of how to acquire virtue. And yet there is something suggestive about Socrates' exaggeration. When he says that wisdom now lives among the Thessalians, having previously lived in Athens, he points to the fundamental difference between Thessaly and Athens. Thessaly has just discovered its "wise man." It is in the full flush of giving answers. The Thessalians were previously well known for horsemanship and wealth. Two parts of their soul, their spiritedness (*thumos*) and their desire (*epithumia*) are already well developed. Now they are confidently completing themselves as human beings. Athens, more sophisticated, is the home of many sophists. As a place where the tradition can be openly doubted and debunked, it is aware that its *nomoi* are *its nomoi*. The seeds have been planted for doubt about the finality of its own laws and their ability to answer all questions. It looks, and this is a bit anticipatory, as though *nomos* operates perfectly only when we are unaware that it is operating. That is the significance of its absence from the *Meno*. This hint is the first indication of the tension which runs throughout the dialogue as a whole between being virtuous and knowing what virtue is. The opposition between Thessaly and Athens anticipates the tension later in the dialogue between statesmen and sophists, between those who do but do not know and those who know but do not do. Of course what the statesmen do will be affected by the fact that they do not know and what the sophists know will be affected by the fact that they do not do. It will prove impossible to be virtuous without knowing what virtue is. Thessaly is brutish, Athens self-conscious and corrupt. Putting the two together is the problem. And yet each is only the extreme of the two possibilities necessarily present in all law. Laws, and the gods supporting them, can render us perfectly confident in our own virtue, or, by comparison to the gods, perfectly humble.

By claiming not to know what virtue is Socrates avoids Meno's question and substitutes what looks like a genuine Socratic "what is" question, "What is virtue?" The example Socrates chooses for showing the priority of his question over Meno's is significant.

> Or does it seem to you to be possible that one who knew not at all who Meno was would know whether he was handsome (*kalon*), wealthy or well born, or the opposite of these? (71b)

Now on the one hand it does not seem possible to identify the qualities of Meno without knowing who Meno is. But on the other hand it would be rather difficult to say what precisely this "knowledge" of Meno consisted in apart from knowledge of these qualities. One has to know something of Meno in order to determine who he is, and so to know more precisely what sort of qualities really belong to him. There are obviously different kinds of knowing implicated here as Socrates' introduction of the verb *gignōskō* (to know, recognize, perceive, etc.) suggests. Socrates will use this example to argue for the necessity to answer a "what is" question with the *eidos*, idea or species, of the object of the inquiry. But in order to do so he will have to make a demand which is in its way just as unreasonable as the argument Meno will later present against the possibility of learning at all (80d). What could Socrates' example mean but that we must know Meno before we can ask about Meno? Of course, the example itself suggests the solution to the problem. We frequently "know" whether men are beautiful, rich, or well-born before seeing them. Those are precisely the sorts of qualities we cannot resist gossiping about. Meno is "known" before he is known because his reputation precedes him. That reputation (*eudoxia*) is what makes it possible to wonder about him at all. This fact is highlighted by Meno's response to Socrates' declaration of ignorance. He asks whether Socrates wants him to return home with this report of him. Does Socrates want to be known by his knowledge of ignorance? Meno finds it unlikely.

There is something peculiar about Socrates' procedure here. Meno asks a question about the genesis of virtue—how it is produced. Socrates slowly begins moving him toward another sort of question—a question about the *eidos* of virtue. Meno, of course, will resist; insofar as Socrates succeeds it will be because Meno becomes convinced of the necessity to know what virtue is in order to become virtuous. Only because Meno is persuaded to understand the *eidē* in terms of *archai*, origins or sources, will he be willing to entertain Socrates' new question at all. Only when *eidos* is understood as a cause of *genesis* is it of interest to Meno. The apparent shift in the argument from a "*genesis* question" to a "what is" question is therefore illusory. Meno's motives remain constant; he continues to care very little about disinterested analysis. Why then is he chosen as the interlocutor for this dialogue?

By allowing the question "Who is Meno?" to stand as an example of a "what is" question, Socrates alerts us to the importance of Meno's identity. There will be something about the question, "Who is Meno?" that will shed light on the origin of "what is" questions. There will be a connection between Meno and *eidos*. To discover what that connection is we have to turn briefly to the three answers that Meno gives to the question, "What is virtue?"

Meno's first answer is an extended account of the varieties of virtue.

> But it is not hard to say, Socrates. First, if you want the virtue of a man, it is easily said that this is the virtue of a man: to be competent to manage the affairs of the city, and, managing them, to do well by one's friends and badly by one's enemies, and to take care to suffer no harm oneself. But if you want the virtue of a woman, it is not difficult to describe, that she ought to order the house well, both maintaining the things within and being obedient to her husband. And the virtue of children is different, and of female and male, and of old men, and, if you want, of free and slave. And there are many other virtues. So that there is no lack of means to say about virtue what it is. For according to each deed done by each of us there is virtue. And similarly, I think, Socrates, also vice.
>
> (71e–72a)

Socrates rejects Meno's answer as no definition at all, but rather an enumeration. We have to be more careful. This would not be the only passage in Plato where an initial definition rejected out of hand for formal reasons turns out to be the deepest of the definitions offered.[10] As an enumeration, Meno's account is not even unproblematic. It leaves out whole classes such as old women, and the classes it includes overlap, such as old men, males, and slaves.[11] Still, on the whole Meno has divided the *polis*, the city, by tasks. The tacit understanding of virtue at work comes very close to one of the definitions of justice in the *Republic* (433a–b), namely, doing one's job well or minding one's own business. That looks at first to mean something like acting in accordance with one's nature. Men do manly things, women womanly things. But Meno's understanding of the things men and women do is expressed in terms of their roles as citizens of the *polis*. It is instructive that no mention is made of the most obvious natural difference between men and women, childbearing. Instead, as the last item in the list hints, Meno takes most seriously the difference between master and slave. That men are virtuous in different ways means primarily that some men will obey others. Minding one's own business is understood in very conventional terms by Meno; he suggests, but does not say explicitly, that virtue is acting in accordance with the *nomos*. The *nomos* prescribes a variety of duties because the city requires a variety of tasks.

Meno unwittingly points to the problem of conventional virtue by beginning his list with the virtue of an *anēr*, a manly man, and ending it with the virtue of a slave. Ruling and obedience are not simply compatible, and yet the *polis*, political society, requires both. It must therefore encourage both; it must call both virtues. Socrates' subsequent attack on this notion of virtue as not containing one idea, one *eidos*, is therefore an implicit attack on the *polis*. The *polis* must praise mastery, ordering, and ruling as the virtues of an *anēr*, and it must simultaneously praise servility and obedience as the virtues of slaves. But to be virtuous in one regard will mean to be necessarily defective in the other.

The one who orders the things of the city perfectly will not be subject to his own orders. A founder of a regime, as the source of the law, is not in any ordinary way subject to the law. He is a godlike man. Gorgias, playfully presented as the founder of a new regime in Thessaly, is necessarily a foreigner. On the other hand, the perfectly obedient citizen is not so much a member of the *polis* as a tool for its efficient functioning. Slaves are not citizens.

This tension within political virtue need not be experienced. The *polis* requires both mastery and obedience, as well as other forms of "virtue" which are required for maintaining the whole. Each instance of virtue therefore does share with the others that it contributes to the proper functioning of the city. But the proper functioning of each cog does not require that any cog properly appreciate the function of any other cog. In fact, for a citizen with one function to appreciate the standards of excellence that guide any of the other citizens unlike him will dilute his own excellence. It is perhaps impossible to introduce an appreciation of the task of other citizens without at the same time introducing the possibility that a person of one class will wish to be in another. For a slave to appreciate the virtue of a master involves for him the wish to be a master, and if a master is really to recognize servility as a virtue and not simply have contempt for slaves he will in some sense wish to be a slave. All of this ambivalence is certainly possible; perhaps it is even good. But the perfect functioning of each cog in the machine, that is, the perfect virtue of each citizen in the *polis*, would mean that no one within the city could know the whole which his activity supported. Meno's first definition had to be an enumeration, because as a man, an *anēr*, Meno would know the form of virtue proper to himself, and necessarily be unaware that there were any other virtues. This, of course, contradicts what Meno seems to say. He has presented a list of the various forms of virtue. Yet it does not take us long to discover that he does not really mean what he says. Meno does not admire "virtuous" slaves. In fact, it will soon be clear that what he really means by virtue is the virtue of an *anēr*, ruling. But why then is he made to say something different here?

What Meno appears to mean is that virtue is essentially political virtue. However, his motive for saying so is that the role he understands to be his in the *polis* is that of ruler. Meno affirms the *polis* because it is in his own interest to do so. But an affirmation of the *polis* requires the claim that citizen virtue of all kinds is genuine virtue. There is therefore one part in the *polis* which has a motive for affirming the *polis* for essentially selfish and non-political ends. Socrates makes this mock public spiritedness difficult for Meno by asking him to say what one thing in common runs through all of these various kinds of virtue. To answer genuinely Meno would have to stand outside his role as *anēr*. He would have to relinquish his own understanding of virtue.

Were Meno to say that virtue is essentially political virtue, that the content varies, but the goal is to sustain the *polis*, he would have said something like what Socrates implies at the outset of the dialogue in attributing both his and Meno's behavior to the *nomoi* of their respective cities. However, the very act of attributing one's behavior to the *nomos* thrusts one beyond the *nomos*. To say that one's behavior is conventional is to be aware of the possibility of other conventions, and this awareness prevents behavior from being perfectly conventional. Were Meno to say that the proper functioning of the *polis* is the purpose of its various parts he would cease to be a perfectly functioning part. To say that the *nomos* rules the city is to make its rule imperfect and so to have in part transcended the city. Meno is interesting precisely because he does not handle matters in this way. Instead, he elevates a part of conventional virtue to make it the whole. He knows he must mention the virtue of slaves, but he is serious only about the virtue of masters. He thereby indicates both his need of the *polis* and his need to go beyond it. He will be a criminal, but of a peculiarly conventional kind.

The problem with the first definition is that it gives no account of what makes these various virtues the same, although it assumes their sameness in calling them all virtues. The instances of virtue are visible; what Socrates is about to call their *eidos* remains invisible. At first the problem seems peculiar to Meno's enumeration. However, there is more at stake here than Meno's ineptness at definition. Socrates slowly begins to make that clear in a series of objections presented in the form of a hypothetical conversation between himself and Meno about the *eidos* of bee.

> SOCRATES: It's likely that I am in great luck, Meno, if seeking one virtue, I have discovered a swarm of virtues laid down by you. But, Meno, with regard to this image of swarms, if I were to ask you the being (*ousia*) of bee, what in the world it is, and you said them to be many and of many sorts what would you answer me if I asked you "Do you say that they are in this many and of many sorts and different from one another, in being bees? Or, do they not differ at all in this, but in something else, such as in beauty, or in size, or in some other such thing?" Tell me, what would you answer, having been thus questioned?
> MENO: I would say this, that they differ not at all in that by which they are bees, the one from the other.
> SOCRATES: If, then, I said after this, "Tell me this, Meno, that by which they do not differ, but are all the same, what do you say this to be?" You would be able, I suppose, to say something to me?
>
> (72a–c)

The hypothetical character of the conversation allows Socrates to substitute a report of what Meno "would be able to say" for his actually saying what the *eidos* of bee is. The peculiar thing about being able to say something is that "being able" shows itself only in "making actual," in doing. But then it is no longer an ability or power. Being able, or power, is therefore essentially invisible. It shows itself only as what it can do, not as what it is. If the *eidos* of virtue were to be understood as a power or ability to produce instances of virtue, then the invisibility of the *eidos* would be essential and not an accidental feature of Meno's account. The *eidos* of bee shows itself only in bees; the *eidos* of virtue shows itself only in virtues. To ask for the *eidos* of a class is already to acknowledge that the unity of the class is problematic, much in the way that to see the *nomos* of the city at work is to see it working imperfectly. It is only because we see the difference among certain members of a class, that is, because we see that there is some difficulty involved in their being members of the same class, that we find it necessary to wonder about what it is that unifies the class.

Socrates gives a more precise account of what he means by *eidos* at 72c:

> Even if they [the virtues] are many and diverse, they all have (*echousi*) some one *eidos* the same, on account of which they are virtues, and glancing at which the one answering is able (*echei*) nobly [or beautifully] to show the one questioning what virtue happens to be.

An *eidos* is responsible for things being as they are and it is that at which we look in order to know what they are. As a principle of the being of things it cannot be the same as that of which it is a principle. The *eidos* of man is not a man. On the other hand, if the *eidos* is that at which we look to see what something is, then the *eidos* of man must be in some sense a man. Of the two functions of *eidē* Meno is concerned with the former, and therefore tacitly accepts that the *eidos* of man is not a man. Regardless of which of these functions we consider, the *eidos* is presented here as prior to its instances. It is a ruling principle, an *archē*, both of the being of things and of our knowing. On the other hand, it is no more clear how we come to know an *eidos* than it was clear how we came to know Meno. Fortunately, Meno is none too clear about what all of this means either. To explain it to him Socrates proceeds to give an enumeration, a *list*, of various *eidē*. It seems as though the only way to explain what an *eidos* is would be to give examples of it. Contrary to everything that Socrates says one should do, he is attempting to give Meno access to the *eidē* via their instances. One knows an *eidos* by observing what it does; it is itself invisible. It is an invisible power ruling over a visible multitude, and apparently knowable only through the instances over which it rules.[12] At the same time, however, to be what it is the *eidos* must have something like absolute priority over its instances. This tension between the need for the *eidē* to be dependent in order to be known and the need to be independent in order to be ruling principles is reflected here in the tension between what Socrates says *eidē* are and what he does to make clear what they are. The necessary invisibility of the *eidē* is intimately connected with the necessary invisibility of the virtue that Meno wants to possess. The connection becomes clearer in the second definition of virtue.

If some of the variety of virtue is to be sacrificed it is clear where Meno prefers the sacrifice be made. When pressed to identify the same virtue in all of the instances he replies,

> Indeed, what else than to be able to rule human beings? If indeed you seek some one thing over all. (73c–d)

So much for the virtue of slaves, and, one might add, citizens. Virtue has become the virtue of the real man, of the *anēr*. Seeking one *eidos* to rule (*archein*) as a principle (*archē*) over all instances of virtue, Meno chooses to say that the virtue of a man is to be able to rule (*archein*) over human beings (*anthrōpoi*). But that is not quite what Meno says. He surely thinks that it is the virtue of the real man (*anēr*) to rule over mere human beings (*anthrōpoi*), but he answers here in response to Socrates' request for the virtue which is the same in all human beings. What Meno says, therefore, is that it is the virtue of human beings to be able to rule over human beings. Now that would certainly be most reasonably interpreted as the political rule of one man over others. It could also be interpreted to mean self-rule. What underlies Meno's understanding of virtue is autonomy or freedom. But like Ajax his autonomy is only visible to him in others. Meno does not realize what Descartes had seen as the necessity to master one's own nature if one was to be master of nature. Autonomy is for him too simple; he unwittingly depends on others for his sense of independence. It is not a formula for success. Socrates asks for the view shared by Meno and Gorgias here because he knows that even Meno's view of autonomy comes from another. For in response to Socrates' question about the greatest good that he claimed to produce in those he taught, Gorgias had once said,

> That very thing, Socrates, which is in truth the greatest good and cause at once of freedom to men themselves and of ruling over others in their respective cities. (*Gorgias* 452d)

Meno leaves out freedom because, as we shall see, he considers it the same thing as the ability or power to rule. Meno knows that he is free only to the extent that he rules over others. He is unaware that he is enslaved to Gorgias. That is why Socrates' immediate response to this definition is to ask Meno whether it is the virtue of slaves to rule their masters. On the one hand he means to point out that Meno's definition does not apply to all human beings. On the other hand he means that in the sense in which it does apply to slaves it indicates that they rule their masters, who cannot be masters without them. The freedom of the master is dependent upon the servitude of the slave. Socrates can therefore dispense with Gorgias and concentrate on Meno. At the same time, Meno's repeated forgetting of justice is owing to his unwillingness to acknowledge the extent to which he is dependent upon others. This desire for complete autonomy which, however, shows itself only as rule over others, is a desire to be like an *eidos*. The problem of the virtue of slaves is simply the problem of how it is possible for the instances of an *eidos* to share with the *eidos* what is decisive for its being an *eidos*. The two problems of the one and the many in Plato, the one political and the other epistemological, are in fact one problem. Knowledge requires utterly independent *eidē—archai* or ruling principles; virtue requires that a man be an utterly autonomous ruler, or *archon*. Meno is as unaware of the difficulties with the former as he is with those of the latter. Perhaps it is even the desire to be the latter which lies behind the positing of the former. Meno accepts *eidē* only as instruments.

It is ironic that Socrates should force Meno to become aware of the difference between *eidos* and instance by giving instances of the difference, as though they could stand for the whole problem. It was through the example of the *eidos* of bee that Socrates first introduced the problem. From there he quickly moved to the *eidē* of health, size, and strength (72d). The decisive examples for the difference between *eidos* and instance are figure and color.

> MENO: For I am not able yet, Socrates, [to do] as you seek, to take one virtue over all just as in the other cases.
> SOCRATES: Most likely. But I will attempt, if I am able to push us forward. For you understand, I suppose, that it is like this concerning each thing? If someone were to ask you, what I said just now, "What is figure, Meno?" if you should say to him that it is roundness, if he were to say to you, as I did, "Is roundness figure or a figure?" you would say, I suppose, that it is a figure.
> MENO: Quite
> SOCRATES: And on account of this, that there are also other figures?
> MENO: Yes
> SOCRATES: And if he continued to ask you of what sort, you would say?
> MENO: I would.
> SOCRATES: And again if concerning color similarly he asked what it is, and when you answered that it was white, after that the one questioning replied by asking whether whiteness was color or a color, you would say that it was a color, because there happened to be others?
> MENO: I would.
>
> (74b–c)

The richness of color and figure as examples of *eidē* belies Socrates' claim that one cannot move from the instances to the *eidos*. One suspects, for example, that we are meant to see that color is that which makes all else visible but is itself visible only as *a* color, and that particular colors are incompatible with one another. One also suspects that the mutual entailment, but nonidentity, of color and figure is meant to shed light on one of the major issues of the dialogue, the relation of virtue to knowledge. For now, however, it is sufficient to follow Socrates in his attempt to induce Meno to make a trial run and give an account of figure. When Meno cannot do so, Socrates gives his own definition. Figure is "what alone of the beings always happens to follow color" (75b). Meno is not impressed, thinking the definition silly because it presupposes that we know what color is. However, had we ever occasion to doubt it, Socrates' earlier examples show that Meno knows what color is. Meno only feigns ignorance "for the sake of the argument." Like everyone else, Meno makes presuppositions as Socrates points out in his remarks on the difference between eristic and dialectic.

> And if one of the eristic or contentious sophists should be the asker, I would say to him that I have spoken, and if I do not speak correctly, it is his task to take the speech and refute it. But if like you and I now, being friends, they should want to converse (*dialegesthai*) with one another, it would be necessary to answer more gently and dialectically. But perhaps the more dialectical is not only to answer the truth, but also by way of what the one asking acknowledges that he knows. (75d)

Both dialectic and eristic make presuppositions; the question is of what sort. Socrates' definition of figure was not silly or naïve. To say that there is no color without figure and no figure without color is to say that the two go together necessarily. Granted that it is an analysis of what one already knows, it is done so as to make clear the fundamental character of the relation between figure and color. It is like the law of noncontradiction, at which nobody is amazed, but the formulation of which nevertheless teaches one about the world. Socrates' definition gives us a glimpse at the look (*eidos*) of things.[13] Meno is only interested in their origin (*genesis*).

Meno's objection implies that no definition is good unless it has an absolute beginning point, an *archē* in the strictest sense. That would be fine if he could really be so rigorous, but it quickly becomes clear that he cannot. Socrates' second definition of figure, that it is the "limit of solid" has a certain pseudo-exactness that appeals to Meno, but it is in fact less revealing than the original definition. The solid in question cannot be a closed surface of a visible thing, because such a solid would be colored. It must therefore be a geometrical solid. But as Jacob Klein has pointed out, "There is hardly anything in the world less solid than a geometrical solid."[14] Meno accepts the second definition because it defines an unknown in terms of a known, but in what sense is solid more known than color? Meno accepts it because its mathematical form is familiar to him. That does not mean the definition is without presuppositions; it merely means that its presuppositions are sufficiently comfortable to Meno as to be invisible to him.

The problem is still clearer in the final sample definition offered by Socrates, the definition of color as "an effluence of figures commensurable with sight and perceivable" (76d). As Socrates intimates, this definition could apply to any of the senses. It singles out sight only if you already know the difference between sight and, say, smell. More important, the definition contains *figure* within it, and thereby indicates the difficulty with Meno's "rigorous" approach. Once defined, figure is taken as a given, as an *archē* from which one argues and to which one does not return. But, if, as we saw, the definition of figure was not so lacking in presuppositions as at first appeared, then the definition of color, and everything following from it, will be infected by the inadequacies of the definition of figure.

It is at this point that Socrates calls Meno's pseudo-rigor "tragic" (76e). Tragedy is built upon the necessity of an initial mistake that later exacts an enormous price. It is not that the mistake is to be avoided; as we have seen, definitions require presuppositions. We can never start from scratch, from the *archai*. The serious attempt to behave as though we can begin at the beginning ultimately leads to tragedy. To the extent to which the need to treat certain things as fixed is a fixed condition of human nature, tragedy will be a perennial possibility for human beings. It is no accident that Socrates chooses to address Meno here for the only time in the dialogue by his patronymic. Meno is no more self-generated, autonomous, no more an *archē*, than the definitions he prizes. His desire for autonomy, for being self-generated, has the ingredients of tragedy. He avoids it only by taking so much for granted. It remains to be seen what happens when one ceases to take one's beginning points for granted.

Meno began with a question about the *genesis* of virtue. Socrates attempted to transform this question into one about the *eidos* of virtue. Meno seemed to acquiesce for a time, but all the while his sights were set on the practical question. That became clear when he rejected Socrates' first definition of color. To converse (*dialegesthai*) Socrates had to meet Meno halfway; he had to change the character of his definitions. Accordingly, Socrates' second definition of color was not so much an account of what color is as it was an account of how it comes to be. Socrates adopted the mode of modern science; he identified *eidos* and *genesis*. No wonder Meno finds it the best of the three definitions.

The second definition of color coincides with a significant change in the terms of the argument. Directly after referring to its tragic character (76e) Socrates asks Meno to give him a similar answer about the "whole of virtue" (77a). The notion that virtue is a whole and its instances, parts had been implicit from the beginning of this section of the dialogue (73d–74a) when Meno called justice virtue, and failed to distinguish between "virtue" and "a virtue." It is a necessary consequence of the movement from an *eidos* question to a *genesis* question. Generating virtue means assembling it out of its parts, not simply recognizing its presence and its necessary relations to other things.

The most obvious difference between the *eidos*/instance relation and the whole/part relation is that a whole is not the same as any one of its parts. Justice cannot really be virtue if it is a part of virtue. When Meno responds to Socrates that justice is virtue, he responds as though virtue were adjectival. "Justice is virtue," is a claim of the same sort as "Snow is white." By forcing Meno to distinguish between virtue and a virtue Socrates forces him to treat virtue as substantive. That is necessary to the argument, and yet at the same time, for Meno, it will force him to treat it as a whole with parts.

In effect, Meno's two mistakes are one. To understand virtue as a whole and the particular virtues as its parts means to substitute something "visible" for something essentially invisible. It means to transform an analytic account into a genetic account. Tragedy proves to be the result. On the other hand, Meno's initial inability to distinguish between the particular instance and the universal, a difficulty, as we saw, built into the final definition of color (the Empedoclean account of color as an effluence of figures easily could have been an account of anything perceived), is also tragic. Tragedy arises from thinking that the whole is available to us in the same way that the parts are available—from failing to distinguish between the universal and the particular. Socrates' second definition of color is a formula which allows a universal form to appear to determine a particular while in fact presupposing the particular. The definition is unintelligible unless one already knows what color is.

Meno, of course, had promised to follow Socrates' definition of figure with a definition of virtue. His unjust refusal to keep his promise causes the following exchange:

> SOCRATES: Anyone would know even having been blindfolded, Meno, from your conversation, that you are beautiful (*kalos*) and still have lovers.
>
> MENO: Really, why?
>
> SOCRATES: Because you do nothing but lay down the law (*epitatteis*) in speech, just as spoiled pets do, being tyrannical while they are in the bloom of youth. At the same time perhaps you have heard about me, that I am helpless before the beautiful. I will gratify you then and answer.
>
> (76b–c)

With this remark Socrates has added another piece to the puzzle. Meno is not only suspiciously like an *eidos*. He is *kalos*, noble or beautiful. We must now wonder about the connection between virtue understood as a whole, knowledge, and the *kalon*.

Why does Meno have to be beautiful? What we have seen so far is a developing parallel between Meno and *eidos*. The dramatic indication of the parallel is that Meno recognizes that to be virtuous means not being dependent or derivative. He wants to be an *archē*, or rather an *archon*. That is why he repeatedly forgets justice and breaks his agreement with Socrates. Justice is the virtue which calls attention to the equality of ruler and ruled, to the fact that they are of the same species or *eidos*. It is his refusal to be like other men which constitutes Meno's *hubris* (76a).

It is precisely in this context that Socrates calls him *kalos*. The *kalon* would seem to have something to do with *eidos* understood as the ruling principle of a class, that is, ruling while remaining wholly apart from what is ruled, wholly determining the particular while remaining itself unaffected. This is rather ironic. Meno has repeatedly depended on Gorgias. Gorgias, in his theory of color, depended on Empedocles, and, one must suppose, Empedocles depended on someone else; they all begin with someone else's *logos*.[15] They converse (*dialegesthai*), or engage in dialectic, that kind of argument that depends not only on saying the truth, but also on arguing by way of what your interlocutor acknowledges (75d). And yet they do not realize that they converse. The *kalon* has something to do with this spurious sense of autonomy, of being whole.

But why should Socrates claim that he can tell even by Meno's conversation that he still has lovers, and why does he go on to claim to be weak before *tōn kalōn* (either the beautiful men or the beautiful things)? Why does Socrates need the beautiful? Perhaps it is well to begin with a speculation. Let us suppose the world were a perfectly ordered whole. If each part of the whole were to have its function and fulfill that function perfectly, no single part would itself point to the whole. The whole would be like a clock. From the inside it would look like chaos—could anyone think to ask what it looked like. Let us suppose, however, that within this perfectly ordered clock we introduce a perfect miniature, a model of the whole clock. If an accurate model, it would have to look utterly detached from any of the other parts. It would be as though it were framed so as to ensure that we did not attempt to see it as connected to anything else. The cost of having such a model, hence some access to the wholeness of the whole from within the whole, would be the loss of the perfect order of the whole, since there would now be one part serving no purpose and unrelated to all other parts. What is true of this model would be true of anything within the whole which looks like a whole itself, anything so utterly complete and autonomous as to be self-justifying. On the other hand, without these "wholes" it is hard to see how we could even have an idea of the whole. It looks therefore as though *the* condition for the knowability of the whole is the imperfection of the whole. This need not deny that the knowable whole is more perfect than the unknowable whole; these wholes within the whole do make it more rather than less perfect. Nevertheless, their presence ensures the incompleteness of the very knowledge which they make partially possible.

Now, if the *kalon*, the beautiful, is what allows us to have the experience of things within the whole as not needing any justification, as being themselves sufficient to themselves, as being whole, then the *kalon* is also a sign of imperfection within the whole; it is something like a criminal element. The beautiful is, on the one hand the manifestation of something as perfect; on the other hand this very appearance ensures the imperfection of what appears. There is a connection between this understanding of the beautiful and Socrates' reference to the tragic character of the definitions preferred by Meno, the beautiful. The wholeness of the *kalon* is spurious; it does not and cannot give us the true whole, although it is our only access to the whole. To treat this spurious whole as though it were the true whole, as though it were simply nonderivative, is in part what we all do. But to take its every detail to be an exact representation of the details in the whole is like reading a metaphor literally. It is to mistake an instance for the *eidos*. The power of the *kalon* is that it seems to us to make the *eidos* visible as a whole. The ultimate result of simply accepting what the *kalon* makes visible as the *eidos* is tragedy.

Just what this all has to do with Meno becomes clear in the third definition of virtue.

> Accordingly, Socrates, virtue seems to me to be just as the poet says, "to rejoice in beautiful things and to be able for them." And I say this to be virtue: desiring the beautiful things, to be able to procure them. (77b)

This definition is of a piece with the previous two. The first had said that a man's virtue was to be capable of managing the affairs of the city. The second had said that virtue was to be able to rule human beings. Here virtue is the ability to procure the beautiful things that one desires. In each case Meno understands virtue to be an ability or power rather than whatever the power is a power for. Power is the underlying *eidos* linking Meno's three definitions of virtue. It remains unstated because power is always power for something. It shows itself only when it is actualized, and so is no longer potential. Like the *eidē* it is necessarily invisible.

While Meno's definition is once again borrowed, he does make crucial changes. By changing *rejoice* to *desire*, Meno is forced to change the ambiguous "to be able for them" of the poet's version, something which could mean being up to the level of the beautiful things, to the unambiguous "to be able to procure" of his version. The changes go together. Desire is for Meno the desire to possess (77c). Power is the power to get. Meno has turned the beautiful things from things to be looked at into things to be consumed. Some people go to art galleries to look, others to buy. Meno is a buyer. For that reason it is easy for Socrates to get him to agree to the substitution of "good things" for "beautiful things." And yet the difference is substantial. One can say no to the beautiful things; one can refuse to do one's duty. But it is more questionable that one can say no to what seems good. It is appropriate that Meno should have borrowed his definition from a poet. In refuting it, Socrates will point out the consequences of the fundamental principle of tragedy, the mistaking of the beautiful for the good. Tragic poetry is concerned with the effects of this mistake; the mistake, however, is characteristic of our day-to-day lives. It is what Descartes understands as the error of "good sense"—natural egoism.

The gist of Socrates' refutation is as follows. No one desires bad things because to desire means to desire something you think is good for you. To desire bad things would mean to want to harm yourself, and so to be wretched or *kakadaimonia*—the opposite of *eudaimonia*, happiness or having a good (*eu*) god (*daimōn*) within. The first part of Meno's definition, to desire good things, is therefore common to all men, and so does not differentiate the virtuous from everybody else. The differentiation must then be accounted for by the second part of Meno's definition, the ability to procure good things. When Socrates presses Meno on just what he means by goods, and suggests health and wealth, Meno replies,

And to possess gold, I say, and silver, and honors and offices (*archas*) in the city. (78c)

Socrates then summarizes without any objection from Meno.

Very well. Virtue is really to procure gold and silver; so says Meno, the ancestral guest-friend of the Great King. (78d)

With Meno's tacit approval Socrates has confirmed the omission of health from good things to be procured and seems to have understood the possession of offices and honors in terms of the possession of gold and silver. Meno models himself on his ancestral guest-friend, the Great King of Persia, who is famous for his wealth, and whose power is so frequently measured in terms of that wealth.[16] For Meno everything is understood in terms of gain; Xenophon's account has been confirmed. This issue is signaled by the very first word of the dialogue, a form of the verb *echō*. Its primary meaning is to have or hold, but it also means to be able. For Meno virtue is power, but power is understood as having.

Why, though, is wealth so important? The key is that for the first time in Meno's account of virtue power is omitted (78d). That is because wealth is something like power objectified. Meno's love of gold and silver points to his love of gain in general, and not gain of any specific object. For Meno, virtue is power because to be good is to be utterly independent, autonomous. But power is invisible. One does not acquire it. In fact, it seems as though one cannot acquire it. It is now perhaps easier to see why the dialogue begins as it does. The question, how virtue is acquired, follows naturally from the identification of virtue and power. If virtue is power, then the ability to acquire it, as a power, is also virtue. To acquire virtue means to presuppose its presence. Either you have the power to acquire good things or you do not. If you do you are virtuous by nature. If you do not, since virtue is itself a good thing (87d), you cannot acquire it. Virtue understood as autonomy therefore has this difficulty. To lack it is to lack the ability to get it. To want it is to need something, and to need something is to fail to be autonomous. To put the point in a slightly exaggerated way, Meno seeks out Socrates to ask the following question: How is it possible to become a god?

Meno's love of wealth has nothing erotic about it. He does not acquire as a means to pleasure; he acquires as a means to show his ability to acquire. One can imagine him as a rapist, but not as a lover. The problem with Meno's understanding of virtue is that he thinks that to be virtuous is to rule, but he must acknowledge that he is not a ruler. The way out of this dilemma is for him to say to himself that virtue is not actual ruling, but rather the hidden ability making it possible to rule. But how does Meno, himself so superficial, understand this hidden power? He is forced to make an external object of it; it is transformed into wealth. Consequently, Meno, who now sees the need for distinguishing between the internal and invisible and the external and visible, constructs an inside, an invisible realm, for himself. But he does so as though it were an outside, a visible realm. This is not only Meno's failure however. It is in a way what we all do and must do. It is a tendency which, for example, lies behind conventional Platonism and its treatment of Platonic *eidē* as though they were beings in time and space like all other beings. This need to reconstruct the inside as an outside, the need to think metaphorically, is simply another way of pointing to the role the *kalon* plays in our understanding. What Descartes noticed and sought to overcome by the invention of a new science, was understood by Sophocles to be the limiting condition of human nature. The question is whether the condition is simply tragic. We apparently have to *mis*understand in order to understand at all. We misunderstand because metaphor is always incomplete. Wealth, for example, is not really power externalized; it is an image of power. To treat it as power would be to ignore its conventional character. Money, *nomisma*, is money only to the extent that it is believed or held (*nomizō*) to be valuable. Its value is therefore the result of convention, *nomos*. Whoever fails to understand this and reads the metaphor of money literally will misunderstand the extent to which his power depends upon others.

If virtue is power, then it is invisible much in the way that the *eidē* are invisible. It is therefore not surprising that, having initially forced Meno to ask what virtue is, Socrates then leads him to ask what *eidē* are. The latter question is explored in this dialogue only in terms of particular *eidē*, notably, color and figure. But suppose one were to ask what *eidos* as such was, that is, what the *eidos* of *eidos* was. Every particular *eidos* is an *eidos* of something. To understand what *eidos* as such is would mean to make its power visible without making it specific. That would be possible only if we could get a sense of power which did not willy-nilly cause us to confuse it with what it is power for. This in turn would be possible only if there were some discrepancy between the power in question and that for which it was the power, in other words, only where there was some difference perceived between what something was and what it appeared to be. Now this sort of discrepancy is first apparent in human beings, the beings who are not what they seem to be, the beings who can say to themselves what they ought to be. Accordingly, Socrates' first example of the sort of question to which an *eidos* is the appropriate answer is not "What is X?" but "Who is Meno?"[7] It is the idea of self-realization present in the attempt to acquire virtue which is the source of our insight into the necessity of *eidē*. Or, as the dialogue later makes clearer, while it first appears that there is no virtue without knowledge, the underlying theme of the *Meno* is that there could be no knowledge without virtue. The price we pay for this visibility of the *eidē* is, however, not negligible. To be able to "see" power means that power is not perfectly operating. The price one pays for the awareness of the good is the existence of evil or defect. This is why Socrates' conversation on virtue takes place with *the* defective man. Plato has in mind to examine the necessity of defect. All of this has to do in turn with the question of Meno's beauty. The *kalon* is what allows us to get a look at the wholeness of the whole, but only by being itself a false or spurious whole. All visible wholes are of necessity specious. No wonder Meno, so purely beautiful, is so purely defective.

What happens after the refutation of Meno's third definition is the turning point in the dialogue. Meno, not very happy, refuses to continue the argument (79e–80b). His rebellion is in its way understandable enough. Socrates has been asking Meno throughout for the sort of account he himself seems to have no inclination to give. In his insistence on *eidē* Socrates has given no end of instances to serve Meno as paradigms. What is important for us is the manner in which Meno handles his frustration. In response to Socrates' questioning, Meno has been forced to say *"ouk' echō,"* "I am not able"(80b). Meno has been made to feel powerless, that is, without virtue. His confidence in his own virtue made him not at all hesitant to seek Socrates out even though he had heard about Socrates' ways. This virtue is now rendered dubious. In his helplessness Meno attacks Socrates in an image. Socrates has "bewitched," "drugged," and "sung incantations" to him. All of this implies that Socrates is more than he appears, that he has invisible powers. In Meno's image, Socrates is like the torpedo fish in looks (*eidos*). These fish look harmless, although quite ugly, and yet are surprisingly powerful. So far Meno has done no more than Socrates has done a number of times. He has tried to understand what something is by likening it to something else. The problem with Meno's image is that it is pushed too far.

> And you seem to me to be completely, if one must scoff at something, most like the flat torpedo fish in the sea both in looks and in other ways. (80a)

Meno has made literal his own metaphor in his rush to have something to scoff at. Socrates is "completely" (*pantelōs*) "most like" (*homoiotatos*) a torpedo fish, not only in certain respects similar but in all respects similar. The sign of what Meno has done is that Plato has him reverse what is by this time the standard use of *eidos* in the dialogue. In the expression *"eidos kai t'alla,"* Meno means to say that Socrates is like a torpedo fish in looks and in other ways. The use of *eidos* to mean "looks," its original meaning, is startling given its previous use to mean something like "essence." What Meno has done is to put the inside (*eidos* as essence) on the outside (*eidos* as looks). He has been moved to do so by his sense of powerlessness. However, the fact that Meno needs to use an image to describe Socrates is a sign that there is more to Socrates than meets the eye.[18] Socrates cannot be "completely most like" the image meant to represent him. One could even say that it is because men are not what they appear to be that we become aware that things are not what they appear to be. That, in turn, leads us to see that things are only images of what they "want to be." Philosophical idealism is rooted in, and depends on, frustrated idealism in the ordinary sense.

Meno's newly discovered powerlessness is also the occasion for the first use of the word *psuchē*, or soul, in the dialogue (80b1). One discovers one's soul as a consequence of being aware of what one lacks, a fact beautifully illustrated by Meno's complaint that he has previously given myriad speeches on virtue to all sorts of people and quite successfully *hōs ge emautō edokoun* (80b3). The phrase can mean either "as indeed they [the speeches] seemed to me," or "as indeed I seemed to me." As long as Meno succeeds, the difference between his speeches, the external product of his soul, and his inside, his soul, is obscured. Only when his speeches fail does he discover himself.[19]

Meno claims that he has previously shone everywhere, in all cities. He warns Socrates against going anywhere but Athens (80b). It is a threat forewarning us that Anytus will soon be on the scene, and that Socrates will eventually be tried and put to death for asking questions about virtue. Socrates' remarks on the relative safety of Thessaly (*Crito* 53d–54b) not withstanding, the man who questions virtue is safe nowhere. Even in the midst of disorder and lawlessness men can be offended. Meno, however, is apparently free of the problem of Socrates. The *kalon*, for which he stands, shines in every city. And yet the beautiful itself will not be beautiful when measured against any one of the instances in which it appears. Socrates will call Meno *panourgos* (80b). A "doer of everything" is on the one hand at home in every regime and on the other a criminal in every regime. The *kalon* is the universal particular. It will not be the same everywhere, but it will be everywhere. Meno can make fine speeches in Thessaly and in Athens, and he can enjoy the admiration he calls forth in both cities even though his speech in one city may contradict his speech in another. But he can behave in that way only so long as he remains unself-reflective. If he were at any time to reflect on what makes him able to be admired in both Thessaly and in Athens, that is, if he were to reflect on the power of the beautiful rather than simply being the vehicle for the production of its instances, he would cease to be at home in any regime. He would become like Socrates. Reflecting on the power of the *kalon* to appear everywhere differently also means reflecting on the inadequacy of any of its particular appearances. Meno is beautiful; Socrates is ugly.

To become like Socrates would mean to recognize how partial is the character of the images in the ten thousand speeches that Meno produces. It would be to recognize that the perfection of the *kalon* is local, and so not really the perfection that it appears to be. And yet to understand this fact is also to understand that our awareness of the possibility of perfection is dependent on these partial images. We need the *kalon*, but to understand that need is to understand that we can never quite achieve for ourselves what it represents to us. As a reminder of our imperfection, of our lack of autonomy, the beautiful is not beautiful. Plato understands what Descartes was to think through in the *Discourse on Method* as the problem of God.

Meno is unwilling to recognize the consequence of his desire to be beautiful everywhere. He does not realize that it is because there are beautiful things everywhere that *the* beautiful cannot be recognized anywhere. Socrates is therefore correct in saying that what Meno really wants is for Socrates to make an image of him in return. Meno wants to have the kind of perfection and autonomy that beautiful things seem to have. But Meno is sufficiently sophisticated to wish to combine all of the "perfections" of all of the beautiful things. In this he imitates the beautiful itself. The beautiful "rejoice in being imaged" (80c). That they do so is the sign of the spuriousness of their autonomy and perfection. The *kalon* deceives us by making us think of it as the independent and autonomous source of the many *kala*, the many beautiful things. In fact, the ugly truth of the *kalon* is the necessary imperfection of the beauty of the beautiful things. Meno no more sees that beautiful people need lovers than he had seen that rulers needed those whom they rule. That the beautiful rejoice in being imaged means that they are not beautiful independent of the power they have to generate a plurality of images. Beautiful human beings therefore need admirers. The beautiful itself needs the plurality of beautiful things. But just as the need of beautiful human beings for admirers casts doubt on the very "perfection" which is the source of their being admired, the dependence of the beautiful itself on the many beautiful things casts doubt on the perfection it is supposed to possess. The beautiful is the sign of the necessity of human incompleteness. Because he is blind to that necessity, Meno misunderstands his own image of Socrates. Meno thinks that torpedo fish numb others alone, with their arguments. He does not realize that it is possible to numb oneself as well, that we are no more in a position to see our own inside without images, without the outside, than we are to see the inside of others. He thinks that Socrates' speeches numb others, thus proving their power, and so the power of Socrates. It does not occur to him that, as there is a difference between Socrates and the speeches of Socrates, the speeches can have a numbing effect on Socrates himself. It does not occur to him that one can recognize the power of images, of metaphor, as the fundamental form of human understanding while at the same time being aware of metaphorical understanding as essentially defective. For Meno speech must be a vehicle for transporting thoughts, and not a way of thinking. It is hard to imagine him as talking to himself.

It is because Meno is too much the "Platonist," too much preoccupied with the dependence of speech on *eidē* and insufficiently appreciative of the dependence of *eidē* on speech, that it is possible for him to formulate his famous paradox of learning.

And in what way will you seek, Socrates, for that about which you do not know at all what it is? For what sort of thing, of the things you do not know, will you seek, setting it up as a goal? Or even if at the very best you should happen upon it, how will you know that this is what you did not know? (80d)

We are reminded of Socrates' response to the question of how to acquire virtue. If learning is to be understood as a kind of acquisition of knowledge, then according to Socrates' earlier position, it will be impossible to settle the question of acquisition until one has settled the question of what knowledge is. But to settle that question means to learn. We cannot learn unless we know what we are to learn, but in that case we already know and so do not need to learn. Learning looks to be impossible. It is true that Socrates chides Meno for putting forth such an eristic argument, but we must not let that distract us from the fact that it is Socrates' introduction of the *eidē* that makes this argument seem so plausible. In calling Meno's paradox eristic Socrates reminds us of his earlier distinction between dialectic and eristic (75c–e), according to which in the case of eristic one takes a position and dares others to attack. This proved to mean that one assumed an absolute *archē* without ever returning to question its absoluteness. Eristic is characteristic of that sort of deductive argument that takes the declarative sentence as the fundamental unit of *logos*; it is an understanding of *logos* as answering fearlessly in the manner of Gorgias (70b). It is characteristic of that epideictic or show-off mode of speech that Socrates once asked Gorgias to forego in favor of questions and answers (*Gorgias* 449b). Dialectic seems rather to take an *archē* to be always provisional, something to which one returns, which is to be questioned. By calling the argument eristic Socrates suggests that Meno has been too quick to take the *eidē* as answers. The sign that he has done that is that he begins with the metaphor of learning as seeing, and then shows that learning cannot be seeing. Meno then concludes that learning must be impossible, which he *learns* ironically enough from the metaphor of learning as seeing. Of course he might simply have concluded that learning is not really like seeing; the looks (*eidē*) of things are not visible. The whole section is an example of that way Socrates had earlier characterized as tragic, the way of taking the *kalon* as simply true without realizing that there is inevitably a discrepancy between an image and that of which it is the image. Meno has fundamentally misunderstood the character of the invisible *eidē*, but his misunderstanding is only the most extreme version of the way in which the invisible is inevitably misunderstood. The inevitability of this misunderstanding and its connection to political life is the concern of the remainder of the dialogue. This is why Socrates' response to Meno's attack is a myth in which learning is understood as recollection, a myth also in which Hades figures prominently. As we know from the *Ajax*, Hades is both a place and the name of the god who rules that place, the god of wealth whose name comes from the Greek, *a-eides*, or invisible. The criminality of Ajax was to be unable to understand the invisible, the inside. The same will be true of Meno.

II

The problem of the *Meno* stated most generally is this: What does it mean to learn, and what does that have to do with virtue? This problem leads in a variety of directions. It leads to the question "What is an *eidos*?" because the answer to this question will determine whether there is anything to be learned. However, the *eidē*, the "looks" of things, turn out to be invisible and necessarily invisible powers. Thus the question of the *eidē* leads us to the problem of visibility and invisibility, which is the same problem hinted at by the ambiguity of the first word of the dialogue, *echeis*. "Are you able?" can also mean "Do you have?" In other words, a power is not something had, and yet it always comes to sight as something had. This is the difficulty hidden in the meaning of Hades. It is an invisible realm necessarily presented as though it were visible.

Put somewhat differently, the question of visibility and invisibility comes to sight only by way of a reflection on human beings. The crucial example of an invisible power is the soul. Consequently, the first *eidos* question in the dialogue is not a "what is" question, but rather "Who is Meno?" Meno, however, proves to be something of a caricature of a man. What he knows he knows secondhand, whether it is from Gorgias, from Empedocles, or now from Socrates. As nothing seems to come from within, it is poetic justice that Meno should fail to distinguish between himself and his speeches (80b). Meno is identical with his speeches and his speeches come from Gorgias. Meno is so utterly superficial that he comes very close to having no inside, no invisible power, hence no soul. Why, then, should he have been chosen to converse with Socrates in this dialogue? Plato has contrived to show us the necessity to get at the inside by way of the outside, to show us that the crucial element of learning is metaphor or imaging, likening something to what it is not. This is the reason for Meno's connection to the *kalon* for his vice. Plato presents the utterly superficial man so that he can give an account of the necessity to begin with the surface.

If learning is something like getting inside, then Socrates introduces the account of learning as recollection in order to show how it is possible to get inside. At the same time we must not forget that it is a metaphorical account with its own superficiality. Socrates presents the myth as secondhand knowledge, handed down by priests and priestesses and by poets, specifically Pindar. Although the reason for its introduction is Meno's attack on the possibility of learning, Socrates first uses it to raise a moral issue. He begins with the claim that the soul is immortal; it dies, but it does not perish. One ought, therefore, to be concerned about the next life where Persephone (the wife of Hades) will reward the virtuous with wisdom. Virtue here (80b–c) seems to consist in acknowledging one's defectiveness. Wisdom is available only to those who have "sinned" and been forgiven. There is no knowledge without the Fall.

Socrates' explanation of Pindar's poem is entirely in terms of knowledge. Having been born many times (we do not even know whether this might be our first time), the soul has *seen* everything in Hades and elsewhere. The soul has seen the *eidē* and their instances according to Socrates' account. If, however, this were its first birth, it would have seen only the *eidē*. Therefore either the instances are not really necessary to knowledge, or else the soul is never born for a first time. According to Socrates there is nothing the soul has not learned, but if the purpose of the myth is to explain learning as recollection, how can he say that the soul "learns" in Hades? Is learning in Hades also recollection, and does it therefore presuppose another "having seen"? Or if it is not recollection, is there a learning which need not, indeed cannot, be understood as recollection? If so, then why do we need to account for any learning as recollection? Why do we need Hades at all? Could we not simply have learned in this other way, in this life?

Socrates goes on to say that since the soul knows everything, and since all things are related, whenever one thing is remembered there is nothing to stop the soul from moving from it to everything else. However, if that were the case, why would not everybody know everything? Socrates' answer is that to recollect requires one to be courageous and not to grow weary. In other words, knowledge depends on virtue. But how do we acquire virtue? Here Meno's problem becomes a real one. Are all men equally able to recollect? Socrates seems to mean that they are, but Meno is clear proof that they are not. Still, the purpose of Socrates' speech is not to make Meno smarter but by an implied threat and by holding out the lure of fame to make him less lazy. The problem of the *Meno* is not so much that learning is impossible but that it may prove to be impossible to teach people to learn. Socrates' story is the beginning of an attempt to get around this difficulty. That is the purpose of his long exchange with the slave boy.

In what follows we observe Socrates "teach" a slave of Meno the solution to a problem in geometry by asking him a series of very leading questions. The ostensible purpose of the exchange is to show that someone who has never learned geometry can find the correct answers to these questions "within" himself without being taught. The slave is shown a square with sides of two feet in length. He is then asked what would be the length of the sides of a square twice the area of the two-foot square. The slave boy gives two incorrect answers, four feet and three, and then ends by pointing to the diagonal of the two-foot square. In terms more familiar, but not used by Plato here, the line in question is twice the square root of two in length.

The solution to this geometrical problem requires an irrational magnitude, a magnitude literally unspeakable, *alogon*, and so one to which we can only point. And it is possible to point to it only because the line is part of a larger whole, and can be seen and known in relation to that whole. That in turn presupposes that the whole of which it is a part is known. In this instance that means knowledge of the size of the two-foot square and of the four-foot square. But the assumption about the length of the side of the first square was just that, an assumption. Only by making an essentially arbitrary assumption does a necessary relation become clear. However, this arbitrary assumption is also the source of the slave boy's first error. The side of the first square was assumed to be two; in his first answer the slave boy confused the area of the square, side multiplied by side, with side multiplied by two. This is merely an example of what is always the difficulty. The slave confused an accidental attribute of the particular instance with an essential character. He confused the instance with the *eidos*.

The very first question which Socrates had asked Meno about the slave was whether he spoke Greek and was Greek (82b4). We are meant to see this precondition for the geometrical conversation as very much like the assumption of the length of the side in the demonstration. Socrates could not have spoken with the boy at all had he not spoken Greek, but the boy's language and what we would now call his "culture" are surely accidental attributes. Greekness, or one might say *nomos*, is an accidental assumption that proves necessary in order to make a necessary relation manifest.

The purpose of the geometrical demonstration is supposed to be to provide an example of learning as recollection of something which could not have been learned during this life. Knowledge is supposed to be within the boy, just waiting to be recollected. There is something to that. However, Socrates' questions are very pointed, indicating that the boy needs—and receives—

considerable prompting. While it is clear that the slave's assent is important, it is not clear what that assent means. He is, after all, a slave; he has been told to answer. He therefore has very practical reasons for answering, reasons altogether unconnected with an attempt to learn. Meno probably does not suffer disobedience very well. But even granting these practical reasons for conversing with Socrates, once the slave has begun answering there is little reason for him not to answer as honestly as possible. Practical reasons serve to encourage theoretical honesty. That is something like the way in which knowledge depends on virtue. Nevertheless, had Socrates not been present to force the slave boy to realize his errors, the slave would have been content to go away thinking that the square root of eight was three. We "recollect" as much error as we do truth. What is not yet clear is how we are supposed to distinguish between the two.

So far, there are two parts to the account of recollection, Socrates' myth and the instance of recollection which is meant to help Meno understand the myth. In Socrates' explanation of his exchange with the slave boy the crucial change is that he describes the boy's answers as opinions, *doxai*. At first *opinion* seems to be interchangeable with *knowledge*, but the change is necessary because Socrates had also discovered false things in the slave. The difference between knowledge and opinion is further elaborated in the sequel:

SOCRATES: In the one not knowing, then, concerning what he may not know, there are true opinions concerning these things which he does not know?

MENO: It appears.

SOCRATES: And now, just like a dream these opinions have just now been stirred up in him. But if someone were to ask him at various times and in various ways the same things, you know that in the end he will know these things no less precisely than anyone.

MENO: It is likely.

SOCRATES: Therefore, no one having taught him, but by being questioned, he will know, recovering the knowledge himself from himself (*autos ex hautou*).

MENO: Yes.

SOCRATES: And to recover knowledge himself in himself (*auton en hautō*), is this not to have recollected?

MENO: Certainly.

(85c–d)

The opinions seem always to be in the boy. When they are stirred up, or put in motion by questioning, this stirring up leads to knowledge. But then the truth of the myth of recollection would be in these wise opinions which we have without knowing that they are wise.

It is hard to believe that we had these opinions in us before we were born. The problem, then, is to understand what it means to have opinions "in us." What, exactly, are these opinions in? The ambiguity of this self in which opinions are contained and which comes to know is revealed by Socrates' use of two expressions to describe the recovery of knowledge. It is recovered himself from himself (*autos ex hautou*) and it is recovered himself in himself (*auton en hautō*). The difference between the two depends on what is being emphasized. The first emphasizes the taking out, and so the self that is doing the retrieving. The second emphasizes the recovery in oneself, and hence what one might call the primordial self receives the emphasis. The problem is that for learning to be possible the "real" self must be both. We must have knowledge in us and hence "know" in our primordial selves, but we must also seek it and hence not have it in our seeking selves. Any learning or questioning self is therefore necessarily two selves. The recollection myth is an attempt to render this split self in time so as to avoid the need for the self to be simultaneously both selves. It is an attempt to replace knowledge of ignorance by a history of the soul, to replace an eidetic by a genetic account. It is therefore essentially metaphorical in character. The metaphor needs only to be read literally to see why learning cannot be recollection, and so, to see in an indirect way what learning must be. The recollection story divides learning into various "moments," thereby suggesting that learning might be constructed out of these moments as though out of its parts. The construction fails owing to the incompatibility of certain of these "parts," but the failure reveals the fundamental ambiguity of the *eidos* of learning.

Socrates' use of the present tense to describe the knowledge the boy "now has" (*hēn nun houtos echei*, 85d) is a sign that the temporal account will not do. The problem is really the same as the ambiguity of *echō*, to have and to be able. If throughout this section Socrates had substituted "to be able" for "to have" then the tension between always "having" knowledge and learning would have been invisible. To be human would have meant to be able to know, but there would have had to be no time at which we acquired the knowledge we now "have" and can "recollect." By describing knowledge as something had, however, Socrates is pointing to a real opposition within "to be able." He seems to be using the myth of recollection as an example, an instance, of one of those opinions which when stirred up lead to knowledge.

Where did this opinion about recollection come from? Socrates said that he had heard it from priests and priestesses, and from poets. That is, it seems to have come from the tradition. The time before we were born seems to refer to a time when these opinions were in us, but before we were stirred up enough to turn them into knowledge. The time before we were born is the time before we began to question opinions, the time when we were in the cave.[20] If being born means becoming a questioner, then what we "always knew" must mean what precedes our questioning and makes it possible. Our "prenatal" glimpse of all things is simply the tradition into which we are born, the city and its *nomos*. For all of this to be true means that the temporal argument cannot be the real argument here. That becomes clear in the sequel:

> SOCRATES: But if he did not get them in the present life isn't it already clear that he had them in some other time and had learned them?
> MENO: It appears.
> SOCRATES: Isn't this the time when he was not a human being?
> MENO: Yes.
> SOCRATES: If then, during the time when he is a human being and when he isn't a human being true opinions will be in him which will become knowledge when awakened by questions, then his soul will at all times be in a state of having learned. For it is clear that at every time he either is or is not a human being.
>
> (85e–86a)

There seems to be a confusion in the argument. Did we learn before we were human beings, or did we always know? The confusion is compounded in two places. At 86a1 Socrates says that the boy "had learned" (*ememathēkei*) in some other time. At 86a8 he says that "at all times his soul will have learned" (*memathēkuia*). By coupling the perfect tense with *always* Socrates shows that he cannot have a temporal account in mind. It is not possible for the soul to exist for all time in a state of having learned. What Socrates must mean then is that strictly speaking there is no time at which the soul learns. Socrates has given an indirect definition of what it means to be human. If the time before we were human is the time before we learned, then to be human means "already to have learned," already to have moved away from the beginning, the *archē*.

Put somewhat differently, if being human means questioning, could not the time frame of the act of "recollecting" be rather like fading in and out of humanity? Sometimes we are human, sometimes not. Or, in order to recollect we need sometimes to take things for granted. Consequently, in order sometimes to be human we sometimes need not to be human. That would mean of course that there could be no perfect humanity. By presenting human life in two stages, Socrates makes it appear as though having passed through one we then enter upon another. But what is presented temporally here is really an account of the soul divided against itself at all times. Sometimes we act, and sometimes we reflect upon what we have done. But we cannot reflect on what we have done unless we have done something. If reflection is the essence of our humanity, then pure humanity is out of the question. The problem of the connection between doing and reflecting will emerge later in the dialogue as the question of whether we go to statesmen or to sophists to learn virtue (91a–96b). There it will have to do with the question of whether it is possible both to know what virtue is and to be virtuous. Here it has to do with the necessarily dual character of the human soul as always in a state of having learned—always recollecting what has come before. Were it to stop being in that state it would stop being human. That is the meaning of Socrates' remark that he is willing to fight in word and in deed for the fact that believing we ought to seek what we do not know will make us better, braver, and less lazy. This belief keeps us seeking and so keeps us two. The alternative is seeking to be an *arché* oneself, that is, seeking to be not at all derivative. That is what Meno wants; what he fails to notice is that the primordial soul to which he is so attracted is referred to throughout in the singular. It is not a human soul. Meno is too ready to leave his humanity behind in his desire to be nonderivative. This is his criminality.

In this section of the dialogue (81a–86c) Socrates has purported to show that learning is possible if it is understood as recollection of what we know in some other life. His central thesis, that the soul "will at all times be in a state of having learned" (86a), is a way of saying that while there is no beginning to learning, no *arché*, there is a coming to be of knowing. It is a way of saying that the human soul is forever split in two. Learning, which presupposes a primordial knowing, equally presupposes something like a primordial ignorance. It may be the case that in order to learn we need to know what we are looking for so that we will know it when we find it. But it is also true that learning involves a sense of not having known, which is a necessary part of discovery. Meno has said that there can be no learning if we know and no learning if we are ignorant. He had taken that to be a proof of the impossibility of learning. However, in its serious version his paradox seems rather a proof that neither knowledge nor ignorance is possible; learning is what is possible.

But how is learning possible, if it is not to be had tragically, that is, from the beginnings? Since the *Meno* will connect virtue and knowledge, one is tempted to wonder whether there is not only a deeper level to the paradox of learning but also a deeper level to the paradox of virtue. Would it make sense to describe human beings as "always in a state of having acquired virtue?" This would of course mean that just as learning requires a sense of discovery which ensures that one does not already know completely, acquiring virtue would involve not being completely virtuous.

This peculiar situation becomes somewhat clearer in light of Meno's understanding of what it means to rule. Meno thinks that ruling means complete freedom (86d–e). Ruling others means that one does not have to rule oneself. Socrates, on the other hand, claims that ruling requires self-rule. But self-rule implies that there is a part of oneself which is ruled, a slavish part. To the extent that rule is self-rule, rule is necessarily incomplete, just as if knowledge is self-knowledge or discovery, it is necessarily incomplete. Were rule complete the self which rules would be utterly unaware of itself. It would be quite literally superficial.

All of this makes some new sense of the opening of the dialogue. When Socrates gives Meno an account of the origin of his desire for knowledge of the origin of virtue he points to the connection between the desire for knowledge of the *archē* and virtue. What underlies both is the will to rule (*archein*), the link between ancient tragedy and modern science. Socrates had presented himself and Meno as perfectly ruled, as perfect instances of their respective traditions. Had that been true they would have been slaves. But, as Meno's first definition of virtue reveals, the *polis* requires that men be both masters and slaves. In the terms of the *Ajax*, it is an association for the mutual benefit of "the great and the small." The combination is necessary for the *polis* to be an autonomous whole. Meno has from the very beginning failed to understand this fact about the *polis*. On the one hand, he has modeled his notion of autonomy after ruling in the *polis*; on the other, he thinks it possible to have this sort of rule without the *polis*. Meno wants to be a ruler independent of the ruled; he always forgets justice. He seems unlike Ajax, who thinks of nothing but justice, but they are alike in being unaware of their dependence on those over whom they think themselves fit to rule. Ajax' pursuit of complete virtuosity leads him to bestiality. Meno's complete unconcern for others, his complete selfishness, leads him to understand virtue as perfect autonomy. Both are unlike Socrates who claims only to rule himself, and so models himself on the *polis* as a whole and not simply on its highest part. The result, however, is imperfect virtue.

The whole matter may be seen somewhat differently. In his desire to rule absolutely, Meno has the soul of a pure tyrant. That is what it means to want to be an *archē*. Meno's ambition is therefore unbounded; it is pure. However, this pure wilfullness makes the desire for or attraction to any particular thing seem inconsequential. Meno's desires are not erotic but always for the sake of something else. He wants things as a sign of his power to get them. Yet Meno is only a much purer version of what all human beings are to some extent. Our humanity means that we reflect on what we are doing, and that we take as much pleasure in the reflecting as in the doing. Meno is a man whose desire for *pure* satisfaction, that is satisfaction in the reflection, leaves him nothing to reflect on.

The man who wants everything and who can be satisfied with no less is the tyrant. In desiring what is characteristically human the tyrant becomes inhuman, just as by pushing the political to its limit he becomes essentially a private man. The transformation from the human to the inhuman in this way does not occur in the imperfectly tyrannical tyrants of the real world. It is rather the subject of tragedy.[21] Meno has been called tyrannical by Socrates (76b).

In various ways the dialogue makes repeated references to *the* tyrant of Greek tragedy, Oedipus. Just after Socrates has ostensibly proven the immortality of the soul (86b) Meno says to him, "You seem to me to speak well, Socrates, I know not how." However, the "I know not how" is in the Greek "*ouk oid' opōs.*" With the pun translated the remark would read, "You seem to me to speak well, Socrates, not Oedipus." Meno unwittingly acknowledges that Socrates' account of learning as recollection has been an attack on the tragic understanding alluded to earlier in the dialogue. It is meant to show that the *archai*, the first beginnings or principles, are not to be grasped. There is no possibility of an account from the beginning. Finally, that Socrates is waging a battle with Oedipus is playfully alluded to by the entire conversation with the slave boy. In the geometrical demonstration there is constant repetition of the phrases "two feet," "three feet," and "four feet." The *Meno* of course had all but begun with the problem of how to reconcile the variety within the human species. To ask why the virtue of men, women, old men, slaves, children, and so forth, while being all different, are still the same—that is, virtue, is really to ask what it is about the diverse instances of human being which makes them all nevertheless human beings. This issue parallels the problem of *Oedipus the Tyrant*. Oedipus comes to Thebes. To end the plague he must solve the riddle of the sphinx: What walks on four feet in the morning, two feet at midday, and three feet in the evening? Oedipus can answer the question because his deformity, his swollen foot, forces him to use a staff. Because he does not fit the description of the sphinx he understands that the answer to the riddle is man. His not fitting, his criminality, is the key to learning. At the same time, in a deeper sense Oedipus' not fitting has to do with his attempt to combine in himself the whole of the definition of man. He tries to be the perfect and complete man. It is this desire that ultimately leads to tragedy.

At first it looks as though Meno wants to be a god, but that is not quite correct. Even Zeus acquired rule from his father. In wanting to rule absolutely Meno does not quite realize that he wants to be nonhuman and nonanthropomorphic. He wants to be like an *eidos*. This substitution of the *eidē* for the gods, the crucial Platonic substitution, describes a whole in which there is no perfect satisfaction for the desire to rule. The human soul is characterized by the desire to be free which means ultimately a desire to be an *eidos*. But the *eidē* remain essentially outside of soul, something toward which soul is directed but different from it. There are two results. The world thus described makes self-awareness possible; yet at the same time it makes alienation inevitable. The alternative is the possibility of which Meno is the caricature, the tyrannical soul which in wanting everything is condemned to superficiality, or the soul that is not a soul because it tries to be the perfect soul. This is the final result of changing a "what is" question into a "who is" question. The difference between *Oedipus the Tyrant* and the *Meno* is perhaps that Sophocles begins with the longings of one of the deepest sort of men. Oedipus, who attempts to be just, ends by being tyrannical. His "superficiality" is therefore tragic. Plato, on the other hand, begins with a very superficial man in order to show how perfectly he is suited to the life of tyranny, and so in this way to show the deeper implications of the superficiality of tyranny for human nature generally.

The critical addition to the argument of the dialogue as a whole in the section on recollection is the split in the human soul. Tragedy results from the attempt to make the soul whole while not wanting to lose any of its attributes as split. It results from wishing to rule perfectly while still being aware of oneself as ruling, and from the desire to have known always while not relinquishing the pleasures of learning. It results from the attempt to be perfectly human. To ignore the impossibility of this perfection is to take the *kalon* as an *archē* rather than as a hypothesis. It results in what Sophocles in the case of Antigone refers to as her "criminal piety."[22] At the same time, such human virtue as there is seems to require this origin in criminality. Conventional virtue originates in a literal understanding of metaphor. It is ultimately destroyed by the same thing. For this reason Socrates attempts to show that perfect virtue and perfect knowledge are in principle impossible, thereby making virtue and knowledge possible.

III

The issue of the *Meno* is the issue embedded in "having learned always." It is the issue of the split soul as the condition for the possibility of learning and of virtue, and as the condition that makes pure knowing and pure virtue impossible. Socrates has shown us, although he has not shown Meno, the impossibility of perfect rule; he has shown us the tragedy of tyranny.

There is another way to see the problem. Meno is essentially lazy. He wants to know without learning, and he wants to be virtuous without trying.

His laziness is not simple, but rather points to what lies behind serious laziness, that there is something necessarily effortless about perfection. When we try to make ourselves look beautiful part of what that means is to try to make it look as though we have not tried very hard. The art of cosmetics must conceal its work so that the result of the art looks natural. There is something imperfect about having to strive for perfection. Children know that. When they do well on tests they are torn between saying how much they studied and claiming not to have studied at all. Meno's laziness, his reluctance to try, has a foundation in his awareness that there is something ugly in trying. To work is to admit one's incompleteness, one's lack of autonomy.

On the other hand, effortless activity does not point to anything inside. Effortless order is superficial; one does not know that there is any ruling going on. In a strange way, then, it is good that we lack perfection. If our souls were not split we would have no souls. In order to make this split in the human soul visible Socrates will turn to its manifestation within the *polis*. For that, however, Meno will not serve as an interlocutor. It will require Anytus who "fortunately" happens to be present (89e). This *fortunately* (*eis kalon*) rendered more literally would be something like "for beauty" or "in keeping with beauty." Plato inserts Anytus into the dialogue just when he is needed, and that perfect timing must look like an accident. The wholly purposive and the wholly accidental tend to look identical. This identity is marked by a reference to the beautiful.

Socrates turns to Anytus in order to ask to whom Meno should go to learn virtue. To see why the question comes up in this way we must go back a bit. The myth of recollection and its immediate sequel seem to succeed in convincing Meno that it is necessary to inquire once again into the question "What is virtue?" Socrates has convinced the lazy Meno that he should try. But Meno in his way is quite right in pointing out that a general resolution to try does not get you very far. He wants to know whether this virtue whose nature they are trying to discover is to be regarded as something acquired by teaching, by nature, or in another way. Meno still thinks that to look for something you must have some sense of what it is.

At first Socrates' response simply appears to be a repetition of the priority of the "what is" question to the "what sort" question, but in his reply Socrates indicates that if he ruled over Meno as he ruled over himself he could begin with the "what is" question. He does not, and so he cannot. He goes on to say that since Meno does rule over him, he will oblige him. And so, in the space of no more than ten lines Socrates has affirmed both his own self-rule and Meno's rule over him. The two claims can be rendered consistent only if there is some sense in which Socrates' self-rule is identical to Meno's rule over him. Socrates recognizes the need for a certain boldness characteristic of the *kalon* in order to begin an inquiry at all. The question "What is virtue?" could come to sight in the *Meno* only because Meno thought he already knew what virtue was and was interested in its acquisition. Socrates' question may be logically prior to Meno's answer, but Meno's wrong answer is the necessary condition for the coming to be of Socrates' question. Just as boldness was the necessary precondition for the acquisition of knowledge in the myth of recollection, a bold error is the necessary condition for Socratic correction. It is in this sense that Meno rules Socrates.

To illustrate what this rule means Socrates proposes that Meno relax his rule a bit to allow them to proceed by hypothesis, an instance of boldness which does not have our full confidence, a cautious boldness (86d–e). If virtue were knowledge, or were like knowledge, then it would have to be teachable. So all they have to do is ask whether virtue is knowledge. Socrates has not simply restored the "what is" question which Meno refused to answer. The new question is not "What is X?" but rather "Is X Y?" Meno's bias was the necessary ingredient for making a general question into a specific inquiry.

There is much more to this introduction of the hypothetical method. Jacob Klein points out the peculiarities of the mathematical example (86e–87b) used to introduce it, and also points out the queerly ambiguous use of the word *hoion* throughout the section.[23] It is used to mean "it is possible," "for example," "such as," and "similar." The last use could be the strong *homoion* of Euclid, that is, mathematical similarity, or it could simply mean "like." If the latter, then the extent and nature of similarity is not indicated, and Socrates rather cavalierly would have assumed that to be like knowledge was the same thing as to be knowledge. The whole argument is based on this assumption. Socrates is aware of his sloppy argument, as is implied by his remark at 87b–c that there should be no differing among them (Socrates and Meno) about which of two names to use, teaching or remembering. The difference is of course far from unimportant, since if the distinction between the two is allowed to stand, then knowledge would be precisely what can never be taught, but has to come from within. What is taught is opinion.

Be that as it may, the substitution of "to be" for "to be like" is allowed to stand, and so Socrates seems to make precisely that sort of mistake he had earlier attributed to tragedy, namely, reading metaphor literally. The difference is that Socrates' willingness to make the mistake is because of his recognition of their beginning point as a hypothesis. Any hypothesis is only provisionally an *archē*, a fact about which Meno is altogether unclear, as is indicated by his later surprise that Socrates returns to question the validity of their hypothesis (89c).

Socrates' proof that virtue is knowledge seems rather straightforward. Virtue is good, but the good is the profitable or useful. Consequently, virtue is profitable or useful. However, everything that can profit can also harm. What makes the difference is that things be used rightly. Only with the mind are things used correctly; without mind they harm. Therefore, if virtue is profitable it must be prudence or practical wisdom (*phronēsis*). Virtue, as consisting in whole or in part of *phronēsis*, must be acquired by learning. From the very beginning of this argument there are difficulties. By identifying the good with the useful Socrates excludes the *kalon* from virtue. Nevertheless, the argument seems to have a certain commonsensical power. Virtue surely has something to do with knowing how to act. At the same time, this argument works only because Socrates shifts first from *epistēmē*, knowledge or science, which is most likely to be thought of as teachable, to *nous*, mind, which seems rather to be given to one by nature, and finally to *phronēsis*, apparently to be acquired by experience. While it may be that virtue has something to do with knowledge, their identity has hardly been shown, a fact signaled in Socrates' conclusion by the substitution of "learning" for "teaching" (89c).

The underlying difficulty of the proof is further indicated by the fact that according to the myth of recollection we needed virtue in order to learn. Here we need knowledge in order to become virtuous. The relation between virtue and knowledge now seems to be something like the earlier relation between figure and color (75b). Given this mutual dependence of virtue and knowledge, Socrates is forced to make two revisions in his argument, both unnoticed by Meno. The "knowledge" needed for virtue becomes *phronēsis* instead of the much more rigorous and teachable *epistēmē*. And the virtue we need in order to learn is not "courage" but "boldness." At 86b Socrates had used the participle *tharrounta*, being bold, for that quality of soul necessary if we are to try to know what we do not know. But at 88b he calls courage without wisdom mere *tharros*, mere boldness. Recollection, or learning, requires courage, but courage for that very reason cannot yet be accompanied by wisdom. It is mere boldness. Yet courage without wisdom is one of those "attempts and endurances of the soul" which when led by thoughtlessness (*aphrosunēs*) ends in the opposite of happiness (88c). Learning is consequently a very risky thing. It requires a kind of stupid boldness; it requires that criminal quality of soul of which Meno is the pure representative.

Socrates casts doubt on their conclusions by pointing out that if virtue is taught there ought to be teachers of virtue (89d); he neglects to point out that virtue might be learned without having been taught. Since the *polis* has an interest in the virtue of its citizens, the *polis* ought to know how conventional virtue is to be fostered. Socrates therefore turns to Anytus in the expectation that the representative of the *polis* will tell them who teaches virtue (89e). He looks to Anytus to tell him what the origins are of the opinions about virtue fostered by the political community.

Of Anytus, Aristotle tells us that he bribed the judges at his own trial to escape punishment for the loss of Pylos.[24] Xenophon has Socrates describe Anytus as a vicious man angered at Socrates' having told him that he ought not to confine his son's education to the tanning business. Xenophon also remarks that the son turned out rather badly.[25] Anytus, of course, was the chief of the prosecutors of Socrates. He was the son of a successful tanner, Anthemion, and one of the leaders of the democratic faction in Athens; he became influential after the overthrow of the Thirty Tyrants. Anytus was powerful and, it seems, not particularly virtuous. He is presented in this dialogue as the guest-friend of Meno, although Socrates introduces him as though he were a stranger. Like Meno, Anytus is proud and greedy. He also possesses some of the qualities associated with being *nouveau riche*. Anytus is a bit embarrassed by his origins.

This last makes it particularly nasty of Socrates to dwell so much on Anytus' father. Anytus' "virtue" is explained in terms of his father in the very section of the dialogue in which the influence of fathers on their children is brought radically into question.

> And indeed, often inquiring whether there were any teachers of it [virtue], doing everything, I am not able to find out. And yet I seek with many, and of them the best, whom I believe to be the most experienced in the matter. And really now too, Meno, what beautiful luck for us (*eis kalon*), sitting here next to us was Anytus, with whom let us share our inquiry. And he is likely to share it; for Anytus here is first of all the son of a rich and wise father, Anthemion, who became rich not by accident (*apo tou automatou*), nor by some gift, like Ismenias the Theban, the one recently having received the wealth of Polycrates, but rather having acquired by his own wisdom and care, and further with regard to other things not seeming to be an overbearing citizen, nor full of himself and annoying, but an orderly and well-mannered man. Further, he nurtured and educated him well, as it seems to the multitude of Athenians, for they choose him for the greatest offices (*archas*). It is indeed just to seek teachers of virtue with such men, to inquire whether there are or are not any, and who they are. You then, Anytus, inquire with us, with me and with your guest-friend Meno here, concerning who would be the teachers of this matter. (89e–90b)

There are a variety of puzzles in this passage. Anthemion is said not to have acquired his money *apo tou automatou*, but rather by his own wisdom and care. In the context the phrase clearly means "by accident." However, it can also mean "by one's own efforts." Completely autonomous behavior is indistinguishable from completely automatic behavior. Therefore, in the case of Anytus the son, either Anytus will be noteworthy because his father was noteworthy owing to having acquired his wealth *on his own* (*apo tou automatou*), in which case Anytus is not really noteworthy since his wealth is derivative. Or, Anytus is noteworthy because of the automatic (*apo tou automatou*) character of his wealth, in which case his father would not be noteworthy. In either case the conditions necessary to acquire (*ktaomai*) will be at odds with the conditions necessary to possess (*ktaomai* in the perfect tenses). This opposition will place teaching virtue at odds with having it.

This section of the dialogue is replete with fathers and sons. Anytus is paired with Anthemion (90a1–2). Socrates presents Meno to Anytus as one who wants to learn virtue for the sake of serving his parents (91a4). Anytus will be concerned with sons who go to the sophists (92a7–b4), and statesmen will be presented and criticized in terms of how well they have succeeded in teaching their sons (93c–94e). The issue arises partly because it is the natural sign of the problem of autonomy. That we have parents means that we are not self-originating.[26] The issue also arises because the existence of parents points to the tension between two ways of teaching. We learn by imitating our parents, and we learn by doing what they tell us to do. Insofar as we imitate them as self-governing rulers, our attempt is to be masters. Insofar as we obey them our behavior is slavish. Virtue requires that we both imitate our parents as free agents and that we obey them in order to act well. But it is not at all clear how the two are to be combined. Fortunately, parents are not perfect beings. Were they perfect, imitating them in their freedom would necessitate doing something bad. The precondition of virtue in human beings is either the imperfection of the parent or the imperfection of the child. It is, of course, really both. The connection between virtue and imperfection is the fundamental insight of the *Meno* as a whole, and certainly the central issue in this last section.

Anytus is not only introduced and praised in terms of his father. There is a crucial ambiguity in the introduction: Is Socrates referring to him or to Anthemion? If it refers to Anytus then he seems to be the one who is not overbearing, and the Athenian multitude chooses him for the highest offices because he raised his son so well. But if the reference is to Anthemion, then Anytus is chosen for the highest offices because he has been so well raised. The tension between being well educated and educating well is in a way simply the dual function of *eidos* as it was articulated at 72c, as well as the duality of *eidos* more narrowly understood and *genesis*. An *eidos* is what makes something what it is; an *eidos* is also what we look at to see what something is. Put still differently, the question is whether a virtuous man is good in the sense of being useful, as Anthemion's wealth was acquired by his own efforts, or *kalon* understood as something self-justifying and without use, as Anytus' wealth is his through no efforts of his own. The problem of Anytus and his father has turned out to be the problem of the unity of the expression which will figure so prominently in Anytus' understanding of virtue, *kalos te k'agathos*, beautiful and good, or the Greek for gentleman.

Anytus' discussion with Socrates concerning whom to ask about learning virtue will therefore be divided into two. First they will discuss those who teach but do not seem to have virtue themselves, the sophists; then they will turn to those who do not teach but appear to have virtue, the statesmen. The difficulty will be that the sophists' knowledge cannot be real knowledge without virtue, and the statesmen's virtue cannot be true virtue without knowledge. The problem of putting together the sophist and the statesman which first appears to be only an accidental element of the discussion of the *Meno* points to several deeper problems: the unity of *eidos*, the unity of virtue, and the unity of man.[27]

There is something queer about the question Socrates puts to Anytus. He asks to whom they ought to send Meno if he is to learn virtue. One wonders why they are so worried about sending Meno rather than sending themselves. The difficulty is alluded to elliptically by Socrates when, in a series of questions designed to determine where Anytus would send Meno to learn certain arts, Socrates asks "And if we should want [him] to become a good cobbler?" (90c). Given the context, the sentence seems to contain an ellipsis. Socrates has left out the third person accusative pronoun. Still, as it stands, it points to the fact that Socrates and Anytus are in the same position as Meno. This fact is emphasized by Anytus' rather close connection to the art of cobbling. At 90d, Socrates will ask Anytus where they should send Meno in order to be sending him sensibly or moderately or wisely. Should there not be some relation between wisdom and the wisdom necessary to learn where to go for wisdom? Socrates begins his conversation with Anytus by circumventing another paradox. By "choosing a teacher for Meno" he covers up the troubling fact that choosing a teacher means knowing where you are going before you get there.

The matter is yet more complicated. After saying that they would be right to send Meno to a doctor if they wanted him to learn to become a doctor, Socrates adds "Whenever we may say this do we say (mean) this (the following)" (*houtan touto legōmen tode legomen*—90c). This is the first indication that the act of saying makes a difference. Meno would not be sent simply to cobblers to learn shoemaking, but to those who profess to be cobblers. The word used for them here is *antipoioumenous*, "those claiming."

But as a compound of the prefix *anti* and the verb *poieō* it has the etymological sense of resisting or setting up an opposition, and indeed this is one of its alternative meanings. Those who lay claim to being doctors are when they do so precisely not doing what doctors do. The sayers are not the doers. The sign of this is Socrates' apparently gratuitous addition of "for a fee" to his description of those who lay claim to an art as those to whom one would send Meno. Doing something for a wage means stepping outside of what you are doing in order to say, "This is what I do." Wage earning points to our capacity to say of ourselves, "I am a doctor." This self-reflection in its pure form was the source of Meno's tyrannical desire to rule the whole. Meno was the pure wage earner. On one level, of course, Socrates means it when he tells Anytus that it would be an absurdity, an *alogia* to send Meno to one who has no students and does not make himself out to be a teacher. On another level, he means that it would be *alogos*, or speechless, to send Meno to such a man. The difficulty is that one who speaks, that is, the man who can justify his every move as a doctor, is to that extent not the perfect doctor for whom the ability to say what he is doing would be a mark of imperfection. Explanations are for those who are aware of alternatives to what they are doing; This would presumably not be the case in the effortless activity of the perfect artisan.

With this as a preparation, we are not so shocked as Anytus that Socrates proposes the sophists as the teachers to whom they should send Meno. Anytus' response to the suggestion is "Heracles, Socrates, don't blaspheme." (91c). Anytus is shocked because the sophists both lack virtue and do not seem to teach it as he understands it. By this time, however, it is clear that this is the necessary condition of their being teachers at all. Nevertheless, Anytus has a point. The sophists are certainly not teachers of local virtue. They do not teach men to be Athenians. For that reason Anytus is not soothed by Socrates' description of the sophists as the "common teachers of the Greeks" (91b). Anytus prays that this madness should seize none of his, whether of his household or friends, nor any townsman or stranger (or guest-friend, i.e., *xenos* which can mean either). In his excitement Anytus reveals the principle of his attachments: love of his own. He lists people in order of the closeness to him. Meno's relation to Anytus is, as we have seen, ambiguous. On the one hand he is tied to him as a guest-friend (*xenos*—90b); on the other Socrates introduces Anytus as though he were a stranger (*xenos*—89e–90b). Anytus proves considerably more conventional than Meno in the way in which he defines what is his own; his harshness toward what is other than his own is mitigated by the particular conventions of the *polis* he calls his own.

Socrates' long speech describing the sophists (91c–92a) makes matters as difficult as possible for Anytus. In pointing out that the sophists do quite well in terms of money Socrates makes clear that Anytus' view of them is not simply the prevailing view. There is obviously a market for their product, and so a strong body of public opinion in support of them. At the same time we are made aware that the sophists are not the real issue here. By likening them to menders of clothing and shoes Socrates makes it clear that their education of men is merely reeducation.[28] Another teacher of virtue has preceded them. Anytus enters the dialogue to reveal this teacher to be the *polis*.

Socrates points to the *polis* as the real issue here in his repeated references to Protagoras.[29] The references remind us of the dialogue bearing his name, where the question of the teachability of virtue is also raised by Socrates. Protagoras responds to Socrates' question with a long myth of the origin of men and animals, the terms of which are remarkably similar to the terms of the *Meno*. The brothers Prometheus and Epimetheus have as their task the apportioning of the various powers or *dunameis* among all the animals. When men are left helpless because of Epimetheus' lack of forethought, his brother whose very name means forethought steals wisdom and fire from the gods, and so men are given a *theia moira*, a divine share. But as men do not yet have any political art they are being killed off and killing each other off. Zeus, therefore, tells Hermes to give men justice and shame in order to bind them together. Most important, he tells Hermes to give them equally to all men unlike the other arts. For there can be no cities unless all men are bound together within each city. Protagoras then remarks that while some may be more able by nature, it is still true that all men teach virtue the way all men teach Greek. In effect Protagoras answers the question which Socrates will put to Anytus. The *polis* which needs virtue to survive teaches virtue; it is the original of which the sophists are only pale copies.

The *polis* requires of its citizens that they have knowledge of virtue, and it condemns all those who question that knowledge. It is therefore hostile to the sophists. But how can Anytus, who admits that he has never met a sophist, be so sure that they are so bad? The problem is yet another version of Meno's paradox. Anytus is like the slave who has no previous experience in geometry and yet can answer Socrates' geometrical questions. He has no previous experience of the sophists and yet he can claim to know all about them. Socrates is sufficiently filled with wonder about all of this to suggest that Anytus is a prophet. And so the resolution to this version of Meno's paradox is, like the account of recollection, dependent upon some supernatural assistance. Yet in calling Anytus daimonic and a prophet (92c) Socrates is surely being ironic. There is no mystery to Anytus' knowledge. What he "knows" he has gotten not by direct experience, but by hearsay. Anytus can "know" without experience because of the collective tradition of the city in which he was reared. The *polis* and its laws are the truth of the "time before we were born" of the myth of recollection.

As an alternative to Socrates' sophists Anytus suggests that all human beings teach virtue, although it becomes quickly apparent that he really means all Athenian *kaloi k'agathoi*, all Athenian gentlemen. The problem with this response is that it simply forces the further question about where these men learned virtue. Anytus responds that they learned it from the previous generation, but this sort of answer cannot go on endlessly. Secondhand knowledge presupposes that at some point someone had firsthand knowledge. Any appeal to the tradition is like saying that men have always been in a position of "having learned." It is both to claim that there are *archai*, first beginnings, and to render them obscure.

Socrates therefore shifts the issue, much as he had with the myth of recollection. Rather than pressing Anytus for an account of the beginning of the tradition as the origin of virtue Socrates tries to turn Anytus' attention to the best of those gentlemen in the *polis* as the contemporary source of virtue. He therefore turns from a temporal account of origins to something less straightforward. The best of the gentlemen are the rulers, the great Athenian statesmen. By showing that none of the sons of these statesmen amounted to much, and by assuming that their fathers were concerned with their benefit, since that after all is the *nomos*—that fathers look after their sons, Socrates undermines the claim that they are able to teach virtue. Clearly, if they could teach virtue to their sons they would do so, presuming that their actions are governed by the *nomoi*, of which they are the chief custodians. But perhaps the activity of being a custodian is so absorbing that it leads to the neglect of those who are one's own. We ought to remember that Socrates was not a particularly successful teacher of his own sons.[30] In the most extreme case the act of ruling a regime is the act of founding it. The founder of a tradition that forms men is not formed by the tradition he founds. He is extralegal and in a way criminal. Fratricide is the origin of political life in traditions as diverse as the biblical and the Roman. Agamemnon had to sacrifice Iphigeneia in order to lead the Greeks to Troy.

It is also worth noting about Socrates' line of argument here that it presumes that the sons of the great are capable of being taught. Socrates seems intentionally to have minimized the extent to which becoming virtuous requires a certain nature. The argument is as forceful as it is because one expects that the children of the great are more likely to be great since they are more likely to share something of the nature of their parents. Socrates thus tacitly admits that there is something to the third of Meno's possibilities for the way virtue is acquired, namely that it comes to be by nature. However, the dialogue never treats this alternative openly. To do so would mean to acknowledge that some are more able to be virtuous than others. On the one hand this is obvious; on the other it can never be acknowledged so long as virtue is understood as conventional virtue. If people are of unequal natural ability there would be something particularly unjust about expecting all to meet the standards of conventional virtue. In addition, those more able and hence more virtuous would be deprived of some of the responsibility for being what they are. Anytus and the *nomos* cannot acknowledge nature because it undermines the claim of the *polis* to be just. Meno cannot acknowledge nature because it undermines his understanding of himself as autonomous.

Socrates cites four examples of Athenian statesmen. He begins with Themistocles, the "best of all" according to Anytus, and Aristeides, Themistocles' rival within the democratic faction. He concludes with Pericles, the greatest Athenian democrat, and Thucydides, his aristocratic rival. Socrates calls Pericles wise in a way fitting to the great (*megaloprepōs*, 96b). *Megaloprepeia* was the virtue which seemed to be Meno's favorite (74a), and which was used to characterize Gorgias' answering style (70b). It is peculiar as a virtue in that it takes greatness as its standard or source. That is why it is so attractive to Meno, whose desire is to be great, but without much thought about what the content of his greatness will be. Any content, really, would do. If *megaloprepeia* is the virtue which makes the *polis* possible, then a certain kind of man becomes the standard for the *polis*. The tradition originates in imitation of the peculiarities of the men who found it. The men of Thessaly had become lovers of wisdom for Gorgias' sake, and proceeded to imitate him in their answering of questions. If the founders' peculiarities are lionized by the regimes they found, then the understanding of virtue in the *polis* will of necessity be the absolutizing of a partial view. Virtue of this sort is not simply partial; it is potentially brutal to men other than the founder who are his rivals and are equally *megaloprepeis*. Socrates' examples make this clear. Not only is there enmity between virtuous men in opposing factions, Pericles and Thucydides, but also within the same faction, Themistocles and Aristeides. Neither the *polis* nor its internal factions speak so univocally about the question of virtue as Anytus seems to think. The source of the discord is that virtue is not simply a horizontal principle by which men are bound together as Athenian citizens. It is also a hierarchical principle by which men seek to distinguish themselves from their fellow citizens. Anytus does not realize how problematic his principle, love of one's own *polis* simply because it is one's own, is as a principle of virtue. The *polis* makes man the measure of all things. On the other hand, the sophists who owe loyalty to no *polis* say that man is the measure of all things. The saying has the effect of emptying the content for the measure. One aspect of virtue requires blindness to the partiality of one's view, and one aspect of virtue requires openness to the partiality of one's view. The question is how the two can be combined.

On the one hand virtue is connected to knowledge since it seems to be necessary to know what you are doing if you are to be responsible for what you are doing. It looks, therefore, as though you ought to be able to *say* what you do, and so being virtuous seems to imply being able to teach virtue. On the other hand the meaning of the split between sophist and statesman is this: the conditions making it possible to be virtuous are at the same time conditions making it impossible to *say* what virtue is, to teach it. There is apparently no virtue without taking things for granted and no virtue if things are simply taken for granted.

Anytus' way out of this problem is to appeal to the tradition, to what is taken for granted. But the problem with an *appeal* to the tradition is twofold. It is always secondhand, and so always implies firsthand knowledge. Hence, any appeal to it will always, automatically, be an appeal beyond it. In the second place any tradition is ambiguous and contains inconsistencies within it, as is made clear by Socrates' examples of statesmen paired in rivalry. An unequivocal tradition could not contain Thucydides and Pericles. Anytus does not understand what has happened to him in this exchange with Socrates, but Plato presents his angry response in language which is meant to make us understand.

> Socrates, you seem to me easily to speak badly of human beings. Now I would advise you, if you will be persuaded by me, to take care. Because perhaps in another city it is easier to do bad to men than good [or perhaps "make men badly than well," that is, fashion them badly—perhaps as poets do?], but in this one certainly. And I think you know it. (94e–95a)

Anytus collapses the difference between speaking badly of others and doing bad to them, or perhaps on another reading, making them badly. If Anytus thinks that bad-speaking is the same as bad-doing does that mean he also identifies good-speaking and good-doing? Strangely enough, this attacker of the sophists seems to take talking very seriously. One wonders why. It may have to do with the fact that Anytus considers himself one of the *kaloi k'agathoi*. And yet he has no more direct experience of the noble and good than he does of sophistry. Anytus points to the danger of any tradition insofar as it is memory divorced from its object. He is a product of the tradition, and inadvertently indicates as much when he collapses, on the alternate reading of this passage, speaking well or badly with making men well or badly. Without his realizing it, Anytus is ruled by those who articulate the tradition— the poets, those who do well by making well. He can therefore say that anyone at all teaches virtue and yet be unable to mention a single man who does so. Anytus knows only *that* all who are called Athenian *kaloi k'agathoi* are virtuous. He uses a sort of syllogism: Virtuous men are like Pericles; I, Anytus am virtuous; therefore, I am like Pericles. But all of this involves no direct experience of virtue. Like Meno, Anytus begins from the top. Virtue is for him *megaloprepeia*.

Socrates replies that Anytus would cease to be angry with him if he were ever to know what sort of thing speaking badly of someone really was. Anytus thinks that it is identical with doing harm, and that Socrates was doing these great men harm. That is because Anytus is convinced that the *polis* requires total uniformity to its *nomoi*, to its traditions. Yet if he were ever to see that virtue is possible only because there is rivalry in the *polis*, he would see that speaking ill of others is the necessary condition for them to do well. Only awareness of alternatives makes virtue more than automatic.

The result of the conversation with Anytus is that there still do not seem to be any teachers of virtue. Anytus, we are told, is too angry to continue (95a). Socrates seems needlessly to have antagonized a very powerful man, and so to have brought on himself the prosecution of which Anytus' presence is a constant reminder. If the argument is to continue Socrates must return to questioning Meno, which he does by asking whether there are *kaloi k'agathoi* in Thessaly (95a). That there are means that there are not only rivalries within traditions; there are rival traditions as well. Thessaly, it seems, is also split on the issue of the sophists, and as Meno points out, the same men at one time think virtue is teachable and at other times not. Individuals are therefore split as well. Meno admires Gorgias for avoiding the issue altogether. Gorgias does not promise to teach virtue; he only "thinks he ought to make men clever with regard to speech" (95c). His assumption, the assumption of the sophists generally, is the mirror image of Anytus' assumption. The sophists assume that speech is not a kind of doing or action. While Anytus had failed to understand the extent to which his tradition was a tradition of claims, Gorgias and the sophists fail to understand the extent to which speaking is rooted in what is done.

Meno, for the first time in the dialogue, is relatively modest. He places himself among the many who at one time think virtue to be teachable and at another not. Socrates rewards him by calling him *politikos* (95c). Being political apparently has something to do with recognizing that there are alternatives, and so strangely enough with the less than perfect functioning of the *nomos*. It has to do with being able to say that the *nomos* is a *nomos*, and so with understanding that in the *polis*, speech is a form of action.

This point is driven home, if only indirectly, by the introduction of the poets into the argument. The explicit argument will remain that there are no teachers of virtue. However, we cannot help but notice that to prove his point Socrates will appeal to Theognis, a gnomic poet, a moralist who advises men on how to act. Socrates quotes a poet in order to *teach* Meno about the division of men with regard to the issue of teachability. He appeals to those men whose name (*poiētēs*) literally means "doer," and who are most generally recognized as the teachers of all Greece. Socrates cites a man recognized to be virtuous who also teaches virtue in order to show that there are no teachers of virtue. In doing so he highlights the fact that those teachers of virtue who, like Homer, teach by example (such as Achilles) and so imitate deeds in speeches, have been altogether left out of the argument.

By introducing Theognis, Socrates has pointed to the real origin of the tradition. The poets are the *archai*, the origins of the *polis*, but they are invisible. Their political role is never openly acknowledged in the argument because it can never be openly acknowledged in the *polis*. The poets form the *polis* because the poets are the creators of the gods of the *polis*. However, they cannot claim the honor due them without casting doubt on the gods they have created, and so depriving themselves of the honor of having created the gods. Because they cannot claim the honor due them, the poets must present the gods as the *archai*. This becomes clearer in the sequel.

If there are no teachers of virtue, Socrates argues, there can be no learners, and if there are none who have been taught, there can be no good men. At this point Meno is led to wonder, "What would be the way of coming to be of the coming to be of good men?" (96d). He asks for the coming to be of the *genesis*, the process. But that question amounts to asking how the *polis* and its traditions come to be. This way of questioning is of course typical of Meno. He wants the beginnings. Socrates responds that they run the risk of being contemptible, *phauloi*, because their teachers did not teach them. The model for teaching here, as throughout, is the transfer of goods. If learning is to be understood as the result of a transfer of goods then it is clear that one needs a first teacher. If all men are products of an all-powerful tradition then we have no other access to knowledge than what has been passed down to us. Knowledge is essentially hearsay. Eventually, that means the need to appeal to a teacher unlike anyone else, a nonhuman teacher who was not formed by the tradition. In a world where learning is not possible at all times, for it to be possible at all there must have been a time at which a god spoke.

The puzzle at the end of the *Meno* is this: Why is it necessary to pursue virtue by finding some person to teach it? But this way is the consequence of the substitution of teaching for learning on the very first page of the dialogue, a substitution confirmed in Socrates' misquotation of Theognis (95d–e). The result is something like the replacement of philosophy, which is never mentioned in the *Meno*, by divine revelation. The replacement was prepared by the use of a "who is" question as a paradigm for "what is" questions at the beginning of the dialogue. Divine revelation or something akin to it will replace philosophy wherever knowledge becomes understood as something to be handed down rather than figured out, or wherever it exists only on the level of memory. We have known for some time that the *Meno* was about Meno's desire for autonomy, and that this desire was in effect a desire to be an *archē*, a source. The dialogue is also a reflection on what happens when persons, be they men or gods, become sources. The startling result is that learning and philosophy become impossible so long as an ensouled being is the highest being.

The strange and unsatisfying account of virtue in terms of opinion at the end of the dialogue has therefore been ordained from the very first sentence. Not the least difficulty with the account will be to understand the perspective from which one can know right opinion to be right. That is especially so because Socrates argues that it escaped their notice that not only knowledge but also opinion serves to guide men. He claims that this is why they did not see how men became good. But this very failure to see, that is, to know, was an opinion which they thought to be true. There seems to be no such thing as an opinion one has and does not think to be true and right. Socrates says that their error was

> that it is not possible to rule rightly without prudence (*phronēsis*) has not been rightly agreed. (97a)

Of course they can "know" that now because they claim to know something. Meno's response, "How do you mean rightly?" hits the mark. Which *rightly* does Socrates intend to cast doubt upon? One has to do with the content of their opinion, their *doxa*; the other has to do with the judgment they are making about the content. Right opinion is an attempt to bring together knowing and doing. That is part of the reason for the repeated shifting back and forth in this section between right opinion and true opinion. However, the two are not simply the same. Right opinion is always understood here in terms of results. If it helps you get to Larisa it is a right opinion regardless of its content. Contrary to what Socrates allows us to think, a right opinion need not be true. A false opinion which led us to Larisa through some systematic misinterpretation on our part would be equally "right." But if a right opinion is distinguishable from a wrong opinion only from the results—only from the outside—then Socrates can argue that opinion is as good as knowledge only from the perspective of knowledge. It will therefore be impossible to know that you have a right opinion without knowledge, at which point you no longer have opinion.

Meno does not quite see the problem. He sees that at one time the one with right opinion will act well and at another time not. Socrates corrects him in a subtle but important way. Meno understands right opinion to be something which once had is always possessed. Socrates' correction is that you do not always have it. Its instability does not consist in its not always working as a substitute for knowledge, but rather in the fact that it comes and goes so that one never knows whether one's opinions are right. What Socrates now calls true opinions are like the statues of Daedalus (97d–98a); they are beautiful but if not bound they run away. Consequently, unless bound they are not worth much. What Socrates does not speculate about is the connection between their freedom of movement and their beauty. Are not the statues of Daedalus so very beautiful precisely because they do not stay put? Would they remain beautiful if they were bound? These statues seem to be good only if bound and beautiful only if free. But one must wonder if they ever could exist as free. When they are not bound they go off on their own; they must be indistinguishable from what they image—men. Unbound images are not really images at all; bound images are not perfect images. Images are either useful (or good) or perfect, but never both. The problem with true opinion is that in any particular situation it is worthless, for one can never know whether one's opinion is true so long as it is an opinion.

Socrates therefore does not know that any of his opinions are right. What he claims is the following:

> And indeed I too speak as one not knowing but imagining (*eikazōn*). But that they are something different, right opinion and knowledge, I do not quite seem to me to imagine, but if I should claim to know anything, and I would claim only a few things, this is one of them I would put among those I know. (98b)

Socrates does not claim to know anything; he only claims that if he should claim to know anything he would claim to know this, that there is a difference between knowledge and right opinion. Socrates seems to have reflected on the connection between claiming to know and making the distinction between knowledge and opinion. The moment he claims to know anything he has tacitly claimed that there is a distinction between knowing and not knowing. That is to make a distinction between things that are true and things that seem (*dokein*) true, or to make the distinction between knowledge and opinion (*doxa*). Consequently, to say one knows something is to identify certain of one's thoughts, which one does not claim to know, as opinions. But to say that something is an opinion is to be no longer satisfied with it. To say one has an opinion is to wish to get rid of it, to transform it into knowledge. It is impossible, therefore, to know that one has right opinion because to know one's opinions as opinions is to consider them defective or wrong. When Socrates says that he does not seem to himself to imagine the difference, but to know it if he knows anything, the "I seem to me" (*dokō moi*) is crucial. That I am aware that things seem to me means that I am aware that they are not what they seem. Furthermore, this awareness that things seem to me is a fundamental awareness of what I am. *Dokō moi* is the Platonic analogue to Descartes' *Je pense, donc je suis*. My awareness of my own defectiveness, my ignorance, and so my lack of autonomy is simply the inverse of my "divination" that there is something more than what seems to be. What Socrates says in the last part of the *Meno* about relying on right or true opinion may be correct, but it is something no one could ever say of himself truly in any specific instance; it must be said of oneself in general, or (what amounts to almost the same thing), it must be said of another.

It is for this reason that in his summary of the argument (98c–99c) Socrates gradually moves away from speaking of true or right opinion until in his conclusion he substitutes *eudoxia*, good opinion or reputation. The word reminds us of the beginning of the dialogue where Socrates spoke of the good repute of the Thessalians and specifically of the Larisaens (70b2). Socrates has just used knowing how to get to Larisa as an example of right opinion. Is there a connection between the two passages? Right opinion of how to get to Larisa was for practical purposes as good as knowledge. We are first introduced to Larisaens as men who fell in love with wisdom for practical reasons. That is, they wanted to impress Gorgias and to gain reputation. But that would mean that they would have to be as satisfied with the appearance of wisdom as they would have been with wisdom. What we have now come to see is that the appearance of wisdom can only be verified from the perspective of the wise, and to them it is useless. Otherwise the "rightness" of opinion will be confirmed by its acceptability to the *polis*. Right opinion is *eudoxia*, reputation. For the *polis* right opinion and knowledge will be the same. The *polis* is a hypothesis which has forgotten its hypothetical character. To confirm itself, it invents *archai*, the gods. Ironically, inventing them means giving their actions a necessarily arbitrary appearance. In the presence of the divine, speaking becomes unself-aware, oracular.

There is more than a little bit of irony in the way the dialogue ends. Anytus was previously called both daimonic and also a *mantis*, a prophet (92c).

Socrates now says that true opinion is founded in the divine and he cites the *theomanteis* to prove his point (99c). The man who is primarily responsible for the death of Socrates will be as able to justify himself by an appeal to the divine as anyone else. It may be that knowledge is unavailable as a political principle. Opinion, however, proves a very dangerous political principle.

If this is so, then Socrates seems foolish to end the dialogue as he does. In announcing that virtue is acquired by divine dispensation, Socrates seems to have given Meno *carte blanche*, an unsettling thought, given what we know of Meno's character. Meno does get the content he wants; to justify himself he need only say that he has had a vision—which is to say he need not justify himself at all. Yet it is crucial to see that he gets this content in such a way as to render it unusable. The content might lead to *hubris*, but the form makes it difficult to accept the content as true. The opinion that virtue is an opinion is revealed to be no more than an opinion. And so the dialogue ends with Socrates' suggestion that Meno "teach" Anytus virtue by persuading him that virtue is true opinion acquired by divine dispensation. However, were Anytus to believe it, he would already have begun to understand that his opinion was a mere opinion, and that he did not know what virtue was. This knowledge of his own ignorance would, as Socrates suggests, make him more moderate, and more virtuous.

IV

On any reading the *Meno* divides, more or less, into two parts. In the first Meno attempts to say what virtue is. After Socrates chides him for giving instances, Meno tries to give an *eidos* of virtue. In each case his efforts point to virtue understood as power, but each fails to make the nature of that power clear. The turning point is Meno's learning paradox—his refusal to go on (80d). Thereafter, Socrates is forced to contribute positively to the dialogue, even if his contribution is presented as having come from someone else. This second part begins with Socrates' account of learning as recollection (81a).

Now the first part can be said to fail because Meno tries to give an account of virtue as power independent of what it is power for. Such an account, like an account of *eidos* independent of instance, or of master independent of slave, is not possible. Meno fails because he wants to have his rule or freedom pure. Rule which was pure would have to be transpolitical, ruling without being ruled, without justice. It would be the most extreme form of tyranny, not real tyranny but tragic tyranny. The first part of the *Meno* is therefore characterized by an ignoring of the central role of the *polis*, its laws and traditions, the *nomos*. The word *nomos* is accordingly not present in the *Meno*.

Its importance is left to be suggested by Socrates' playful reduction of what he and Meno do to the fact that they are from Athens and Thessaly. *Nomos* shows itself most powerfully when it is not mentioned, when it is taken to be *phusis*, nature.

The most important feature of the second part of the dialogue is the necessity of the split in the soul in order that there may be a soul, or the necessity to understand virtue as by necessity imperfect virtue. What that means is that the "time before we were human beings" of the myth of recollection when we were supposed to have seen the *eidē* in reality corresponds to the fact of our having been born into a tradition. It is impossible to give an account of virtue independent of the *polis* and the *nomos*, because the content of virtue depends on them. The truths which we are supposed to have seen in the myth of recollection are in fact the traditional opinions which can be learned from any *kalos k' agathos*. That is why Socrates is forced to move from an understanding of virtue as knowledge to an understanding of virtue as true opinion, and then right opinion, and finally *eudoxia*, good opinion or reputation—what the Thessalians have.

The danger of this understanding of virtue is complete conventionalism, the total, if invisible, rule of the *nomos*. It is Anytus, the man who thinks that any *kalos k' agathos* can teach virtue, Anytus, the man who is so enslaved by the *kalon* as it is understood in his own tradition that he takes *nomos* to be *phusis*, nature. If Anytus represents the attempt to be perfectly political, Meno represents the attempt to be perfectly transpolitical. The latter in turn proves to be merely a reproduction of the political on a "higher" level. Meno is a curious mixture of the totally conventional and the totally unconventional. He is the most extreme result of attempting to transcend the *polis* altogether while continuing to rely on the standards of the *polis*. Meno is the necessary result of taking a "second sailing" (*Phaedo* 96a–100c) as a "first sailing," of taking an eidetic account, which is always parasitical on a prior political convention, to be a genetic account capable of being freed from the *polis*. Accordingly, while we learn the danger of complete conventionalism from the dialogue, we also learn of the necessity of the *polis*. Only when we are provided with a comprehensive *doxa*, or opinion, an orthodoxy, can we come to reflect on the incompleteness of that orthodoxy. The *nomos*, the *kalon*, provides us with a metaphor which can be seen as incomplete. However, it cannot do that without also running the risk that we will read the metaphor literally.

What is really meant by virtue in the *Meno* is therefore something like the mirror image of the myth of recollection. It is true that for us to be able to learn means that we are split in two. We have a primordial self and a learning self. It is necessary to mix a sense of discovery with a sense of eternity. However, the discovery is that what we always thought is not quite what we thought it to be. Discovering the truth of one's tradition is like discovering the truth of a cliché. It means seeing how narrowly we have hitherto understood it, discovering how we have been wrong.

The sign of all of this is the end of the *Meno*. It is of course comical that Socrates should suggest that Meno, with his perfectly tyrannical soul, should teach virtue to Anytus with his slavishly conventional soul. But, by teaching Anytus, understood as the completely powerful and so invisible tradition, that virtue is based on true opinion as a divine gift, Meno, the complete rejection of the *nomos*, would be making Anytus aware of the tradition as a tradition. He would in that way undermine the absoluteness of its control, and so make Anytus gentler. By putting the two together Socrates suggests that virtue consists of the synthesis of the totally political and the total transpolitical; it is consequently inseparable from religion. Or, as his very first and, at that time, utterly bewildering response to Meno's question about how to acquire virtue indicated, the question "How does virtue come to be?" is identical to the question "How does the question 'How does virtue come to be?' come to be?"

The final problem of the dialogue is that this perfect synthesis of Meno and Anytus is never fully possible. Meno will join the Persian expedition and become infamous. Anytus will become the killer of Socrates. Neither acquires virtue. What this dialogue has done instead is to use Meno and Anytus to identify the constituents necessarily present in true virtue. That the two are incompatible points to the imperfectibility of the human soul. The *Meno* is not meant, in the end, to suggest a formula for the production of virtue. It is rather reflection on the fact that the question of the *eidos* of virtue is never simply the same as the question of its *genesis*.

6

Conclusion

What one ought to do depends very much on what one ought to believe, and in everything that is not bound by the first needs of nature our opinions are the rule of our actions.

—Rousseau, *The Reveries of the Solitary Walker*, Third Walk

"For you know, Socrates," he said, "if ever I should consider it to be ugly to philosophize, I would hold myself to be not even a human being, nor any other so disposed."

—Plato, *The Lovers*

I<small>T IS NO ACCIDENT</small> that autonomy should become an issue in a writing concerned with the question of how virtue is acquired. To treat virtue as an acquisition is to view one's own life as though it could at some point become whole and perfect; it is rather like imagining a moment within life at which it would be possible to say "Now I am complete; hereafter I shall live according to what I already am and what I already know." But such a moment is necessarily illusory. The conditions for its possibility are contradictory—like Hades, the invisible place where we are both alive, and so capable of *looking* at our former lives as complete, and dead, and so capable of looking at our former lives as *complete*. Perfect knowing would preclude knowing. The alternative to Hades is prematurely to treat our lives as whole with the result that what we know is incomplete, and our knowing is only opining. Because morality requires this sense of wholeness, it must treat as final what can be only provisional. It requires that we take ourselves to task, and so necessarily mistake ourselves. We are seduced by the impossible command to "get hold of ourselves." For the sake of this self-manipulation we must act as though we are able to grasp our lives as wholes; the soul doing the grasping must, of course, be the same as the soul to be manipulated. Morality demands the illusion of autonomy although were we really autonomous we would have no need to give laws to ourselves.

Nevertheless, it is in the act of making objects of selves which are not exactly objects that we constitute and reveal ourselves. Ajax shows what he is by his own mistaken way of thinking that he knows what he is. However complete his revelation of himself to us, to himself he must remain opaque. This opacity to ourselves is the basis of tragedy. It is at the same time the basis of all learning, for the experience of "rightness" in moral matters depends on some sense of ourselves, however specious, as wholes, and is the origin of our sense of what it means to be a whole. Whereas we tend to think of morality as needing to be validated, in fact the experience of morality is the prior condition for our sense of validation. It is solely because we are moral beings that we are moved to put things together. Only a moral being could have a sense of truth.

That all thinking must take place within a context established by certain presumptions about the whole, and that these presumptions are necessarily inadequate to the whole they purport to describe is the common beginning point for Sophocles' *Ajax*, Descartes' *Discourse on Method* and Plato's *Meno*. All three authors understand that, contrary to our expectations, understanding always depends on a prior misunderstanding. Because we are opaque to ourselves we can see the world. Were we to see too quickly the error of our way, we would not see at all. Nevertheless, this opacity to ourselves ensures that we will see only imperfectly. The name for this combination of under-standing and misunderstanding is the beautiful. The three books are conse-quently concerned both with articulating the nature of the beautiful and with being beautiful. Each must in some way carry with it the false view of the whole which it means to correct. Each is a seductive writing about the nature of seduction, and so exemplifies what it is meant to describe.

One could put the problem somewhat differently. If every attempt to grasp the whole directly yields only a part, that is, a spurious whole, because the attempt fails to take account of its own preconditions and is thus opaque to itself, then perhaps an attempt to grasp a part as only a part is the proper, if indirect, way to approach the whole. Knowledge of ignorance becomes the key to knowledge. It is the realization of this necessity for indirection which is shared by Sophocles, Descartes, and Plato, and which accounts for their modes of writing.

In tragedy this indirection most clearly comes to sight in the irony of those moments when a character's words reveal more than he is aware. In Sophocles' *Trachiniae* Deianira sends her unfaithful husband, Heracles, a robe dipped in what she believes to be a love potion. She conceals her action with a lie, claiming to have made the robe so that if ever Heracles returned home safe he could present himself to the gods freshly clad for a sacrifice. Deianira does not know that her love potion is really a poison, and so will be a means for Heracles to present himself to the gods in a way altogether different from what her lie had intended. That Deianira tells the truth without realizing it is the sign of the "disparity between the horizon of the spectator of the dramatic representation and that of the character represented within it."[1] However, this tragic irony is supplemented by one still deeper. We are led to assume the difference between poison and love charm, but Deianira's erotic goal, to make her beloved one with her, is finally indistinguishable from the complete destruction of her beloved. We who read the *Trachiniae* are at first led to believe that Deianira has made a terrible mistake, but a less trusting look at events within the play forces us to ask whether she might not want to kill Heracles. In this way Sophocles has seduced us into making the mistake that we took her to have made; we consequently become the objects of his tragic irony. Learning means unraveling the reasons why we have been initially taken in.

Tragic seduction lets us believe for a while that our privileged position as spectators allows us to stand outside the whole being described. Furthermore, understanding that whole requires that we assume this privileged perspective. To see what it means that we cannot see inside others it is necessary to accept that we can see inside Ajax. While tragedy therefore forces us to wonder how it is possible for us to see what we have seen, it does not make the possibility of this seeing thematic. The perspective of Sophocles would seem to allow him to avoid the tragic errors of his characters and of us who are seduced into the same errors. And yet this perspective is not made an issue within the plays themselves. Sophocles therefore practices a kind of indirection that his characters never practice. By appearing nowhere in his own drama he leaves himself open to the charge that he "say[s] many beautiful things, but know[s] nothing of what [he] say[s],"[2] which is to say that philosophy nowhere becomes an issue in tragedy.

The formula for tragedy, *ta mathēmata pathēmata* (things suffered are things learned) means both that we must experience things to know them and that our experiences will be painful, that it will not be possible for us to be neutral to them. Descartes is aware that the perspectival character of all experience, natural egoism, is the obstacle to the satisfaction of our desires. The beautiful which is the sign of our deepest longing is the obstacle to its fulfillment. Any question we put to the world is biased from the outset, for in asking after the cause of anything we have unwittingly acquiesced in the prevailing division of the world into specific kinds of things, a division founded on one or another specious understanding of the whole. Only a question which took nothing for granted, and so made no assumptions about the whole, could avoid this difficulty. Descartes, skeptical of the possibility of asking what things are really, therefore devises a method which is neutral to what things are really. The purpose of the method is to establish an altogether impersonal perspective within the whole. It is Descartes' substitute for Hades.

However, the *Discourse* is autobiographical and nonmethodical; the book of the world may be written in mathematical characters, but this book is a history or fable. Cartesian science, then, is not the same as philosophy. Descartes' reflection on the indirect way in which he came to discover that his longing for autonomy was the obstacle to autonomy leads him to devise an artifice for inducing indirection. At the same time it leads him to write the *Discourse on Method* as a mode of introducing the significance of this method indirectly. If to long for an answer is to render it doubtful once one gets it, only what we come upon unexpectedly is to be trusted. We come upon the meaning of the *Discourse* unexpectedly because of the manner in which it is written. Descartes' rhetoric is the sign that his philosophy and his science cannot be understood as the same. In the *Discourse* the message is modern, but the mode is ancient. The latter requires a profound sense of the power of the beautiful in human life; the former requires a deadening of ourselves to the beautiful, and so to the very seductiveness of nature which calls forth the desire to master nature.

Descartes' project aims to create the conditions for widespread contentment, not merely in the sense of a material conquest of nature but more deeply by promoting a way of life in which the idiosyncratic satisfactions of his own life can be reproduced. His book is a serious attempt to do what Plato does only playfully in the *Republic*. Its success would mean the resolution of the tension between philosophy and political life, and therewith the transformation of both philosophy and political life. But the method for mass producing "philosophy" proves much less impressive than the account of how the method was discovered. And the latter account is only possible after the fact; it is intelligible but not predictable. What is most impressive about the *Discourse on Method* proves to be what Plato understood by philosophy.

Like the *Discourse on Method* the *Meno* is concerned with that perspective from which it is possible to know about the partiality of the part, and so in an indirect way know the whole; it is concerned with philosophy. But in embodying that concern in the person of Socrates, Plato preserves the opacity of his own perspective. Like Sophocles, then, Plato manipulates the plot, making necessary and complete what in real life is always contingent and partial for the purpose of revealing the partiality of the part. But the presence of Socrates within Platonic dialogues has a curious effect on all of this. Socrates is not Ajax, and Plato's plot does not consist of speeches somehow serving as imitations of action. Socrates' deeds, and so those of his interlocutors, *are* speeches. Within the *Meno* the inquiry concerns how virtue is acquired, but the *Meno* itself is concerned with the effects of raising the question "How is virtue acquired?" Initially, we quite naturally become interested in the argument as it is articulated within the dialogue, but we then discover that the argument progresses as it does because of the idiosyncracies of its participants. Meno's beauty and Socrates habitual irony must be taken into account. In discovering, without expecting to do so, how these apparently accidental features affect the argument, we discover a new argument related, but not identical, to the first. While the *Meno* appears to lead to the well known "platonic" conclusion that virtue is knowledge (or failing knowledge right opinion), in fact it is an argument for the dependence of knowledge on virtue. On this level the accidental features of the dialogue which undermine the surface argument become necessary features of the revelation of the surface argument's partiality. This is the dialogic equivalent of Socratic knowledge of ignorance.

Platonic philosophy cannot be systematic because in depending on the discovery of how one has erred it gives an account of the world retrospectively. One could never begin with it. Therefore, when it asks the question "What is X?" and not "What is the cause of X?", it does so in full awareness that it is not inquiring directly into the nature of a being so much as asking what it means that a being has been identified in speech in a certain way. A "second sailing" is in this sense a turn to the *logos*, and the *eidē* are the hypotheses of *logos* disclosed in this turn.[3] Platonic philosophy is for the sake of recognition, not prediction; it is eidetic and not genetic. It would therefore be tragic were its principal goal to transform the world. Practicing it we would grow old learning many things, but each new thing would supersede the last and we would always be a step behind. What we learned would never be of use to us, and learning would be no more than suffering. We could not count ourselves happy until we were in a position to stop learning and grasp our lives as wholes so that we could simply know, at which time we would be autonomous were it not for the fact that we were dead. This tragedy is avoided by the fact that unlike modern science Platonic philosophy has as its primary goal not to transform the world, but to understand it.

Notes
Bibliography
Index

Notes

1. Introduction

1. See Plato, *Phaedrus* 264c, in vol. 2 of John Burnet, ed., *Platonis Opera* (1903; reprint, Oxford: At the Clarendon Press, 1977). All references to Plato are to Burnet's text. The translations, where provided, are my own.

2. See, for example, René Descartes, *Discours de la Méthode: texte et commentaire*, Étienne Gilson ed. (1925; reprint, Paris: Vrin, 1967), part 4, paragraph 1 (henceforth references to the *Discours* will be given by part and paragraph number, e.g., IV:1; translations are my own); *Meditations on First Philosophy* (Meditation 1, paragraphs 3 and 5) in E. S. Haldane and G. R. T. Ross, eds. and trans., *The Philosophical Works of Descartes*, 2 vols. (1931; reprint, New York: Dover, 1967), vol. 1, pp. 150, 152; *Principles of Philosophy*, in *Philosophical Works of Descartes*, Principle VII, p. 221.

3. *Discours*, VI:2.

4. Nietzsche, *Ecce Homo*, in *Werke in drei Bänden*, Karl Schlecta, ed. (Munich: Carl Hanser Verlag, 1966), vol. 2, p. 1063.

5. See, for example, Nietzsche, "Von der Erlösung," *Also Sprach Zarathustra*, Zweiter Teil, *Werke*, vol. 2, pp. 392–96 and for the translation, "On Redemption," *Thus Spoke Zarathustra*, part 2, in *The Portable Nietzsche*, Walter Kaufmann, ed. and trans. (New York: Viking, 1954, 1968), pp. 249–54.

6. It is here where I am particularly indebted to the interpretation, already mentioned, of the *Symposium* by Leo Strauss presented in a course on the dialogue at the University of Chicago (transcription).

7. The word *thumos* is not used at the beginning of the *Symposium*. The nameless companion instead accuses Apollodorus of being provoked to anger (*agriainō*) at everyone save Socrates and of wrangling (*erizō*). *Thumos* is a word dying out of the language when Plato rehabilitates it in the *Republic*, where the importance of the phenomenon of anger is made especially clear (see, for example, Book II, 375a-e; Book III, 411a-e; Book IV, 439e–41c; Book VII, 536c; Book VIII, 548c–50b; Book IX, 572a, 588b–92b).

8. Homer, *The Iliad*, A. T. Murray, trans. and ed. (1924; reprint, Cambridge, MA: Harvard Univ. Press, 1971), Book II: ll. 402–10.

9. W. L. Newman ed., *The Politics of Aristotle*, 4 vols. (1887; reprint, Oxford: At the Clarendon Press, 1950), vol. 2, p. 26.

10. For the date of Agathon's victory see R. G. Bury, *The Symposium of Plato* (Cambridge: At the University Press, 1932), p. lxvi. For the participation of Eryximachus, Phaedrus, and Alcibiades in the profanation of the mysteries see D. Macdowell, *Andokides, On the Mysteries* (Oxford: At the University Press, 1962), 15.21, 35.25; as well as Stanley Rosen, *Plato's "Symposium"* (New Haven: Yale Univ. Press, 1968), pp. 7–8; and Strauss, transcript of *Symposium* course, pp. 13–15, 22.

11. Thucydides, *History of the Peloponnesian War*, 4 vols. C. F. Smith, ed. and trans. (London: William Heinemann, 1921), VI.27–28, pp. 230–32.

12. See Plato, *Protagoras*, 315c, for the connection between Eryximachus and Hippias, one of the sophists.

13. For a way in which Descartes' project is both anti-Christian and nevertheless fundamentally Christian in form, see Stanley Rosen, "A Central Ambiguity in Descartes," in *Cartesian Essays: A Collection of Critical Studies*, Bernd Magnus and James B. Wilber, eds. (The Hague: Martinus Nijhoff, 1969), pp. 17–35.

2. Ancient Tragedy: Sophocles' *Ajax*

1. Many of the issues raised in this chapter are also treated in a fine article on the *Ajax* by Bernard Knox ("The *Ajax* of Sophocles," *Harvard Studies in Classical Philology*, vol. 65 [1961], pp. 1–37), in which he sees that the madness of Ajax consists in slaying animals as though they were his foes and does not extend to the desire to attack the army. Knox also understands the importance of enmity in the play and the way in which Agamemnon and Menelaus reproduce the mistake of Ajax after his suicide. However, he concludes that the tragedy of the play has to do with the fading heroic morality that counsels helping one's friends and harming one's enemies. Odysseus emerges as the representative of a new standard of behavior closer to Christian morality. This is a serious mistake, for it prevents Knox from seeing how radical the *Ajax* is. The play has to do with the tragedy, not of a particular morality, but of morality as such. The introduction and notes in Sir Richard Jebb, *The Ajax*, part 7 of *Sophocles: The Plays and Fragments* (Cambridge: Cambridge Univ. Press, 1907) is extremely useful for locating difficulties and puzzling inconsistencies in the text. But after revealing problems, Jebb tends to cover them up again with rather implausible solutions. David Bolotin, "On Sophocles' *Ajax*," *The St. John's Review* 32 (July 1980), pp. 49–57, argues for the importance of friendship in the play in a way that is frequently helpful for understanding the centrality of enmity. Finally, the general understanding of tragedy in this chapter owes much to Seth Benardete's "On Greek Tragedy," *Current Developments in the Arts and Sciences*, The Great Ideas Today 1980 (Chicago: Encyclopedia Britannica, 1980), pp. 102–43. I have also learned a great deal from Benardete's notes for a course he offered on the *Ajax* in the summer of 1981.

2. Throughout I have used Richard Jebb's Greek text of the *Ajax* (Cambridge: At the University Press, 1907). Numbers in parentheses refer to the line or lines of the play.

3. For this use of *endon* (inside or within) see Aeschylus' *Choephoroe* 233 and Aristophanes' *Acharnians* 396. The opposite of *endon*, *ektos* (outside), is used in an interesting way at *Ajax* 636–40: *hos ek patrōas hēkōn geneas aristos poluponōn Achaiōn ouketi suntrophois orgais empedos, all' ektos homilei* (he, who comes on his father's side from the best family of the much-toiling Achaeans, is no longer steadfast in the passions bred within, but dwells without).

4. Compare *The "Oedipus at Colonus"*, part 2 of *Sophocles: The Plays and Fragments*, R. C. Jebb, trans. (Cambridge: At the University Press, 1928) 1370 and 1536–37.

5. Greek lends itself to making a connection between enmity and being outside. In the fourth century B.C. *echthós* even becomes a variant of *ektós*, outside, and of course the Greek for hatred is *échthos*. The result is an almost perfect coincidence in a single word of the two major themes of the *Ajax*, the problem of the inside in relation to the outside and the problem of enmity.

6. For a discussion of the problem of the unity of the play see Knox, "The *Ajax* of Sophocles," pp. 1–2; Jebb, *The Ajax*, pp. xxvii–xlii; and H. D. F. Kitto, *Greek Tragedy: A Literary Study* (London: Methuen, 1939), pp. 120–25.

7. Compare Plato's *Laws* Book VII, 817c, where the Athenian Stranger warns of the danger of letting tragic poets enter the city to set up their *skēnas*, that is, the backdrops for their stages (although with the same results as if they had been an invading army setting up its *skēnas*, or tents), with *Laws* Book XII, 944a where *skēnēn* is used unambiguously to mean the tent of Patroclus.

3. The Origin of Modern Science: Descartes' *Discourse on Method*, I–III

1. See Richard Kennington, "Descartes," in *History of Political Philosophy*, Leo Strauss and Joseph Cropsey, eds. (Chicago: Rand McNally, 1972), pp. 397–400. In general this chapter is especially indebted to Kennington's work on Descartes. His emphases on natural egoism, on Descartes' rhetoric, and on the problem of knowledge based on images, to name only a few crucial issues, have been invaluable guides to what is important in the *Discourse*. The interpretation offered here differs from Kennington's in its emphasis on the role of the beautiful in Descartes and in its claim that it is the character of Cartesian rhetoric to make assertions which are intentionally problematic on one level, but turn out to be true in an odd way at a deeper level. For example, interpreters other than Kennington tend to fail to see the importance of Descartes' use of rhetoric to undermine his apparent assertion of the equality of reason in the first paragraph of the *Discourse*. Kennington sees it and argues persuasively for its connection to the problem of natural egoism. Unless one takes this denial of the equality of reason seriously one is unlikely to understand the real equality which is being asserted, that we are equally influenced by our passions. It nevertheless remains the case that in another sense Descartes does mean to affirm the equality of reason. While this other sense is not necessarily at odds with the interpretation of Kennington, the two differ. It is this third level of Cartesian rhetoric with which this chapter and the one following are particularly concerned. It has consequently been necessary in several cases to summarize Kennington's arguments for rejecting the surface of the *Discourse* in order to make intelligible the reconstitution of the surface presented here. Finally, Kennington has pointed out a great deal about Descartes which has not been published. I have occasionally cited him in the text where I have used his formulations for certain problems.

2. Richard Kennington, "The Teaching of Nature in Descartes' Soul Doctrine," *The Review of Metaphysics*, vol. 26 (1972), p. 97; and "Descartes and Mastery of Nature," in *Organism, Medicine, and Metaphysics*, S. F. Spickler, ed. (Dordrecht, Holland: D. Reidel, 1978) pp. 211–12.

3. Kennington, "Descartes," pp. 396–97.

4. Stanley Rosen has seen this problem quite clearly.

The classical conception of reason is inseparable from the notion of "good." This notion in turn contains two dimensions which we may call the "noble" or "beautiful," and "useful." Modern philosophy generally, and its empiricist branch particularly, tends to begin with a radical separation of these terms (although sooner or later the "beautiful" is redefined as the "useful").

Rosen goes on to point to the connection between this separation and Christianity (*Nihilism*, [New Haven: Yale Univ. Press, 1969], pp. 60–65).

5. See Kennington, "Descartes," p. 401.

6. See "Descartes," p. 398.

7. See, for example, Plato, *Hippias Major* 295a–297d, and *Phaedrus* 250b–e, as well as Aristotle, *Politics* Book VII, 1323a24–1323b29, and *Poetics* 1450b37–1451a16. Also compare *Nicomachean Ethics* Book I, 1094a19–29 with 1094b10–17.

8. "Descartes," pp. 398–99.

9. I owe this observation to Richard Kennington.

10. *Les Passions de l'Ame*, part 2, art. 69, in René Descartes, *Oeuvres et Lettres*, André Bridoux, ed. (Paris: Éditions Gallimard, Bibliothèque de Pléiade, 1953), pp. 727–28.

11. See Plato's *Symposium* 207a. *The Passions of the Soul*, art. 90 leads one to believe that Descartes even had in mind Aristophanes' speech in the *Symposium*:

But the principle one [delight] is that which comes from the perfections that one imagines in a person whom we think could become another self; for with the difference of sex, which nature has placed in men as well as in animals without reason, she has also placed certain impressions in the brain which have the effect that at a certain age and at a certain time one considers oneself as defective, and as if one were only half of a whole of which a person of the other sex should be the other half, with the result that the acquisition of this half is confusedly represented by nature as the greatest of all imaginable goods. (*Passions*, p. 737— the translation is my own.)

12. Kennington, "Descartes," p. 401.

13. Ferdinand Aliquié understands the difference between the two books in terms of the more narrowly mathematical understanding of method in the *Rules for the Direction of the Mind*. In the *Discourse*, Aliquié argues, the method has become more supple (*Descartes* [Paris: Hatier, 1969] pp. 20–23. However, it is not so much the method itself that has been changed in the later book as the understanding of how it originates. Mathematical method must have a source in something premethodical.

14. See Plato, *Phaedo* 96a–102a, where Socrates gives an account of how he abandoned his "pre-Socratic" attempts to look directly at beings themselves, and instead turned to speeches (*logoi*) to inquire into the truth of beings. He calls this his "second sailing for the purpose of seeking the cause." A second sailing was what one had recourse to when the wind failed—namely, rowing.

15. Whether Descartes is actually correct about Aristotle's logic is of course an entirely different question. But there can be no doubt that Aristotle is the enemy he has in mind. For example, in the author's letter serving as the preface of the French translation of his *Principles of Philosophy*, Descartes says first that in order to make clear his intention in publishing he wants to explain the order necessary for self-instruction. After

choosing a morality, the next step is to study logic, but he emphasizes "not that of the School, because it is, to speak properly, only a dialectic which teaches the means of making understood to others the things which one knows, or even to say without judgment several words touching on those that one does not know, and hence it corrupts good sense rather than augmenting it" (Descartes, *Oeuvres et Lettres*, [Paris: Éditions Gallimard, 1953] p. 565). Several paragraphs later, in discussing the fruits of the study of this new logic, Descartes says the following:

> thus when one has true principles in philosophy one cannot fail in following them at times to encounter other truths; and one cannot better prove the falsity of those of Aristotle than by saying that no progress could be made by their means during the several centuries that they have been followed (*Oeuvres et Lettres*, pp. 568–69).

And in a letter to Mersenne concerning his *Meditations* Descartes comments that he hopes that readers will see the truth of his principles before seeing that they destroy those of Aristotle (Descartes, *Oeuvres*, ed. C. Adam and P. Tannery [Paris: Léopold Cerf, 1910], vol. 3, p. 265). For a discussion of the difference between ancient and modern logic in connection with mathematics, see Jacob Klein, *Greek Mathematical Thought and the Origin of Algebra* (Cambridge, MA: M.I.T. Press, 1968), especially chaps. 6–9 and 12B.

16. Kennington, "Descartes," pp. 403–8 and "Teaching of Nature," pp. 105–10.

17. Compare this with the second thesis of *Idea for a Universal History from a Cosmopolitan Point of View*, where Kant argues that it is in the race and not in the individual that human reason is fully developed. Mortality is the obstacle to the full development of our natural capacities. Kant even goes so far as to suggest that were it not possible for one generation to pass the fruits of its rational labors on to another in the hope of a stage of final enlightenment, human life would be without purpose and contemptible.

18. Kennington, "Descartes," pp. 400–401.

19. Ibid., p. 400.

4. The End of Modern Science: Descartes' *Discourse on Method*, IV–VI

1. Kennington's work is an exception. Much of what follows on the relation between part 4 and part 5 is dependent on it, and especially on his having seen the importance of Descartes' claim at the end of the first paragraph of part 5 that the truths he had discovered in physics were more useful and more important than any he had previously learned or hoped to learn (Richard Kennington, "Descartes," in *History of Political Philosophy*, Leo Strauss and Joseph Cropsey, eds. [Chicago: Rand McNally, 1972], p. 402).

2. Richard Kennington, "The Finitude of Descartes' Evil Genius," *Journal of the History of Ideas*, vol. 32, no. 3 (1971), pp. 441–46.

3. See the "Preface to the Reader" in Descartes' *Meditations on First Philosophy*; and Richard Kennington, "The Teaching of Nature in Descartes' Soul Doctrine," *The Review of Metaphysics*, vol. 26 (1972), pp. 105–10.

4. Clarity and distinctness, everywhere used by Descartes to characterize truth (see for example the fourth of the *Meditations on First Philosophy*, Rule V of the *Rules for*

the Direction of the Mind, and Principle 45 of the *Principles of Philosophy*), are very difficult to understand. Descartes defines *clarity* as "that which is present and apparent to an attentive mind" and *distinctness* as "that which is so precise and different from all other objects that it contains within itself nothing but what is clear" (Principle 45). Distinctness is therefore derivative from clarity. And yet the nature of this clarity is none too clear. On the one hand it seems to mean that which operates on our understanding with "sufficient strength" (Principle 45); it is a psychological criterion. On the other hand it is meant to be a logical criterion; Descartes claims that the clear and distinct would not be true "if it could ever happen that a thing I conceived so clearly and distinctly [i.e., that I am a thinking thing] could be false" (Meditation III, paragraph 2). In addition there is a third aspect of clarity and distinctness. They apparently admit of degrees— "From this point I began to know what I am with a little more clearness and distinction than before" (Meditation II, paragraph 9). What is common to all three aspects of clarity and distinctness, however, is that they describe truth in terms that never involve a correspondence between an object and its description. The clear and distinct are rather criteria of a truth which always remains within the subject. The problem with obscure and involved propositions is that they are useless. Thus without a method for clarifying and simplifying, "study seems to be harmful rather than profitable" (Rule IV). For this reason Descartes opposes error to truth in Meditation III, thereby tacitly identifying error and falsity. Falsity finally becomes something like unprofitable activity.

5. This analysis of the biblical accounts follows Leo Strauss' "On the Interpretation of Genesis," *L'Homme*, vol. 21, pp. 5–20.

6. In this connection one might start with an examination of Aristotle's *De Anima* and Plato's *Phaedo*.

7. For Harvey's account see William Harvey, *On the Motion of the Heart and Blood in Animals*, Willis's translation revised and edited by A. Bowie (Chicago: Regnery, Gateway Editions, 1962), especially chaps. V, XV, and XVII. Gilson (*Discours de la Méthode: texte et commentaire*, Étienne Gilson, ed. [1925; reprint, Paris: J. Vrin, 1967], pp. 405–12) provides a useful discussion of Descartes' disagreement with Harvey.

8. Descartes' claim about the inequality within the species even with regard to what differentiates it from all other species should be compared with his remarks about the equality of reason in men in part 1, paragraph 2.

9. Kennington, "Descartes," p. 410.

10. Ibid., p. 396.

11. That the treatises are the *Dioptrics*, *Meteors*, and *Geometry* is probably not accidental. We have already seen that *The World* was an account of the world from the perspective of the problem of light. Hiram Caton (*The Origin of Subjectivity*, [New Haven: Yale Univ. Press, 1973] p. 76) points out that

> Descartes requires foundations for physics because he is animated by the notion that the relation between idea and object is the point at which ontology, or the principles of nature, intersects with epistemology, or the principles of knowledge. His optical studies are the framework in which Descartes works out his methodological answer to the question of the relation between thinking and being.

Caton then quotes Thomas Huxley (*Method and Results* [New York: Appleton, 1897] p. 210) to the effect that Descartes' optics "is the physiological foundation of the doctrine of the relativity of knowledge and a more or less complete idealism is a necessary consequence of it." Caton goes on to argue that Cartesian physics is meant to challenge the traditional centrality of the study of heavenly bodies (*ta meteōra*) for the science of nature. His *Meteors* is therefore closely connected to his *Dioptrics*, and given the mathematical character of the projected science of nature, the connection to the *Geometry* should be clear.

12. See chap. 2, n. 15 above.

13. Kennington, "Descartes," p. 402.

14. See *Republic* VII 514a–521a.

5. The Limit of Autonomy: Plato's *Meno*

1. I have used Burnet's text of the *Meno* throughout (1900; reprint, Oxford: At the Clarendon Press, 1977). The translations are my own. References are to the standard Stephanus pagination.

2. *The Anabasis of Xenophon*, A. C. Kendrick, ed. (New York: Sheldon & Company, 1878). The translation is my own.

3. The importance of this question has been seen by others, notably Jacob Klein (*A Commentary on Plato's "Meno"* [Chapel Hill: Univ. of North Carolina Press, 1965]); Paul Friedländer (*Plato*, 3 vols., Vol II, *The Dialogues: First Period*, Hans Meyerhoff trans. [New York: Pantheon Books, 1964]); and Leo Strauss, to whom this interpretation is most indebted (Plato's Political Philosophy: The *Meno* [a transcript of a course given in the Spring Quarter of 1966 in the Department of Political Science of the University of Chicago]).

4. See *Nicomachean Ethics* Book X, 1179b4–1180a14.

5. See Strauss, Plato's Political Philosophy: The *Meno*, lecture 13, p. 4.

6. There are only two other Platonic dialogues in which *nomos* and words cognate with it (*nomizō, nomisma*, etc.) are not present, the *Theages* and the *Lysis*.

7. Compare Plato's *Apology* 23a–e with 29d–30a.

8. See Plato's *Republic* 435e–436a.

9. The connection between this opening section and the later substitution of right or true opinion or *eudoxia* for knowledge as virtue is also hinted at later (97a) by the example Socrates uses to indicate that knowledge and right opinion are for practical purposes interchangeable. Those especially well known for wisdom are the Larisaens (70b); the example of right opinion is opining vs. knowing the road to Larisa. See also section 7 above. I am grateful to Ronna Burger for pointing this connection out to me.

10. See for example the first "definition" of piety at *Euthyphro* 5d–6a.

11. See Strauss, Plato's Political Philosophy: The *Meno*, lecture 3, p. 6.

12. Compare 95d and 78d.

13. The word *eidos* derives from the verb "to see" and means originally that which is seen, the look, form, or shape of a thing. When applied to people it can mean beauty of form. It later comes to mean form, kind, or class. It is comparable in this way to the word *species*.

14. Klein, *A Commentary on Plato's "Meno,"* pp. 65–66.

15. There is a long, if inconclusive, tradition connecting Emedocles and Gorgias. Diogenes Laertius cites the *Lives* of Satyrus to the effect that Gorgias was actually a student of Empedocles (*Lives of Eminent Philosophers*, R. D. Hicks trans. [New York, 1935], vii.58). Socrates' attribution of the theory of effluences to Gorgias at the same

time that he mentions Empedocles certainly suggests such a connection. In the context, however, all that is important is the second hand nature of the teaching.

16. See, for example, Plato's *Alcibiades I* 123a–e.

17. Compare with Plato's *Gorgias* 447c.

18. That there is more to Socrates than meets the eye is also the subject of the image fashioned of him by another rebellious and beautiful young man. At *Symposium* 215a–b Alcibiades says Socrates is "most like" the figures of Silenus in the statuary shops which, while ugly on the outside, prove when opened to contain images of the gods.

19. See, for example, the later exchange with the slave boy. At 82e Socrates points out to Meno that he has not been teaching, but that the slave boy has been learning (i.e., recollecting). But that has become visible at precisely this moment because the slave boy has made his first *mistake*.

20. See *Republic* 514a–21b; chap. 3, sec. 3 above; Leo Strauss, *Natural Right and History* (Chicago and London: Univ. of Chicago Press, 1953), chap. 4, "Classic Natural Right," pp. 120–52; and Allan Bloom, *The Republic of Plato* (New York and London: Basic Books, 1968), pp. 402–6. That the cave is the city becomes clearest in the description of what will happen to the one who tries to release the prisoners and lead them out of it (517a). The whole of the *Republic* is designed to make clear the connection between appearance (*doxa*) and opinion (*doxa*).

21. I owe a good deal of this analysis to Seth Benardete.

22. Sophocles, *Antigone* l. 74.

23. Klein, *A Commentary on Plato's "Meno,"* pp. 210–11.

24. Aristotle, *Athenian Constitution* 27:5.

25. Xenophon, *Apology of Socrates to the Jury* 29–31.

26. See Socrates' use of Meno's patronymic at 76e and chap. 4, sec. I.4 above.

27. Compare with Seth Benardete, *The Being of the Beautiful: Plato's "Theaetetus," "Sophist," and "Statesman"* (Chicago: Univ. of Chicago Press, 1984), pp. II 71–II 75.

28. See Strauss, Plato's Political Philosophy: The *Meno*, lecture 10, pp. 8–9.

29. See *Protagoras* 320c–328d.

30. See, for example, Xenophon, *Memorabilia* II.ii.

6. Conclusion

1. Ronna Burger, "To See with Parted Eye: Tragic Irony and Dramatic *Mimesis* in the Greek Tragedies," unpublished manuscript, p. 2.

2. Plato, *Apology of Socrates* 22c.

3. Plato, *Phaedo* 99d–102a.

Bibliography

Aeschylus. *Seven Tragedies*. Edited by Denys Page. Oxford: Oxford Univ. Press, 1972.

Alfarabi. *Philosophy of Plato and Aristotle*. Translated by Mushin Mahdi. New York: The Free Press of Glencoe, 1962.

Aliquié, Ferdinand. *Descartes*. Paris: Hatier, 1969.

Aristotle. *Opera*. Oxford: Clarendon Press, 1956–64.

———. *The Politics of Aristotle*. Edited by W. L. Newman. 4 vols. 1887. Reprint. Oxford: Clarendon Press, 1950.

Aristophanes. *Plays*. Edited by F. W. Hall and W. M. Geldart. 2 vols. Oxford: Oxford Univ. Press, 1906.

Benardete, José. "Metaphysics for Lovers." *Graduate Faculty Philosophy Journal* 11 (1986):37–48.

Benardete, Seth. "Achilles and Hector: The Homeric Hero." *The St. John's Review* 36 (1985):31–58, 85–114.

———. *The Being of the Beautiful: Plato's "Theaetetus," "Sophist" and "Statesman."* Chicago: Univ. of Chicago Press, 1984.

———. *Herodotean Inquiries*. The Hague: Martinus Nijhoff, 1969.

———. "On Greek Tragedy." In *Current Developments in the Arts and Sciences*, The Great Ideas Today 1980, 102–43. Chicago: *Encyclopedia Britannica*, 1980.

———. "On Interpreting Plato's *Charmides*." *Graduate Faculty Philosophy Journal* 11 (1986):9–36.

———. "Physics and Tragedy: On Plato's *Cratylus*." *Ancient Philosophy* 1 (1981):127–40.

———. "A Reading of Sophocles' *Antigone*." *Interpretation* 4 (1975):148–97, 5 (1975):1–57, 148–84.

———. "Sophocles' *Oedipus Tyrannus*." In *Ancients and Moderns: Essays on the Tradition of Political Philosophy in Honor of Leo Strauss*, edited by Joseph Cropsey, 1–15. New York and London: Basic Books, 1964.

Bloom, Allan. *The Republic of Plato*. New York and London: Basic Books, 1968.

————. *Shakespeare's Politics*. New York: Basic Books, 1964.

Bolotin, David. "On Sophocles' *Ajax*." *The St. John's Review* 32 (July 1980):49–57.

Burger, Ronna. *The "Phaedo": A Platonic Labyrinth*. New Haven and London: Yale Univ. Press, 1984.

————. *Plato's "Phaedrus": A Defense of a Philosophic Art of Writing*. University: The Univ. of Alabama Press, 1980.

————. "To See with Parted Eye: Tragic Irony and Dramatic *Mimesis* in the Greek Tragedies." Paper presented at Sarah Lawrence College (Jan. 1986).

Bury, R. G. *The Symposium of Plato*. Cambridge: At the University Press, 1932.

Caton, Hiram. *The Origin of Subjectivity*. New Haven: Yale Univ. Press, 1973.

Dannhauser, Werner J. *Nietzsche's View of Socrates*. Ithaca and London: Cornell Univ. Press, 1974.

Davis, Michael. "Aristotle's Reflections on Revolution." *Graduate Faculty Philosophy Journal* 11 (1986):49–64.

————. "Philosophy and the Perfect Tense: On the Beginning of Plato's *Lovers*." *Graduate Faculty Philosophy Journal* 10 (1985):75–97.

————. "Plato and Nietzsche on Death: An Introduction to Plato's *Phaedo*." *Ancient Philosophy* 1 (1980):69–80.

————. "Socrates' Pre-Socratism: Some Remarks on the Structure of Plato's *Phaedo*." *Review of Metaphysics* 33 (1980):559–77.

Descartes, René. *Discours de la Méthode: Avec Introduction et Notes*. Edited by Étienne Gilson. Paris: J. Vrin, 1946.

————. *Discours de la Méthode: texte et commentaire*. Edited by Étienne Gilson. 1925. Reprint. Paris: Vrin, 1967.

————. *Oeuvres de Descartes*. Edited by Charles Adam and Paul Tannery. 13 vols. Paris: Vrin, 1957–68.

————. *Oeuvres et Lettres*. Edited by André Bridoux. Paris: Éditions Gallimard, Bibliothèque de Pléiade, 1953.

————. *The Philosophical Works of Descartes*. Translated by E. S. Haldane and G. R. T. Ross. 2 vols. 1931. Reprint. New York: Dover, 1967.

Diogenes Laertius. *Lives of Eminent Philosophers*. Translated by R. D. Hicks. 2 vols. New York: Loeb Classical Library, 1935.

Doney, Willis, ed. *Descartes: A Collection of Critical Essays*. New York: Doubleday, 1967.

Else, Gerald F. *Aristotle's "Poetics": The Argument*. Cambridge, MA: Harvard Univ. Press, 1967.

Euben, J. Peter, ed. *Greek Tragedy and Political Theory*. Berkeley, Los Angeles, and London: Univ. of California Press, 1986.

Euripides. *Works*. Edited by Gilbert Murray. 3 vols. Oxford: Oxford Univ. Press, 1901–13.

Friedländer, Paul. *Plato.* 3 vols. Translated by Hans Meyerhoff. New York: Pantheon Books, 1964.

Gadamer, Hans-Georg. *Platos dialektische Ethik und andere Studien zur platonischen Philosophie.* Hamburg: Felix Meiner Verlag, 1968.

Harvey, William. *On the Motion of the Heart and Blood in Animals*, Willis's translation revised and edited by A. Bowie. Chicago: Regnery, Gateway Editions, 1962.

Heidegger, Martin. *Nietzsche.* 2 vols. Pfullingen: Neske, 1961.

Homer. *The Iliad.* Edited and translated by A. T. Murray. 2 vols. 1924. Reprint. Cambridge, MA: Harvard Univ. Press, 1971.

————. *The Odyssey.* Edited and translated by A. T. Murray. 2 vols. 1919. Reprint. Cambridge, MA: Harvard Univ. Press 1966.

Huxley, Thomas. *Method and Results.* New York: Appleton, 1897.

Kant, Immanuel. "Idee zu einer allgemeinen Geschichte in weltburgerlicher Absicht (1784)." In *Kleinere Schriften zur Geschichtsphilosophie Ethik und Politik.* Hamburg: Felix Meiner Verlag, 1973.

Kaufmann, Walter. *Tragedy and Philosophy.* Garden City, NY: Doubleday, 1968.

Kennington, Richard. "Descartes." In *History of Political Philosophy*, edited by Leo Strauss and Joseph Cropsey, 395–413. Chicago: Rand McNally, 1972.

————. "Descartes and Mastery of Nature." In *Organism, Medicine, and Metaphysics*, edited by S. F. Spicker, 201–23. Dordrecht, Holland: D. Reidel, 1978.

————. "The Finitude of Descartes' Evil Genius." *Journal of the History of Ideas* 32 (1971):441–46.

————. "The Teaching of Nature in Descartes' Soul Doctrine." *The Review of Metaphysics* 26 (1972):86–117.

Kirkwood, G. M. *A Study of Sophoclean Drama.* Ithaca and London: Cornell Univ. Press, 1958.

Kitto, H. D. F. *Greek Tragedy: A Literary Study.* London: Methuen, 1939.

Klein, Jacob. *A Commentary on Plato's "Meno."* Chapel Hill: Univ. of North Carolina Press, 1965.

————. *Greek Mathematical Thought and the Origin of Algebra.* Cambridge, MA: M.I.T. Press, 1968.

Knox, Bernard. "The *Ajax* of Sophocles." *Harvard Studies in Classical Philology* 65 (1961):1–37.

————. *The Heroic Temper: Studies in Sophoclean Tragedy.* Berkeley, Los Angeles, and London: Univ. of California Press, 1964.

Krüger, Gerhard. *Einsicht und Leidenschaft: Das Wesen des platonischen Denkens.* Frankfurt am Main: Vittorio Klostermann, 1939.

Macdowell, D. *Andokides, On the Mysteries.* Oxford: At the University Press, 1962.

Nietzsche, Friedrich. *The Portable Nietzsche*. Edited and translated by Walter Kaufmann. New York: Viking, 1954, 1968.

———. *Werke in drei Bänden*. Munich: Carl Hanser Verlag, 1966.

Plato. *Opera*. Edited by John Burnet. 5 vols. 1900–1915. Reprint. Oxford: Clarendon Press, 1977.

Rosen, Stanley. "A Central Ambiguity in Descartes." In *Cartesian Essays: A Collection of Critical Studies*, edited by Bernd Magnus and James B. Wilber, 17–35. The Hague: Martinus Nijhoff, 1969.

———. *Nihilism*. New Haven: Yale Univ. Press, 1969.

———. *Plato's "Symposium."* New Haven: Yale Univ. Press, 1968.

Rousseau, Jean-Jacques. *Oeuvres Complètes*. 3 vols. Paris: L'Intégrale, Éditions du Seuil, 1967.

Schiff, Janet. *A Word Index to Descartes' "Discours de la Méthode."* University Park: Pennsylvania State Univ., 1970.

Schleiermacher, Friedrich. *Platons Werke*. Berlin: Realschulbuchhandlung, 1817–28.

Sesonske, Alexander, and Noel Fleming. *Meta-meditations: Studies in Descartes*. Belmont, CA: Wadsworth Publishing, 1965.

Sophocles. *Sophocles: The Plays and Fragments, with Critical Notes, Commentary, and Translation in English Prose by Sir Richard C. Jebb*. 7 vols. Cambridge: Cambridge Univ. Press, 1883–96.

Strauss, Leo. *The City and Man*. Chicago: Rand McNally, 1964.

———. "Jerusalem and Athens: Some Preliminary Reflections." (The Frank Cohen Public Lecture in Judaic Affairs.) The City College Papers, no. 6. New York: The Library, The City College, The City Univ. of New York, 1967.

———. *Natural Right and History*. Chicago and London: Univ. of Chicago Press, 1953.

———. "On the Interpretation of Genesis," *L'Homme: Revue francaise d'anthropologie* 21 (1981):5–20.

———. *On Tyranny: An Interpretation of Xenophon's "Hiero."* Revised and enlarged, including Alexander Kojève, "Tyranny and Wisdom." New York: Free Press of Glencoe, 1963.

———. *Persecution and the Art of Writing*. Glencoe, IL: Free Press, 1952.

———. "Plato's Political Philosophy: The *Meno*." Transcript of a course given in the spring quarter of 1966 in the Department of Political Science of the University of Chicago.

———. "Plato's *Symposium*." Transcript of a course given in the Department of Political Science of the University of Chicago.

———. *Political Philosophy: Six Essays by Leo Strauss*. Edited by Hilail Gildin. Indianapolis and New York: Bobbs-Merrill/Pegasus, 1975.

———. *Socrates and Aristophanes*. New York: Basic Books, 1966.

―――. *Studies in Platonic Political Philosophy.* Chicago and London: Univ. of Chicago Press, 1983.

―――. *What is Political Philosophy?* Glencoe, IL: Free Press, 1959.

―――. *Xenophon's Socrates.* Ithaca: Cornell Univ. Press. 1972.

―――. *Xenophon's Socratic Discourse: An Interpretation of the "Oeconomicus."* Ithaca: Cornell Univ. Press, 1970.

Taylor, A. E. *Plato: The Man and His Work.* London: Methuen, 1929.

Thucydides. *History of the Peloponnesian War.* Edited and translated by C. F. Smith. 4 vols. London: William Heinemann, 1921.

Vlastos, Gregory, ed. *Plato: A Collection of Critical Essays.* 2 vols. Garden City, NY: Doubleday, 1971.

Xenophon. *The "Anabasis" of Xenophon.* Edited by A. C. Kendrick. New York: Sheldon & Company, 1878.

―――. *Xenophon in Seven Volumes.* Vol. 4, *Memorabilia and Oeconomicus—Symposium and Apology.* Cambridge, MA, and London: Loeb Classical Library, 1968.

Index

Michael Davis teaches philosophy at Sarah Lawrence College and is also an adjunct member of the graduate faculty of The New School for Social Research. His research interests lie in ancient philosophy and political thought, and he has written numerous articles on Plato and Aristotle.